FINAL DRAFT

4

Series Editor: **Jeanne Lambert**
The New School

Wendy Asplin
University of Washington
Monica F. Jacobe
The College of New Jersey
Alan S. Kennedy
Columbia University

with
Lindsay Hansen, University of Arizona

CAMBRIDGE
UNIVERSITY PRESS

CAMBRIDGE
UNIVERSITY PRESS

32 Avenue of the Americas, New York NY 10013-2473, USA

Cambridge University Press is part of the University of Cambridge.

It furthers the University's mission by disseminating knowledge in the pursuit of education, learning and research at the highest international levels of excellence.

www.cambridge.org

Information on this title: www.cambridge.org/9781107495579

First published 2016

Printed in Dubai by Oriental Press

A catalog record for this publication is available from the British Library.

Cataloging in Publication data is available at the Library of Congress.

Jacobe, Monica F. author.

Final draft. 4 / Monica F. Jacobe ; Alan S. Kennedy.
pages cm ISBN 978-1-107-49557-9 (Student's Book Level 4) -- ISBN 978-1-107-49558-6 (Student's Book with Writing Skills Interactive Level 4) -- ISBN 978-1-107-49559-3 (Teacher's Manual Level 4) 1. English language--Rhetoric--Problems, exercises and etc. 2. English language--Textbooks for foreign speakers. 3. Report writing--Problems, exercises and etc. I. Kennedy, Alan S., (Language teacher) author. II. Title. III. Title: Final Draft four. IV. Title: Final Draft 4.

PE1408.J23 2015
808'.042--dc23

2015004565

ISBN 978-1-107-49557-9 Student's Book Level 4
ISBN 978-1-107-49558-6 Student's Book with Writing Skills Interactive Level 4
ISBN 978-1-107-49559-3 Teacher's Manual Level 4

Additional resources for this publication at www.cambridge.org/finaldraft

Art direction, book design, and photo research: emc design limited
Layout services: emc design limited

CONTENTS

SCOPE AND SEQUENCE

All academic vocabulary words appear on the Academic Word List (AWL) or the General Service List (GSL). 👁 All academic collocations, academic phrases, and common grammar mistakes are based on the Cambridge Academic Corpus.

WRITING SKILLS	GRAMMAR FOR WRITING 👁	AVOIDING PLAGIARISM	DO RESEARCH
Thesis statements	Gerunds and infinitives	Citing sources to avoid plagiarism	Developing key words for an Internet search
Parallel structure Sentence variety	Past tense forms	Common knowledge	Choosing a quotation for an essay
Paraphrasing Avoiding sentence fragments, run-on sentences, and comma splices	Present perfect and present perfect progressive	Paraphrasing to avoid plagiarism	Choosing a text to paraphrase for support in an essay
Words and phrases that show similarities and differences Coherence	Appositives	Choosing credible sources	Evaluating Internet sources
Introduction to summarizing Acknowledging and refuting opposing solutions	*It* constructions	Time management	Finding up-to-date information
Language for summarizing Neutral and unbiased language Avoiding overuse of key words	Noun clauses with *wh-* words and *if / whether*	Note taking	Taking clear notes to avoid citation mistakes
Audience and appeal Language for introducing counterarguments and refutation	Complex noun phrases	Citing graphs and charts	Using non-textual sources in research
Steps for timed writing: • plan time • analyze prompt • brainstorm • write outline • write essay • proofread essay			

TOUR OF A UNIT

ACADEMIC WRITING AND VOCABULARY

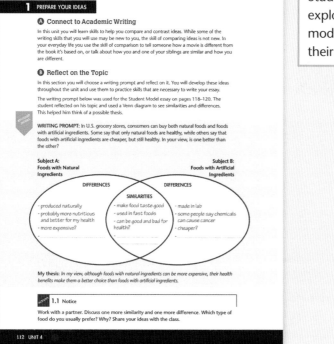

1 PREPARE YOUR IDEAS

Ⓐ Connect to Academic Writing

In this unit you will learn skills to help you compare and contrast ideas. While some of the writing skills that you will use may be new to you, the skill of comparing ideas is not new. In your everyday life you use the skill of comparison to tell someone how a movie is different from the book it's based on, or talk about how you and one of your siblings are similar and how you are different.

Ⓑ Reflect on the Topic

In this section you will choose a writing prompt and reflect on it. You will develop these ideas throughout the unit and use them to practice skills that are necessary to write your essay.

The writing prompt below was used for the Student Model essay on pages 118–120. The student reflected on his topic and used a Venn diagram to see similarities and differences. This helped him think of a possible thesis.

WRITING PROMPT: In U.S. grocery stores, consumers can buy both natural foods and foods with artificial ingredients. Some say that only natural foods are healthy, while others say that foods with artificial ingredients are cheaper, but still healthy. In your view, is one better than the other?

Subject A:
Foods with Natural Ingredients

DIFFERENCES

- produced naturally
- probably more nutritious and better for my health
- more expensive?

SIMILARITIES

- make food taste good
- used in fast foods
- can be good and bad for health?

Subject B:
Foods with Artificial Ingredients

DIFFERENCES

- made in lab
- some people say chemicals can cause cancer
- cheaper?

My thesis: In my view, although foods with natural ingredients can be more expensive, their health benefits make them a better choice than foods with artificial ingredients.

1.1 Notice

Work with a partner. Discuss one more similarity and one more difference. Which type of food do you usually prefer? Why? Share your ideas with the class.

112 UNIT 4

Students begin to explore a rhetorical mode and connect it to their everyday lives.

Next, students prepare for their writing by learning corpus-informed academic vocabulary, collocations, and phrases.

Ⓑ Academic Collocations

Collocations are words that are frequently used together. Research tells us that the academic vocabulary in Part A is commonly used in the collocations in bold below.

2.2 Focus on Meaning

Read the sentences. Decide the meaning of the phrases in bold and circle the correct answer.

1 Among high school students, there is a **popular perception** that joining many school clubs will make their college applications stronger, but some people say that being very active in one club is better. **Popular perception** means
 a the way most people see something.
 b an uncommon belief.

2 Being in a **stable relationship** can help people stay sane during stressful situations because they know that they can depend on a partner for support. **Stable relationship** means
 a a difficult relationship that ends quickly.
 b a relationship that lasts a long time.

3 The study by the Work and Family Research Center at Boston University presented **strong evidence** that mothers in the workplace were less likely to get promoted than fathers. It documented this trend in companies all over America for ten years. **Strong evidence** means
 a many facts that support many different conclusions.
 b facts obviously leading to a single conclusion.

4 Researchers **drew a conclusion** from several studies that all showed the same facts: cyberbullying has the same effects as real world bullying on young people. **Draw a conclusion** means
 a to decide on a single idea based on evidence.
 b to sketch out an idea based on a guess.

5 It seems obvious that principals **have the capacity** to change the behavior of their students, but they do not always realize that their impact spreads beyond the classroom. **Have the capacity** means
 a to be unable to do something.
 b to be able to do something.

ARGUMENTATIVE ESSAYS 217

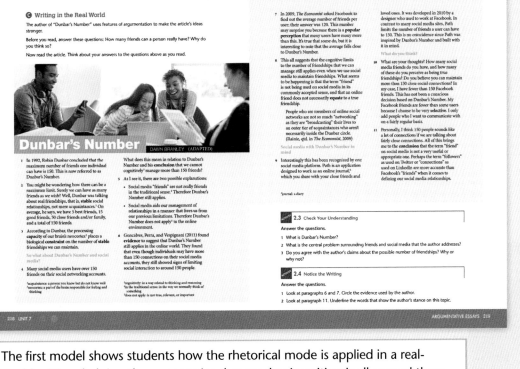

The first model shows students how the rhetorical mode is applied in a real-world setting, helping them recognize that academic writing is all around them.

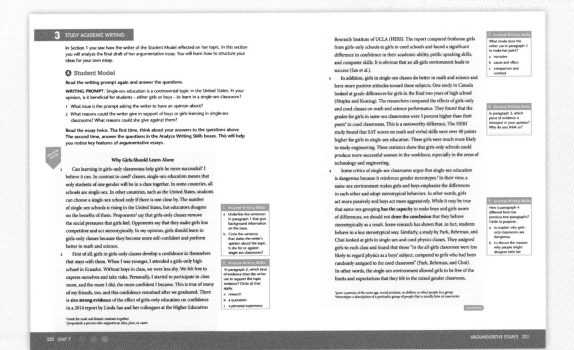

The second model shows a typical assignment from a college writing course. Students analyze this in detail, preparing for their own writing.

THE SKILLS AND GRAMMAR EVERY WRITER NEEDS

In this section you will learn the writing and grammar skills that will help make your writing more sophisticated and accurate.

A Writing Skill 1: Parallel Structure

Writers use parallel structure when a sentence has a list of words or phrases that are all the same form and part of speech. This pattern can involve single words, phrases, or clauses and can be used with different grammatical patterns, which are in bold below. If the part of speech and form don't match, this is not considered good writing. Here are some examples of different kinds of parallel structure.

Adjective phrases:

*Immigration can be **not only** very exciting **but also** quite stressful.*

Verb phrases:

*My father knew he had to **either** find work **or** return home.*

He had never spoken English, been to a supermarket, or eaten fast food before he came here.

Clauses:

Albert Einstein emigrated from Germany because he wanted to work in America, he was worried about the war, and his future there was uncertain.

4.1 Using Parallel Structure

Read the information. Complete the sentences using parallel structure. You may have to add some words of your own.

1 Supreme Court Justice Sonia Sotomayor's parents were born in Puerto Rico. They came to the United States during World War II. During the war, they got married.

   Supreme Court Justice Sonia Sotomayor's parents came to the United States during World War II and _____

2 Sonia Sotomayor is the first Supreme Court Justice of Hispanic heritage. She is also one of the youngest Supreme Court Justices.

   Sonia Sotomayor is not only the first Supreme Court Justice of Hispanic heritage, but she is also _____

3 Sotomayor graduated from Princeton University. She also received a degree from Yale Law School. She served as editor of the *Yale Law Journal*.

   Sotomayor graduated from Princeton University, received a degree from Yale Law School, and _____

> Students develop an extensive skill set, preparing them for every aspect of academic writing.

---

5 One kind of cheese which can only be made in Italy is Parmigiano-Reggiano. Parmigiano-Reggiano is a kind of hard cheese. (appositive at end)

_____

Avoiding Common Mistakes

Research tells us that these are the most common mistakes that students make when using appositives in academic writing.

1. Remember to use an article for an appositive when necessary.

   Alice Waters is the owner of Chez Panisse, a California restaurant famous for its organic ingredients.

2. Don't use a relative pronoun in an appositive.

   Big Food, which the food production industry in the United States, resists movement toward sustainable practices.

3. Always use a comma, a dash, or parentheses with an appositive when it provides extra information.

   Americans, a people not often acclaimed for their culinary traditions, are experiencing a watershed moment in their attitudes toward the food they eat.

4.6 Editing Task

Find and correct four more mistakes in the following paragraph.

Because of the United States' special history of immigration, American food has been influenced by cuisines from all over the world. A melting pot, large pot used to melt multiple ingredients together over heat, has often been used as a symbol of American society and culture. It's true that some food considered "American" did not originate here. Hamburgers and hot dogs, very common American sandwiches were brought by German immigrants. Sometimes, food brought by immigrants adapts to American life just as the immigrants do. Chop suey, dish of mixed meat and vegetables in a thick sauce, is served at Chinese restaurants in the United States but was not eaten in China. Mayonnaise, that a very common American condiment, actually comes from Europe. These are just a few examples of culinary adaptation in the United States.

> Students study specific applications of grammar for the writing task and learn to avoid common mistakes (informed by the Cambridge Learner Corpus).

E Avoiding Plagiarism

It is helpful to take notes when you do research, but keeping track of your sources can be a problem.

I worked hard on the essay I wrote about Bill Gates. I read a lot of articles and took a lot of notes. I thought my paper was good, but my instructor said I plagiarized some information! I guess I mixed my notes with the word-for-word ideas from sources. I didn't mean to plagiarize! I'm really sorry. How can I be better at taking notes? – Ruby

Dear Ruby,

Good note taking does not have to be difficult, but you do need a system to organize your notes. Notes can come from many places, for example, your own ideas, common knowledge, or other sources. If you organize your notes from the beginning, you'll know which ideas are yours and which ones need to be cited. You'll also know which notes are quotations and which ones are paraphrases. The important thing is to have a simple system that you can use for <u>all</u> your notes.

Good luck!

Professor Wright

CREATING A NOTE-TAKING SYSTEM

In order to avoid plagiarizing, you always need to quote your sources. It is important to be able to distinguish between your sources, quoted material, and your ideas in your notes. Organizing your notes from the beginning makes it easier to locate your sources and correctly cite them in your writing.

Here are some suggestions for creating an effective note-taking system.

1 **Take notes** in a notebook, on index cards, or in a document on the computer. Keep notes together. Use a separate page in your notebook, a separate index card, or a new page in a word document for each source. Write all the source information at the top: authors, titles, dates, medium, page.

2 When you write down the **exact words** from a source, write the words in big quotation marks ("…"). Write the word *quote* after the quotation. Highlight all quotations in the same color, for example, in blue.

3 When you **paraphrase** someone's words or ideas, write the word *paraphrase* next to the information you paraphrase. Highlight all paraphrases in the same color, for example, in yellow.

SUMMARY-RESPONSE ESSAYS 205

> Students learn to acknowledge others' work and ideas and appropriately incorporate them into their writing.

> Now fully prepared, students move from brainstorming and doing research to writing their final draft.

STEP 2: DO RESEARCH: CHOOSING A TEXT TO PARAPHRASE FOR SUPPORT IN AN ESSAY

Selecting appropriate texts from credible sources is an important part of doing research. Some credible sources are educational institutions, government agencies, and respected news organizations. You choose texts to paraphrase based on the importance of their **evidence**, like details, explanations, or examples, and how that evidence supports the main ideas in the body paragraphs of your essay.

Sue needed to choose a text to paraphrase for support in an essay response to this prompt: *The populations of most countries are becoming less rural and more urban. What are some reasons for this trend?* Read and find out how she did it.

After identifying the main points in my thesis, I read several sources and identified texts with main ideas related to my thesis. Next, I compared the evidence in the texts to see which one provided the best support for my main ideas. Last, I paraphrased the text into my own words and added a citation for the source.

Sue's Results

Thesis: Primary causes of the rapid urbanization of sub-Saharan Africa are changes in the environment, increased economic opportunities, and population growth.

Focus of research: population growth due to rapid urbanization

Source	Text	How it supports my point.
1 Time, "Urban Planet: How Growing Cities Will Wreck the Environment Unless We Build Them Right" (Bryan Walsh, 2012)	"… the wave of urbanization isn't just about the migration of people into urban environments, but about the environments themselves becoming bigger to accommodate all those people."	shows direct link between population growth & larger cities (more people = more space)
2 http://www.afdb.org/, "Urbanization of Africa" (Mthuli Ncube, 2012)	"In the developing world, Africa has experienced the highest urban growth during the last two decades at 3.5% per year and this rate of growth is expected to hold into 2050."	statistic; general reference to African population growth, but no cause/effect given

Paraphrase of chosen text: Sizes of cities are growing in two phases: first, more people move into the cities, and then the city space must grow to fit all of the new people (Walsh).

5.1 Apply It to Your Writing

Follow the steps Sue took to choose a text to paraphrase for support in your essay.

THE TEAM BEHIND *FINAL DRAFT*

SERIES EDITOR

Jeanne Lambert brings 20 years of ESL classroom, teacher training, and materials writing experience to her role as series editor of *Final Draft*. Jeanne has taught at Columbia University, City University of New York (CUNY), and The New School, specializing in academic writing and English for Academic Purposes. While at Columbia University, she taught writing courses in both the American Language Program and for the School of International and Public Affairs. At CUNY, she co-designed a faculty development program to help high school teachers align their ESL reading and writing curriculum with college standards. She has worked as an ESL Methods Practicum instructor and currently teaches academic writing at The New School.

AUTHORS

Wendy Asplin has taught international students and teachers-in-training in Turkey and the United States. For the past 20 years, she has been a lecturer at the University of Washington in Seattle and is an author of the Cambridge academic reading series Read This!

Monica F. Jacobe is Director of the Center for American Language & Culture at The College of New Jersey. She has 15 years of experience teaching multilingual writers and supporting teachers of multilingual students. She has published and presented widely on a variety of issues in higher education, including pedagogy, instructional support, and writing.

Alan S. Kennedy is a lecturer in language in the American Language Program at Columbia University, where he is also the coordinator of the International Teaching Assistants program. He has presented at several national and international conferences on linguistics and language teaching.

ACADEMIC WRITING ADVISORY PANEL

The Advisory Panel is comprised of experienced writing instructors who have helped guide the development of this series and have provided invaluable information about the needs of ESL student writers.

Laszlo Arvai, Borough of Manhattan Community College, New York, NY
Leo Kazan, Passaic County Community College, Paterson, NJ
Amy Nunamaker, San Diego State College, San Diego, CA
Amy Renehan, University of Washington, Seattle, WA
Adrianne Thompson, Miami Dade College, Miami, FL

Final Draft was influenced by the opinions and insights of classroom teachers from the following institutions:

UNITED STATES Alabama: Cleburne County High School, Gadsden State Community College, University of Alabama; **Arizona:** Arizona State University, Northern Arizona University, Pima Community College; **Arkansas**: Arkansas State University, University of Arkansas, University of Central Arkansas; **California:** Allan Hancock College, Berkeley High School, California State Polytechnic University, California State University East Bay, California State University Fullerton, California State University Long Beach, California State University Los Angeles, City College of San Francisco, College of San Mateo, De Anza College, Diablo Valley College, East Los Angeles College, El Camino College, The English Center, Evergreen Valley College, Foothill College, Fullerton College, Gavilan College, Glendale Community College, Hollywood High School, Imperial Valley College, Las Positas College, Los Angeles City College, Los Angeles Southwest College, Mendocino College, Mills College, Mission College, Modesto Junior College, Monterey Peninsula College, Palomar College, Pasadena City College, Placer High School, Roybal Learning Center, Sacramento City College, Sacramento State, San Diego Community College District, San Francisco State University, San Jose City College, Santa Ana College, Santa Barbara City College, Santa Monica College, Santa Rosa Junior College, Skyline College, Stanford University, Taft College, University of California Berkeley, University of California Davis, University of California Irvine, University of San Diego, University of San Francisco, University of Southern California, West Valley Community College; **Colorado:** Community College of Aurora, Front Range Community College, Red Rocks Community College, University of Colorado; **Connecticut:** Central Connecticut State University, Enfield High School, Naugatuck Valley Community College, Norwalk Community College, Post University, University of Bridgeport, University of Hartford; **Florida:** Barry University, Florida SouthWestern State College, Florida State University, Hillsborough Community College, Indian River State College, Miami Dade College, Robinson High School, St. Petersburg College, University of Central Florida, University of Florida, University of Miami, University of South Florida; **Georgia:** Augusta State University, Emory University, Georgia Institute of Technology, Georgia Perimeter College, Georgia State University, Interactive College of Technology, Pebblebrook High School, Savannah College of Art and Design, West Hall High School; **Hawaii:** Hawaii Community College, Hawaii Tokai International College, Kapiolani Community College, Mid-Pacific Institute, University of Hawaii; **Idaho:** College of Western Idaho, Northwest Nazarene University; **Illinois:** College of DuPage, College of Lake County, Elgin Community College, English Center USA, Harold Washington College, Harper College, Illinois Institute of Technology, Lake Forest Academy, Moraine Valley Community College, Oakton Community College, Roosevelt University, South Suburban College, Southern Illinois University, Triton College, Truman College, University of Illinois, Waubonsee Community College; **Indiana:** Earlham College, Indiana University, Purdue University; **Iowa:** Divine Word College, Iowa State University, Kirkwood Community College, Mercy College of Health Sciences, University of Northern Iowa; **Kansas:** Donnelly College, Johnson County Community College, Kansas State University, Washburn University; **Kentucky:** Bluegrass Community & Technical College, Georgetown College, Northern Kentucky University, University of Kentucky; **Maryland:** Anne Arundel Community College, Howard Community College, Montgomery College, Johns Hopkins University; **Massachusetts:** Boston University, Mount Ida College, New England Conservatory of Music, North Shore Community College, Phillips Academy, Roxbury Community College, The Winchendon School, Worcester State University; **Michigan:** Central Michigan University, Eastern Michigan University, Grand Rapids Community College, Lansing Community College, Macomb Community College, Michigan State University, Saginaw Valley State University, University of Detroit Mercy, University of Michigan, Wayne State University, Western Michigan University;

Minnesota: Century College, Saint Paul College, University of Minnesota, University of St. Thomas; **Mississippi:** Mississippi College, Mississippi State University; **Missouri:** Missouri State University, St. Louis Community College, Saint Louis University, University of Missouri, Webster University; **Nebraska:** Union College, University of Nebraska; **Nevada:** Truckee Meadows Community College, University of Nevada; **New Jersey:** Bergen Community College, The College of New Jersey, Hudson County Community College, Kean University, Linden High School, Mercer County Community College, Passaic County Community College, Rutgers University, Stockton University, Union County College; **New Mexico:** University of New Mexico; **New York:** Alfred State College, Baruch College, Borough of Manhattan Community College, City University of New York, Columbia University, Fashion Institute of Technology, Hofstra University, Hostos Community College, Hunter College, John Jay College of Criminal Justice, Kingsborough Community College, The Knox School, LaGuardia Community College, LIC/LISMA Language Center, Medgar Evers College, New York University, Queens College, Queensborough Community College, Suffolk Community College, Syracuse University, Zoni Language Centers; **North Carolina:** Central Carolina Community College, Central Piedmont Community College, Duke University, Durham Technical Community College, South Piedmont Community College, University of North Carolina, Wake Technical Community College; **North Dakota:** Woodrow Wilson High School; **Ohio:** Columbus State Community College, Cuyahoga Community College, Kent State University, Miami University Middletown, Ohio Northern University, Ohio State University, Sinclair Community College, University of Cincinnati, University of Dayton, Wright State University, Xavier University; **Oklahoma:** University of Oklahoma; **Oregon:** Chemeketa Community College, Clackamas Community College, Lewis & Clark College, Portland Community College, Portland State University, Westview High School; **Pennsylvania:** Pennsylvania State University, University of Pennsylvania, University of Pittsburgh; **Puerto Rico:** Carlos Albizu University, InterAmerican University of Puerto Rico; **Rhode Island:** Johnson & Wales University, Salve Regina University; **South Carolina:** University of South Carolina; **South Dakota:** Black Hills State University; **Tennessee:** Southern Adventist University, University of Tennessee, Vanderbilt University, Williamson Christian College; **Texas:** Austin Community College, Colleyville Heritage High School, Collin College, Dallas Baptist University, El Paso Community College, Houston Community College, Lone Star College, Northwest Vista College, Richland College, San Jacinto College, Stephen F. Austin State University, Tarrant County College, Texas A&M University, University of Houston, University of North Texas, University of Texas, Victoria College, West Brook High School; **Utah:** Brigham Young University, Davis Applied Technology College, Weber State University; **Vermont:** Green Mountain College; **Virginia:** College of William & Mary, Liberty University, Northern Virginia Community College, Tidewater Community College; **Washington:** Bellevue College, EF International Language Centers, Gonzaga University, The IDEAL School, Mount Rainier High School, North Seattle College, Peninsula College, Seattle Central College, Seattle University, Shoreline Community College, South Puget Sound Community College, Tacoma Community College, University of Washington, Whatcom Community College, Wilson High School; **Washington, DC:** George Washington University, Georgetown University; **West Virginia:** West Virginia University; **Wisconsin:** Beloit College, Edgewood College, Gateway Technical College, Kenosha eSchool, Lawrence University, Marquette University, St. Norbert College, University of Wisconsin, Waukesha County Technical College

CANADA British Columbia: Vancouver Island University, VanWest College; **Nova Scotia**: Acadia University; **Ontario:** Centennial College, University of Guelph, York University; **Québec**: Université du Québec

MEXICO Baja California: Universidad de Tijuana

TURKEY Istanbul: Bilgi University, Özyeğin University

1 ACADEMIC ESSAYS

PSYCHOLOGY: CONSUMER BEHAVIOR

"We live in a world of things, and our only connection with them is that we know how to manipulate or to consume them."

Erich Fromm
(1900–1980)

About the Author:

Erich Fromm was a German psychologist who studied the relationships between sociology, politics, and human behavior.

Work with a partner. Read the quotation about consumerism. Then answer the questions.

1 What kind of "things" was the author referring to? Do you agree that we live in a world of things?

2 Fromm wrote this quote in 1955. Do you believe it is more accurate today or less accurate? Explain.

3 When did you last purchase something for another person? What did you buy, and what motivated you to buy it for that person?

Ⓐ Connect to Academic Writing

In this unit you will learn skills to help you write academic essays. While some of the writing skills that you will use may be new to you, others are not. In your everyday life, you already use many of the same skills when you tell a story about a recent trip or compare different cell phone plans.

Ⓑ Reflect on the Topic

In this section you will choose a writing prompt and reflect on it. You will develop these ideas throughout the unit and use them to practice skills that are necessary to write your essay.

The writing prompt below was used for the Student Model essay on pages 20–22. After reflecting on the topic, the student decided to focus on advantages and used a cluster diagram to help generate and organize ideas. This helped her think of a possible thesis.

STUDENT MODEL

WRITING PROMPT: What are the main advantages or disadvantages of shopping online?

My thesis: *The main advantages are that it is convenient, easy, and can be cheaper.*

 1.1 Notice

Work with a partner. Choose one of the ideas in the cluster diagram. Take turns explaining to your partner why you agree or disagree with it.

1.2 Apply It to Your Writing

Follow the directions to reflect on your topic.

A Choose a prompt:

- In order to make a profit, companies need to promote their products to consumers and convince them to buy. What are three ways companies attract consumers?

- Shopping is sometimes jokingly called "retail therapy," and many people say that shopping makes them feel good. Why do some people shop to feel better?

- Think about a company and/or its products that you like, such as a shoe company or a car company. Explain why the company appeals to you. Consider the way the company does business, how it advertises its products, and the quality of its products.

- A topic approved by your instructor

B Work with a partner and complete the following tasks:

1 Think about your prompt. Decide what you will focus on in your essay.

2 Complete the cluster diagram below. Write down as many ideas as you can. Add more circles if you need them.

3 Write a possible thesis statement.

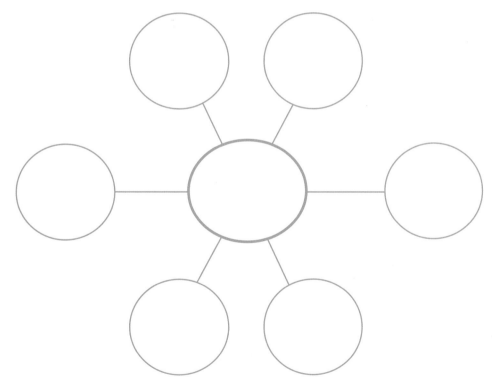

Possible thesis statement:

....

....

In this section you will learn academic language that you can use in your academic essay. You will also notice how a professional writer uses the language and features of academic essays.

Ⓐ Academic Vocabulary

The words below appear throughout the unit. Many are from the Academic Word List. Using these words in your writing will make your ideas clearer and your writing more academic.

alternative (adj)	commitment (n)	excessive (adj)	radical (adj)
coincide (v)	ethical (adj)	expose (v)	widespread (adj)

 **2.1** Focus on Meaning

Work with a partner. Read the sentences. Decide the meaning of the words in bold and circle the correct answer.

1 The new soda commercial tried to show that diet drinks are safe, **alternative** options to higher calorie sodas made with natural ingredients. **Alternative** means

   a better.   b other, different.

2 When signing a new contract for a cell phone service, many consumers must make a two-year **commitment** to the company's services. **Commitment** means

   a a promise to do something.   b a record of something.

3 Many companies have special sales events, such as Presidents' Day sales, during periods that **coincide** with national holidays. **Coincide** means

   a happen at a different time.   b happen at the same time.

4 An important **ethical** concern for any company is treating all employees fairly. **Ethical** means

a   a   relating to what is right or wrong.   b   relating to financial concerns.

5 Many people begin shopping for Christmas gifts just after Thanksgiving, but there is a growing movement questioning this **excessive** focus on gifts and little focus on religion. **Excessive** means

a   a   extreme; unnecessary.   b   very important.

6 Taking children on shopping trips is an opportunity to explain how to get good value for the money they spend. This can **expose** them to good consumer habits. **Expose** means

b   a   change someone's mind about   b   offer an experience.
          something.

7 The company was losing money on traditional ads, so it tried something **radical**. It stopped advertising altogether. **Radical** means

a   a   extreme.   b   small.

8 The **widespread** thinking that organic products are healthier choices grew out of a natural farming and anti-pesticide campaign that has gained national attention and influence. **Widespread** means

a   a   affecting many places or people.   b   providing new knowledge.

B Academic Collocations

Collocations are words that are frequently used together. Research tells us that the academic vocabulary in Part A is commonly used in the collocations in bold below.

ACTIVITY 2.2 Focus on Meaning

Work with a partner. Match the phrases to their meanings. Write the letters.

c   1   The biggest snowstorm of the year **coincided with** Christmas Eve, normally a big shopping day.

a   a different way of doing something

d   2   According to surveys, millions of Americans share the **widespread belief** that genetically modified foods are not healthy.

b   promise to do something

a   3   Some shoppers don't like to carry cash or credit cards. An **alternative approach** is paying by mobile phone.

c   happened at the same time

b   4   You often must **make a commitment** to stay with a phone plan for two years to avoid a fee.

d   a feeling in many places or among many people that something is true

e   5   Many people feel that **excessive consumption** is bad for the environment and can also lead to debt.

e   buying or using too much

C Writing in the Real World

The author of "Buy Nothing Day" uses features of academic essays to strengthen his argument.

Before you read, answer these questions: What does it mean to consume responsibly? How do you think the world would be different if people bought fewer things?

Now read the article. Think about your answers to the questions above as you read.

SCOTT HARRIS (ADAPTED)

BUY NOTHING DAY

1   Some people are trying to change the culture of consumerism in North America. For them, the most important day in their calendar is Buy Nothing Day. On this day, these anti-materialists congregate in shopping malls around the country. They take out their credit cards and cut them up. They wander through department stores in single file, often walking and acting like zombies. They push empty shopping carts and buy nothing. For twenty-four hours, they **make a commitment** to spend no money at all.

2   Buy Nothing Day is scheduled each year to take place in late November so that it **coincides with** the beginning of the busiest shopping period of the year in North America – the month leading up to Christmas day. The idea started in Vancouver, Canada, in 1992 and is now "celebrated" in more than 65 countries. Yet, despite the relative success of the movement, many question whether or not it has any effect whatsoever. They wonder whether it is more than just an empty gesture that makes those who celebrate it feel good about themselves, but has no effect at all on shoppers' habits.

3   One of the organizers of Buy Nothing Day, Tyler Collins of Edmonton, Canada, is aware that "there's a great deal of stigma[1]

surrounding Buy Nothing Day with the average consumer." In the minds of the general public, there is a **widespread belief** that proponents of Buy Nothing Day are trying to "crash the system" and trying to stop people from buying anything. So Collins has made it his goal to change that perception. His goal now is to use Buy Nothing Day as an opportunity to **expose** shoppers to an **alternative** way of thinking about shopping. He wants consumers to be forced to hesitate a moment and think about their buying habits.

4   Ironically, another anti-consumerism activist,[2] Michael Kalmanovitch, is the owner of a general store. He has celebrated every Buy Nothing Day since it started in

[1]stigma: a strong feeling of disapproval that many people have about something

[2]activist: someone who tries to create social and political change

1992. He judges the success of Buy Nothing Day by seeing how much less money he makes in his store on that day. When he first marked Buy Nothing Day, he kept the store open. When shoppers tried to buy something, he told them that there were to be no transactions on that day. He realizes now that this approach was counterproductive.[3] It just made shoppers unsympathetic to his cause because they did not enjoy being told what they could or could not buy. Now he keeps the store open, but when shoppers come in or want to make a purchase, he uses it as an opportunity to raise consciousness. His staff tell the shoppers, "Do you know it's Buy Nothing Day? We'd appreciate it if you didn't buy anything from our store or anywhere else for that matter, but we respect that it's your right or your decision to do whatever you feel is appropriate."

5   Some activists feel that Buy Nothing Day does not go far enough to discourage **excessive consumption**. They think

stopping people from shopping for just one day doesn't achieve much. It simply stops a few well-off individuals from shopping for a day, after which they will simply buy more on subsequent days. Laura Bercovitz, who has promoted Buy Nothing Day since its inception and is worried about being misinterpreted by such critics, is therefore now promoting a **radical alternative**: Buy Nothing Christmas. She wants consumers to stop spending throughout the complete holiday period.

6   Tyler Collins, Michael Kalmanovitch, and Laura Bercovitz may have different strategies, but they have one common goal. They are trying to promote **ethical** consumption. In many cases, this means buying products that are produced locally and sold in small locally owned stores. They want consumers to be made more aware of what they are doing when they are shopping. They want them to ask themselves how their consumerist habits might be having an impact on the environment and the world.

[3]counterproductive: having an effect that is the opposite of what you intended

---

ACTIVITY **2.3** **Check Your Understanding**

Answer the questions.

1   What is Buy Nothing Day trying to change about society? *P 3 lose and over shopping*

2   Why have some people proposed changes to Buy Nothing Day? What are the changes, and which ones do you think would be most effective? *Think before buy*

3   Do you agree with the goals of the Buy Nothing Day organizers? Why or why not?
Yes, companies will give more discont on special day.

ACTIVITY **2.4** **Notice the Features of Academic Essays**

Answer the questions.

1   Look at paragraph 1. Which sentences draw the reader in? *Hook. They tale out.*

2   Look at paragraphs 3, 4, and 5. What is the main idea of each paragraph?
3. Change shopping habits.   *5. how to stop shopping*
4 How Buy Nothing Day success

In Section 1 you saw how the writer of the Student Model reflected on her topic. In this section you will analyze the final draft of her academic essay. You will learn how to structure your ideas for your own essay.

Ⓐ Student Model

Read the writing prompt again and answer the questions.

WRITING PROMPT: What are the main advantages or disadvantages of shopping online?

1 Circle the words in the prompt that you expect the writer to use in her thesis statement.

2 What are some advantages and disadvantages that you think the writer might mention?

Read the essay twice. The first time, think about your answers to the questions above. The second time, answer the questions in the Analyze Writing Skills boxes. This will help you notice key features of academic essays.

STUDENT MODEL

The Benefits of Online Shopping

1   As of 2012, Americans were spending over $1 trillion online ("Ecommerce Sales"). Economists predict that e-commerce will increase another 62 percent by 2016 and continue growing after that. Years ago, people could only shop in stores near their homes or stores that they could drive to. Ordering by mail from catalogs was also possible, but it was time-consuming. The Internet offered a **radical** shift in shopping that has forever changed consumer behavior. While detractors[1] of online shopping often point to its dangers, these risks are exaggerated. There are retailers who are not **ethical** both online and in stores. Overall, online shopping is superior to shopping in stores because it is convenient, it offers consumers a wider range of products, and it saves money.

2   Online shopping is clearly more convenient than in-store shopping. The first reason why online shopping is more convenient is that it takes less time than traditional shopping. Less time shopping means more time to do free-time activities and to be with friends and family. In addition, it takes less time to receive merchandise, as well. Now, ordering and shipping almost **coincide**, because shoppers can order in a single click and send the order right to the warehouse. The number of distribution centers is growing throughout the world. As a result, transactions are faster than ever. Amazon.com is one example of this. As of May 2014, Amazon.com had 108 distribution centers[2] and was planning to build 14 more in the United States and another 11 outside of the U.S. ("Amazon"). In addition, online shopping is extremely beneficial[3] for senior

---

[1]detractors: people who criticize someone or something, often unfairly
[2]distribution centers: places where products are stored, packed, and shipped to customers
[3]beneficial: having a good effect

Analyze Writing Skills sidebar:

last sentence

1 Analyze Writing Skills

Underline the sentences in paragraph 1 that get your attention or make you interested in this topic.

2 Analyze Writing Skills

a What is the writer discussing in paragraph 1?
Circle your answer:
  advantages
  disadvantages
  both.

b Circle the three main points that the writer will discuss to develop her thesis.

3 Analyze Writing Skills

Underline the main point that the writer discusses in paragraph 2. Does it match one of the points you circled in paragraph 1?

1st sentence

citizens, the disabled, and anyone who has limited mobility. One example of this is the world's first Internet shopper, Jane Snowball, who ordered groceries to be delivered when she broke her hip (Winterman and Kelly). It's easy to see that convenience is a key advantage of online shopping.

3   Another advantage of online shopping is that it offers better product availability than stores do. Online retailers can keep a very large number of items in stock[4] at all times. There is often more variety and more actual items available online than in physical stores. For example, retailers such as Target and Walmart carry many more items in their online stores than they do in their physical stores (Fitterman). In addition, shoppers can buy items from anywhere in the world, not just things that are available in their local stores. This can **expose** consumers to new and exotic items that they may not have in their neighborhood stores, such as ethnic foods and foreign language DVDs. Online shopping also allows consumers to know what is in stock at all times. This is because many online retailers can show customers the quantities that are available for many items. Consumers can also sign up for email messages that tell them when items they are looking for become available. Online shopping clearly offers shoppers a wider range of products than traditional retailers can.

4   Finally, online shopping reduces costs. Shoppers are much less likely to practice **excessive consumption** because they are less likely to make last-minute or unplanned purchases than they might make in a physical store. With online shopping, there are no high-pressure salespeople, so online shoppers can think through their purchases independently. Online retailers can also often offer lower prices for products because they have such large quantities stored in their distribution centers, and not just what they can stock in a physical store. Online shoppers also save money on gas and parking because they use their cars less when they shop at home. These conditions make online shopping less expensive overall than in-store shopping.

[4]in stock: available for sale

(CONTINUED)

---

4 Analyze Writing Skills

Read the final sentence of paragraph 2 and the first sentence of paragraph 3. Circle the words that help the writer change from one point to another.

5 Analyze Writing Skills

a   Underline the main point that the writer discusses in paragraph 3. 1st sentence

b   How many supporting ideas does the writer use to explain this subject?

3

6 Analyze Writing Skills

Underline the last sentence in paragraph 4. Does this sentence restate the main point of the paragraph?

Yes

5   Online shopping was once an **alternative approach** to the retail experience, but today it is the most convenient, cost-effective way to shop for a wide variety of products. With these advantages, it seems very likely that economists' predictions about online shopping are correct: online shopping will undoubtedly become even more convenient and popular in the future.

Works Cited

"Amazon Global Fulfillment Center Network." *MWPVL International*. MWPVL International, Inc., n.d. Web. 26 May 2014.

"Ecommerce Sales Topped $1 Trillion for First Time in 2012." *Emarketer*. Emarketer, 5 Feb. 2013. Web. 11 Nov. 2014.

Fitterman, Scott. "The Ultimate Debate: Online Shopping vs. Brick and Mortar Shopping." *Wired Innovation Insights*. Condé Nast Digital, 19 Dec. 2013. Web. 26 May 2014.

Winterman, Denise, and Jon Kelly. "Online Shopping: The Pensioner Who Pioneered a Home Shopping Revolution." *BBC News Magazine*. BBC, 16 Sept. 2013. Web. 11 Nov. 2014.

> **7 Analyze Writing Skills**
>
> a Circle the sentence in the last paragraph that connects back to the thesis. _last sentence_
> b Underline the sentence that contains a suggestion, opinion, or prediction.

ACTIVITY 3.1 Check Your Understanding

Answer the questions. *1. more convenient   2. better product availability   3. reduces cost*

1 According to the writer, what are the main benefits of online shopping?

2 Evaluate the writer's main points. Which do you think is the strongest? Why? *reduces cost   I the amount*

3 Have you or someone you know ever had similar experiences with online shopping? *Yes, out of stock in store, but cheaper & in stock online.*

ACTIVITY 3.2 Outline the Writer's Ideas

Complete the outline for "The Benefits of Online Shopping" using the phrases in the box.

consumers know what's in stock   good for people with limited mobility
saves money on transportation   cost reduction
more variety and items in stock   takes less time to receive goods

ESSAY OUTLINE

I. Introduction

Thesis Statement

Online shopping is superior to shopping in stores because it's convenient, it offers

consumers a wider range of products, and it saves money.

Body Paragraph 1

II. Convenience

Supporting Idea 1

A. Takes less time to shop

Supporting Idea 2

B. takes less time to receive goods

Supporting Idea 3

C. good for people with limited mobility

Body Paragraph 2

III. Product availability

Supporting Idea 1

A. More variety and items in stock

Supporting Idea 2

B. Can buy things not available locally

Supporting Idea 3

C. Consumers know what's in stock

Body Paragraph 3

IV. Cost reduction

Supporting Idea 1

A. Fewer unplanned purchases

Supporting Idea 2

B. Large stock = lower prices

Supporting Idea 3

C. Saves money on transportation

V. Conclusion

B Academic Essays: Essay Structure

Writers use essay structure to communicate their ideas clearly and convincingly. There are several types of essays that you will study in this book, including narrative, comparison and contrast, cause and effect, problem–solution, and argumentative. Academic writers often combine elements from different types of essays, depending on which type is more effective for their purpose. For example, a college writing prompt may ask a writer to argue a specific viewpoint (argumentative), and the writer may choose to do so by comparing two subjects (comparison and contrast) or by examining the causes or effects of an issue (cause and effect).

An academic essay has three parts:

1 An **introductory paragraph** that explains the topic and the writer's purpose in writing. It includes:

- a hook
- background information
- a thesis statement

2 **Body paragraphs** that develop each of the writer's main points. Each body paragraph includes:

- a topic sentence
- supporting sentences and details
- a concluding sentence or transition sentence

3 A **concluding paragraph** that summarizes the main idea of the essay and provides a final comment. It includes:

- a restatement of the main idea
- an insight, prediction, or call to action

 **3.3** Notice

Circle the correct answers.

1 What does an introductory paragraph usually include?

    a a topic sentence

C   b an insight, prediction, or call to action

    c a thesis statement

2 In which part does the writer develop each main point of the essay?

    a introductory paragraph

b   b body paragraphs

    c concluding paragraph

3 A concluding paragraph includes .... the main idea of the essay.

    a a restatement of

a   b support for

    c an introduction to

THE INTRODUCTORY PARAGRAPH

An effective **introductory paragraph** invites the reader into the essay with a hook, provides context for the topic with background information, and presents the writer's point of view in a thesis statement.

The <u>hook</u> is usually the first sentence in the paragraph. It makes the reader interested in reading your essay. A hook can be:

- a surprising statistic

  Online shoppers spent over $1.964 billion during Black Friday sales in 2013.

- a provocative question

  Have you ever wondered why an ad for an item you recently bought online pops up every time you check your social media page?

- an interesting fact or statement

  Some people are trying to change the culture of consumerism in North America.

- a memorable quotation

  "To travel is to shop."

<u>Background information</u> usually consists of three to five sentences. It connects the hook to the thesis statement and provides information the reader needs to know before beginning the essay, including definitions of terms and ideas. Background information can be:

- a story or narrative
  One rainy Saturday, Jen decided to stay home and go online to buy some items she needed for an upcoming business trip. As she clicked her way through her purchases, it never occurred to her that …

- historical information
  Years ago, people could only shop on days when stores were open. In fact, there were days when no one shopped at all. Sundays and holidays, for example, …

- general to specific information
  The goal of many shoppers is finding a good deal. For example, finding something inexpensive and fashionable online gives many of us a thrill. However, do we ever stop to consider what makes these items so inexpensive in the first place?

The <u>thesis statement</u> is the last sentence or two in an introductory paragraph. It presents the main idea of the essay. A thesis statement includes:

- the topic of the essay
- what the writer wants to communicate about the topic

A thesis statement may or may not include the main points that the writer will discuss in the body paragraphs.

- *Online shopping is inferior to bricks-and-mortar shopping because you cannot interact with the merchandise, it's more expensive, and it isn't safe.* (includes points)

- *Bricks-and-mortar shopping will never disappear as it offers significant advantages over online shopping.* (doesn't include points)

You will learn more about thesis statements in Section 4.

3.4 Notice

Read the introductory paragraph of the Student Model on page 20. Answer the questions.

1 Find the hook. What type is it?

   a a surprising statistic

   b a provocative question

   c a memorable quotation

2 What type of background information does the Student Model use?

   a a story or narrative

   b historical information

   c general to specific information

3.5 Notice

Find the thesis statement in the introductory paragraph of the Student Model. Answer the questions.

1 What is the topic?

....

2 What does the writer want to communicate about the topic?

....

3 Does it include the points that the writer will discuss in the body paragraphs?

....

3.6 Practice Writing

Read the prompt. Then complete the introductory paragraph for an essay that responds to the prompt. Write a hook and a thesis statement.

WRITING PROMPT: To save money and pass on the savings to consumers, many clothing companies produce items in developing countries. Should consumers buy inexpensive clothing made in developing countries? Why or why not?

....

HOOK

The goal of many shoppers is finding a good deal. For example, walking out of a store with a bargain makes many of us feel victorious. However, do we ever stop to consider what makes these items so inexpensive in the first place? ....

THESIS STATEMENT

....

3.7 Practice Writing

Work in a group. Read the prompt. Then complete the introductory paragraph with background information about the topic.

WRITING PROMPT: Many companies practice planned obsolescence – intentionally producing consumer goods that rapidly deteriorate or become out of date and require replacing. What are the main advantages or disadvantages of planned obsolescence?

Have you ever wondered why you need to buy a new cell phone every two years or constantly purchase expensive ink cartridges for your printer? ....
BACKGROUND INFORMATION

....

....

Planned obsolescence may help companies increase their profits, but it leads to excessive consumption, it's bad for the environment, and it contributes to a negative corporate image.

 3.8 Apply It to Your Writing

Think about the writing prompt you chose in Section 1 on page 15. Choose a type of hook and a type of background information that you could use in an introductory paragraph for an essay on this topic. Write your ideas below. You can change these later. This is for practice.

Hook type: ....

Type of background information: ....

BODY PARAGRAPHS

Body paragraphs present the main points of an essay. Each body paragraph logically and thoroughly explains, describes, or argues one aspect of the thesis statement.

A body paragraph includes:

- a **topic sentence** that states the main idea of the paragraph. A good topic sentence clearly connects to the thesis by reusing or paraphrasing key words.

   Thesis statement: *People who buy merchandise online tend to fit into three different types.*

   Topic sentence: *One type of online shopper is the researcher.*

- **supporting sentences** that give specific information about the topic sentence. They give information such as facts, examples, explanations, and reasons. **Details** are extra explanations, examples, and facts.

   |———————— TOPIC SENTENCE ————————||———————— EXPLANATION ————————|
   One type of online shopper is the researcher. A researcher does a thorough search of a
   |——————————————||———————————————— EXAMPLE ————————————————|
   product before buying it. For example, before buying a product, a researcher finds out all the

   possible places to buy the product and how much it costs at various online retailers.
   |———————————————— DETAIL THAT GIVES ANOTHER EXAMPLE ————————————————|
   A researcher might even read product reviews or use online product comparison features.

- a **concluding sentence** that ties all the ideas in the paragraph together. Writers signal the conclusion with a word or phrase such as *clearly*, *for these reasons*, *therefore*, and *in brief*.

   *Online shopping **clearly** offers shoppers a wider range of products than traditional retailers can.*

Below are some ways that writers can order body paragraphs within an essay:

- Use chronological order when the essay describes events or steps.
- Start with the strongest or most important idea.
- Start with the idea that is most familiar to the audience.

ACTIVITY 3.9 Notice

Look at the first body paragraph (paragraph 2) of the Student Model on pages 20–22 and answer the questions.

1 What main point of the thesis does this paragraph describe?

2 What key word or phrase connects the topic sentence and the thesis statement?

3 Which supporting sentence gives an example?

4 Which supporting sentence gives a fact?

5 Which supporting sentence gives a reason?

6 Which of the sentences is also a detail sentence?

....

7 What key word or phrase in the paragraph signals the conclusion?

....

 **3.10 Practice**

Work with a partner. Read the thesis statement. Think about the underlined main point in the thesis. Write a topic sentence, two supporting sentences, two detail sentences, and a concluding sentence for a body paragraph on this point.

Thesis statement: Consumerism is good for the economy because it helps keep existing companies in business, <u>creates new jobs</u>, and leads to the development of new products.

Topic sentence: ....

    Supporting sentence 1: ....

        Detail sentence: ....

    Supporting sentence 2: ....

        Detail sentence: ....

Concluding sentence: ....

 **3.11 Apply It to Your Writing**

Look at the thesis statement you created in Section 1 on page 15 for your writing prompt. Write a topic sentence for one body paragraph. Write two supporting sentences and a concluding sentence. You can change these later. This is for practice.

....

....

....

....

CONNECTING IDEAS BETWEEN BODY PARAGRAPHS

Writers choose appropriate words and expressions to connect ideas within an essay. These words remind readers how ideas in body paragraphs connect to the thesis statement. They also show how each body paragraph connects to the one before and the one after. For example, the topic sentence of the first body paragraph in an essay repeats or paraphrases one of the ideas in the thesis statement. The final sentence in this body paragraph also repeats or paraphrases one of the ideas in the thesis, while at the same time reminding the reader of the topic of the paragraph. The topic sentence of the next body paragraph reminds the reader of the topic of the previous body paragraph, and at the same time, repeats or paraphrases another idea in the thesis statement. This continues throughout the body paragraphs in the essay.

Writers also use words and phrases such as *also, another, in addition,* and *finally* to help readers transition smoothly from one paragraph to another.

- Beginning of Student Model body paragraph 1: *Online shopping is clearly more convenient than in-store shopping.*

Notice that "Online shopping is clearly more convenient" reminds the reader of one of the ideas in the thesis statement.

- End of Student Model body paragraph 1: *It's easy to see that convenience is a key advantage of online shopping.*

Notice how this sentence paraphrases one of the ideas in the thesis statement ("convenience") and also reminds the reader of the main idea of the paragraph.

- Beginning of Student Model body paragraph 2: *Another advantage of online shopping is that it offers better product availability than stores do.*

Notice that this sentence reminds the reader of the second idea in the thesis statement. Notice also that the word *another* tells the reader that this paragraph will add an additional idea to the one in the previous body paragraph.

ACTIVITY **3.12** Practice

Work with a partner. Read the thesis statement from an essay on ways retailers can attract local customers. Follow the steps in the numbered list to complete each body paragraph. Use the words and phrases from the box where appropriate.

also	finally	in addition	another (way)	first of all	one (of the ways)

Thesis statement: Some of the ways that retailers can attract potential customers in the areas where they do business include giving back to the community, hiring local residents, and carrying merchandise that appeals to the local market.

For each body paragraph, do the following:

1. Write a topic sentence that repeats or paraphrases a point in the thesis statement. Follow the order in the thesis statement.
2. Write one example that explains the topic of this paragraph.
3. Write a second example that explains the topic of this paragraph.
4. Write a final sentence for this paragraph that repeats or paraphrases the supporting idea in the thesis and reminds the reader what the paragraph is about.

Body paragraph 1

1 ....

Giving back means helping people in the community who can benefit from what a large

company can offer. A typical large company, for example, 2 ....

Companies can also 3 ....

Clearly, there are many ways a large retailer 4 ....

Body paragraph 2

1 ....

When local residents work for large retailers in their community, they become loyal to the company and its products. For example, when people work for a company in their community,

they 2 .... People also

3 .... These reasons

show 4 ....

Body paragraph 3

1 ....

Carrying merchandise that is targeted at the local market shows members of a community that

the company knows who they are and what their needs are. For example, 2 ....

.... Also, 3 ....

.... For these reasons, 4 ....

THE CONCLUDING PARAGRAPH

The concluding paragraph is the final paragraph in an essay. It tells the reader that the essay is
finished by restating the main ideas of the essay and makes a final comment.

The concluding paragraph includes, usually in this order:

- a **restatement of the main idea**, which often begins with a transition word or phrase. This
  part of the conclusion paraphrases the thesis statement of the essay.
  *Online shopping was once an alternative approach to the retail experience, but today it is the
  most convenient, cost-effective way to shop for a wide variety of products.*

- a **final comment** that leaves the reader with something to think about. This can be a
  suggestion, an opinion, or a prediction.
  *With these advantages, it seems very likely that economists' predictions about online shopping are
  correct: online shopping will undoubtedly become even more convenient and popular in the future.*

ACTIVITY 3.13 Practice

Read the following concluding paragraph. Write the final comment.

In conclusion, when a company operates in an ethical way, it increases profits, increases
opportunities to trade with other countries and cultures, and ensures employee satisfaction and
productivity. ....

ACTIVITY 3.14 Apply It to Your Writing

**Think about the writing prompt you chose in Section 1 on page 15. Use the space
below to write two or three possible final comments for your concluding paragraph.**

....

....

....

....

In this section you will learn the writing and grammar skills that will help make your writing more sophisticated and accurate.

A Writing Skill: Thesis Statements

An academic essay always includes a thesis statement that introduces the topic of the essay and the idea or point of view that the writer has about the topic. A thesis statement is a topic plus a point of view.

TOPIC   IDEA/POINT OF VIEW

Online shopping **is superior to shopping in stores because it is convenient, it offers consumers a wider range of products, and it saves money**.

Key words in the prompt help the writer develop a point of view. Read the prompt below:

STUDENT MODEL WRITING PROMPT: What are the main advantages or disadvantages of shopping online?

The topic is "shopping online." The key words _advantages_ and _disadvantages_ help the writer decide on a point of view. Other key words in writing prompts that can help a writer develop a point of view might include _discuss differences/similarities, explain causes/effects,_ or _argue for/against._

Thesis statements often tell the reader the specific points that will be developed in the body paragraphs. Some thesis statements are more general and do not state the points that will be developed in the body paragraphs, but it is clear to the reader what the points could be.

WRITING PROMPT: What are the benefits of shopping in large chain stores?

Stated points: _Shopping in large chain stores is superior to shopping in smaller local stores because the choice of products is greater, product uniformity is more reliable, and prices are lower._

More general: _Shopping in large chain stores offers consumers many benefits._

Effective thesis statements:

* are clear and focused.

   Effective: _Buying locally produced products is good for the environment, improves the local economy, and enhances the shopping experience._ (The topic and point of view are clear and focused.)

   Not effective: _Shopping at some large retailers can be a bad idea._ (The topic is vague and the writer's point of view is unfocused.)

* are debatable.

   Effective: _Shopping in-store is superior to shopping online for three important reasons._ (Debatable; you can argue for or against the superiority of something.)

   Not effective: _The Internet allows you to buy goods from all over the world._ (This is a statement of fact. It's not debatable.)

- help readers understand how the writer will organize his or her ideas and get readers engaged in the topic.

<u>Effective</u>: *Signal Hill Mall should not be torn down for three reasons: it provides local residents with necessary goods and services, it offers many employment opportunities, and it gives families a safe and convenient place to spend free time.* (This is specific. You can see how the writer will organize ideas.)

<u>Not effective</u>: *Shopping is a lot easier nowadays.* (This is too general because it does not indicate how he or she will organize them.)

Some things are NOT thesis statements:

- A question: *What are the benefits of online shopping?*

- A topic that is too vague or broad: *The Internet has changed us.*

- A simple statement of fact: *Many people shop online.*

- A statement that tells what you will talk about: *I am going to discuss online shopping.*

 **4.1** Choose a Thesis

A Read the prompts and the possible thesis statements. For each prompt, check (✓) the most effective thesis statement.

WRITING PROMPT 1: Many people complain about Internet ads. Should they be banned, or do they serve a purpose?

- a Internet ads are everywhere: on news sites, on shopping sites, and on your favorite social media sites.

- b Internet ads are good for businesses because they are the best way to target consumers, they allow popular websites to be free of charge, and they are inexpensive.

- c Internet advertising should be banned for many reasons.

- d Internet ads provide a way for websites and online retailers to increase their revenues.

WRITING PROMPT 2: Many people consider impulse buying – buying things without planning to – a bad habit. However, companies intentionally market products to attract impulse buyers. What motivates us to buy things impulsively? Explain your answer.

☐ a Many people buy things impulsively, and companies market products intentionally to attract impulse shoppers.

☐ b Impulse buying is a bad habit because it leads to excessive consumption, it causes debt, and it's bad for the environment.

☐ c There are three main causes of impulse buying: poor self-esteem, a culture of consumerism, and clever marketing practices.

☐ d There are several things that lead to impulse buying.

B Work with a partner. Explain why the thesis statements you chose in A are effective. Then explain why the others are not effective.

 **4.2** Rewriting Thesis Statements

Choose two of the ineffective thesis statements in Activity 4.1 and rewrite them on a separate sheet of paper to make them more effective. Refer to the information on pages 32–33.

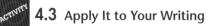 **4.3** Apply It to Your Writing

Look at the thesis statement you created in Section 1 on page 15 for your writing prompt. Revise it and make it stronger. Use the information you learned about writing effective thesis statements to help you. Then compare your thesis to a partner's. Identify the topic and point of view.

B Grammar for Writing: Gerunds and Infinitives

Writers use gerunds and infinitives to connect ideas between sentences and allow for more sentence variety.

GERUNDS AND INFINITIVES

1 A **gerund** is the *ing* form of a verb that functions as a noun. It can appear as a subject or as an object of a verb or preposition. As a subject, it takes the singular form of the verb.	SUBJECT ***Buying nothing*** *is one way in which some activists protest the consumer culture in North America.* *While online shopping can be dangerous, that does* OBJECT *not mean consumers should avoid **buying online**.*
2 Some verbs can be followed only by a **gerund**. These verbs include *avoid, consider, delay, discuss, enjoy, finish, propose,* and *suggest*. These verbs also include verb + preposition combinations such as *believe in, be interested in, be responsible for, care for, insist on,* and *worry about*.	*Some consumers* <u>avoid</u> ***purchasing*** *clothing online because it might not fit.* *Smart credit card users* <u>insist on</u> ***paying*** *their balances in full each month.*
3 **Gerunds** are often used in noun + of patterns. These noun + *of* combinations include *benefit of, cost of, (dis)advantage of, effect of, idea of, problem of,* and *process of*.	*One* <u>disadvantage of</u> ***shopping*** *online is the possibility of ID theft.* *The* <u>idea of</u> ***buying*** *something that you cannot pay for is far too common in modern society.*
4 An **infinitive** is the *to* + base form of a verb. It can appear as the subject of a sentence or as the object of a verb. As a subject, it takes the singular form of the verb.	SUBJECT ***To spend*** *a lot of money with credit cards* <u>is</u> *a poor financial choice.* OBJECT *Some people are trying **to change** the culture of consumerism in North America.*
5 Some verbs can be followed only by an **infinitive**. These verbs include *agree, choose, decide, expect, fail, need, plan, seem, tend,* and *want*.	*Shopping search engines help people find good prices for things they* <u>want</u> ***to purchase**.*
6 Some nouns are often followed by **infinitives**. These nouns include *ability, chance, decision, method, opportunity, time,* and *way*.	*Most retailers think holidays are the best* <u>time</u> ***to get*** *people into the stores.* *An allowance gives children the* <u>chance</u> ***to learn*** *good spending habits.*
7 Both **gerunds** and **infinitives** can be passive. Use *being* + past participle or *to be* + past participle.	*The consumers did not enjoy **being told** what they could or could not buy.* *Many people do not want **to be exposed** to ads while surfing the Internet.*

Complete each sentence with the correct gerund or infinitive form of the verb in parentheses.

1 Many shoppers cannot avoid .... (buy) something during Buy Nothing Day.

2 Although Internet shopping has many advantages for consumers, not everyone wants .... (spend) a lot of their money at online retailers.

3 Some experts believe in .... (teach) consumer awareness to children at an early age.

4 Some people nowadays choose .... (pay) for their purchases with cash instead of credit cards in order to avoid debt.

5 The idea of .... (tell) investors bad news about a company is unpleasant, but it is part of a CEO's job.

6 For the disabled, online grocery stores and pharmacies provide a convenient way .... (purchase) necessary items.

7 Many people enjoy .... (go) to local markets because the shopkeepers know them and they get fresher products.

8 Some consumers are interested in .... (buy) only products that are made locally.

9 Paying with cash is one of the best methods .... (get) out of debt, according to some financial experts.

10 A benefit of .... (grow up) in a poor family is that you know how to survive in difficult financial times.

Complete the paragraph with the correct passive gerund or infinitive form of the verb in parentheses.

The CEO of a small shoe company received an email from a graduate student who was doing a study on ethical businesses. The student wrote: "Your company has a reputation for treating its employees fairly. Would you consider _____ (include) in a
(1)
survey on ethical business practices?" To conduct the survey, the student said, all employees needed _____ (interview). The employees would be asked many questions
(2)
about the CEO's behavior, she added. The CEO agreed _____ (evaluate)
(3)
by her employees. In fact, she saw the survey as an opportunity _____
(4)
better _____ (inform) about what her employees were thinking. She was also interested in _____ (expose) to any new ideas that might result from
(5)
the study. When she read the results of the survey, the CEO was shocked. Many employees described situations in which they felt the CEO had not acted fairly. She called a meeting to discuss the survey. She promised to listen to all of the employees' complaints and to change her behavior. She announced, "We need _____ (see) by our customers as
(6)
a company with the highest ethical standards, and I promise to do everything I can to reach this goal."

Avoiding Common Mistakes

Research tells us that these are the most common mistakes that students make when using gerunds and infinitives in academic writing.

> **1 Always use a singular verb with a gerund subject.**
>
> Talking to consumers ~~help~~ *helps* make them more interested in buying a product.
>
> **2 Do not use infinitives after verbs that require gerunds.**
>
> Some people avoid ~~to be~~ *being* flooded with online advertising by changing their browser preferences.
>
> **3 Do not use gerunds after verbs that require infinitives.**
>
> People who shop at farmers' markets often expect ~~finding~~ *to find* a wider variety of local produce.

ACTIVITY **4.6** Editing Task

Find and correct five more mistakes in the following paragraph.

Email advertising from retail stores ~~give~~ *gives* customers access to great deals, but is it effective? Studies show that filling people's in-boxes with more and more advertising force them to think about the company, but does not always convince them to shop. Many companies think that customers will want buying things when they receive these messages, and that is good enough for them. However, a recent poll showed that consumers choose to delete these messages 65 percent of the time. The same poll showed that people fail to take advantage of the advertised deals 61 percent of the time. Studies also show that consumers tend removing themselves from mailing lists after deleting advertising messages for more than three months. As a result, some companies are considering to change the way they practice email advertising. Many of these companies are discussing to use text messaging and social media as alternatives to email marketing. Clearly, email advertising may not be working well enough for some companies to continue using it.

C Avoiding Plagiarism

Plagiarism is a serious problem at colleges and universities, but you can learn ways to avoid this problem.

On the first day of class, my teacher asked me to sign an academic integrity pledge. There was a section on plagiarism. It said that students can be punished if they use other people's ideas and do not acknowledge their sources. What does all of this mean? – June

Dear June,

An academic integrity pledge is a kind of contract with your school. When you sign the contract, you are saying that you will be honest in your studies. This may be different in another culture, but in North America "being honest" means you won't:

- cheat on exams (including take-home tests);
- have someone else write your papers for you;
- plagiarize, or copy other people's exact words or ideas (including DVDs, CD-ROMs, film, music, and radio);
- forget to cite, or identify, your sources.

Yours truly,

Professor Wright

CITING SOURCES TO AVOID PLAGIARISM

Plagiarism is copying other people's words or ideas without giving them credit. Let's look at how you can avoid plagiarizing by citing sources. There are different styles for citing sources. In this book, we use MLA (Modern Language Association) style, but ask your instructor which style you should use.

Within your essay:

- **Paraphrase** the original writer's ideas and words. In parentheses, write the page number where you found the information.

  According to Michael Norton and Katherine Dunn, if you spend money on others, it will bring more happiness (15).

- Use **quotation marks** when you use the original writer's exact words. Again, write the page number where you found the information.

  Michael Norton and Katherine Dunn report that giving money to others "reliably makes them happier than spending that same money on themselves" (15).

At the end of your essay:

Always **list all of your sources** at the end of the essay. Follow the formats below, paying special attention to the punctuation.

- For **printed books**, write: Author's last name, First name. *Title of Book*. City: Publisher, Year of publication. Medium. (You can often find this information on the first page of the book.)

    Underhill, Paco. *Why We Buy: The Science of Shopping*. New York: Simon, 2000. Print.

- For **online news articles**, write: Author's last name, First name. "Article Title." *Name of Newspaper or Site*. Publisher of site, Date of article. Web. Date *you* got the article.

    Richtel, Matt. "There's Power in All Those User Reviews." *New York Times*. New York Times, 7 Dec. 2013. Web. 31 Mar. 2014.

- For **online government reports** when no author is listed, write: Country. Government agency. *Title of Report*. Date of report. Web. Date *you* got the report.

    United States. Federal Trade Commission. Bureau of Consumer Protection. *Recent FTC Cases Resulting in Refunds*. Feb. 2014. Web. 28 Feb. 2014.

ACTIVITY **4.7** Practice

Circle the correct citation form.

1	Author:	a Wilson, Jim.	b	Jim Wilson.
2	Publisher:	a Java, 2013, Seattle.	b	Seattle: Java, 2013.
3	News article:	a "New Colors in the New Year"	b	New Colors in the New Year

---

ACTIVITY **4.8** Practice

Use the information to write a citation for the book below.

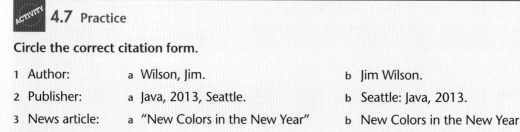

Steven Levitt (author)   *Freakonomics* (book title)   2006 (year of publication)

Morrow (publisher)   New York (location of publication)   Print

---

ACTIVITY **4.9** Writing Citations

Read the information about a source that was used for a paper. Work with a partner. Write a correct citation.

You read an article called "Why Clearance Sales Are Psychologically 'Irresistible'" in *Psychology Today*. You found it on the Internet. On the Web, the date is January 17, 2013. The publisher of the site is Psychology Today. You found it on March 30, 2014. The author is Kit Yarrow.

In this section you will follow the writing process to complete the final draft of your essay.

STEP 1: BRAINSTORM

Work with a partner. Follow the steps below to brainstorm more ideas.

1 Before you start, notice how the writer of the Student Model brainstormed. She wrote many ideas but did not use all of them in her essay. Cross out the ideas that were not used.

STUDENT MODEL

WRITING PROMPT: What are the main advantages or disadvantages of shopping online?

2 Write the ideas that you wrote in Section 1, page 15, in the cluster diagram below. Include ideas from the Your Turns throughout the unit. Brainstorm more ideas.

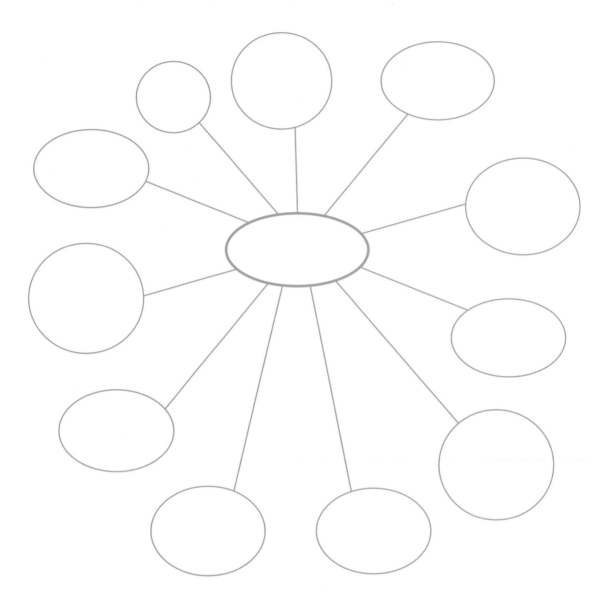

When you are finished, circle the three strongest points that support your thesis and write them here.

1 ....

2 ....

3 ....

Now, circle the best supporting information for each point.

STEP 2: DO RESEARCH: DEVELOPING KEYWORDS FOR AN INTERNET SEARCH

Using the Internet for research is convenient, but it can be challenging because there is so much information. To search for the information you need, use **keywords** about the topic from your writing prompt.

Alex needed to find information from the Internet for this prompt: *The Internet has changed the shopping habits of consumers over the past two decades. What are the advantages or disadvantages of online shopping?* Read and find out how he did it.

First, I identified the content keywords from the prompt. Then, I brainstormed alternative keywords – like synonyms or phrases – for each content word. Next, I typed logical combinations of my keywords into a search engine to find the best information for my paper. Last, I wrote down the title and web address of my results so that I could go back to them later.

Alex's Results

Content Keywords	Alternative Keywords	Search Results
advantages	pros, benefits	The **Pros** & **Cons** of a Retail Store vs. an **Online Store** (http://smallbusiness.chron.com/)
disadvantages	cons, problems, issues	Citizens Advice - **Buying** by **Internet**, mail order, or phone (http://www.adviceguide.org.uk/)
online shopping	Internet buying, store	What's wrong with **online shopping** – TIME.com (http://business.time.com/)

ACTIVITY **5.1** Apply It to Your Writing   **YOUR TURN**

On a separate sheet of paper, follow the steps Alex took to find the best information for your essay. Write the content keywords, alternative keywords, and search results in a chart.

STEP 3: MAKE AN OUTLINE

Making an outline helps you organize your ideas. Complete the outline below with your ideas from the previous steps.

ESSAY OUTLINE

I. Introduction

Thesis Statement

Body Paragraph 1   II.

Supporting Idea 1   A.

Detail   1.

Supporting Idea 2   B.

Detail   1.

Body Paragraph 2   III.

Supporting Idea 1   A.

Detail   1.

Supporting Idea 2   B.

Detail   1.

Body Paragraph 3   IV.

Supporting Idea 1   A.

Detail   1.

Supporting Idea 2	B.
Detail	1.
	V. Conclusion
Ideas for Final Statement	

STEP 4: WRITE YOUR FIRST DRAFT

Now it is time to write your first draft. Here are some suggestions on how to get started.

1 Reread your writing prompt and your outline to make sure that your ideas answer the prompt.

2 Focus on making your ideas as clear as possible.

3 Look back at the Your Turns in the unit and see if you can use them in your first draft.

4 Try to include a reference to one source.

5 Just write! Focus on making your ideas as clear as possible.

6 Remember to add a title.

After you finish, read your essay and check for basic errors.

1 Make sure your thesis statement tells readers what the topic of your essay is and your idea about that topic.

2 Make sure all of your main points support your thesis.

3 Make sure that the essay follows this structure: introduction, body paragraphs, and conclusion.

4 Make sure your introduction has all the necessary parts: hook, background information, thesis.

5 Check that you have used gerunds and infinitives correctly.

STEP 5: WRITE YOUR FINAL DRAFT

1 After you receive feedback on your first draft, review it carefully. Fix any errors.

2 Make a note of errors that were most frequent (misspellings, wrong verb tense, errors in using commas). Try to avoid them as you write.

3 Review the Academic Vocabulary and Academic Collocations from this unit. Are there any that you can add to your essay?

4 Turn to page 270 and use the Self-Editing Review to check your work one more time.

5 Write your final draft and hand it in.

2 NARRATIVE ESSAYS

HISTORY: IMMIGRATION

> *"No matter by what various crafts we came here, we are all now in the same boat."*
>
> Calvin Coolidge
> (1872–1933)

About the Author:

Calvin Coolidge was president of the United States from 1923 to 1929.

Work with a partner. Read the quotation about immigration. Then answer the questions.

1 What does the idiom "in the same boat" mean? In what ways are you and your classmates in the same boat?

2 In what ways are all immigrants in the same boat when they first arrive in a new country?

3 Why do people immigrate to another country? With your partner, make a list of three or more reasons.

A Connect to Academic Writing

In this unit you will learn skills to help you present your ideas in a narrative essay. While some of the writing skills may be new to you, the skill of telling stories is not new. In your everyday life you use the skill of telling stories in order to explain to your manager why it was not your fault that you arrived late to your job, or to retell the plot of a movie you recently saw and explain why it was better than the book version.

B Reflect on the Topic

In this section you will choose a writing prompt and reflect on it. You will develop these ideas throughout the unit and use them to practice skills that are necessary to write your essay.

The writing prompt below was used for the Student Model essay on pages 54–56. The student reflected on his topic and used a chart to help him remember specific events and details that made each event clear in his mind. This helped him think of a possible thesis.

WRITING PROMPT: Choose a significant event in your life that resulted in a change in your view of the world or taught you a lesson.

What happened?	When?	Feelings and descriptive details
grandparents said we were moving to the U.S. from Mexico	when I was 13	upset, didn't want to leave my friends
arrived in the U.S. and started school	a few months later	felt awful, couldn't speak English, didn't fit in at school
things got worse at school and at home	start of school	embarrassed at school, hated it when my grandparents came to school and spoke Spanish, felt lonely
finally my grades improved and I had friends!	before end of school year	working hard at school, feeling more comfortable, didn't feel so lonely

My thesis: *My experience of moving to the United States taught me how to adjust to a new culture.*

 1.1 Notice

Work with a partner. Read the events in the chart above and answer the questions.

1 Do the events have a clear beginning, middle, and end?

2 Do you think this will be an interesting story? What will the writer have to develop?

ACTIVITY **1.2** Apply It to Your Writing

Follow the directions to reflect on your topic.

A Choose a prompt:

- Tell the story of an immigrant who moved to a new country and how he or she felt about that experience.

- When people make changes in their lives, such as moving to a new country or a new town or school, they often are faced with challenges. Think about a time in your life or the life of someone you know that was challenging. Write a story that describes how the challenge was faced.

- Tell the story of a family of immigrants and describe one influential event in their adjustment to a new culture.

- A topic approved by your instructor

B Work with a partner and complete the following tasks:

1. Think about your prompt. Decide what you will focus on in your essay.

2. Complete the chart below. Think of everything you know about the story that you want to tell. Add more rows if you need them.

3. Write a possible thesis statement.

What happened?	When?	Feelings and descriptive details

Possible thesis statement:

....

In this section you will learn academic language that you can use in your narrative essay. You will also notice how a professional writer uses the language and features of narration.

Ⓐ Academic Vocabulary

The words below appear throughout the unit. Many are from the Academic Word List. Using these words in your writing will make your ideas clearer and your writing more academic.

adjust (v)	anticipate (v)	image (n)	security (n)
ambition (n)	complexity (n)	initially (adv)	stressful (adj)

ACTIVITY 2.1 Focus on Meaning

Work with a partner. Match the words to their meanings. Write the letters.

A

.... 1 **Initially**, the first European immigrants to America were from England. They came before anyone else did.

a making you feel worried and nervous

.... 2 When some immigrants arrive in a new place, they are surprised because they did not **anticipate** how different things would be.

b at the beginning

.... 3 Early immigrants to America were not used to the weather and the difficulties of farming in the new land, so they had to **adjust** quickly in order to survive.

c to imagine or expect that something will happen

.... 4 Immigrating can be **stressful**. Getting used to a new life is hard, and immigrants sometimes wonder if they've made a mistake.

d to become more familiar with a new situation

B

.... 1 Craig Ferguson worked hard to become a well-known comedian in Scotland, but his main **ambition** was to be a successful entertainer in the United States.

a the quality of having many parts

.... 2 When he arrived in Hollywood, he was surprised by how different it looked from the **image** that he saw in his mind. He had not realized how big it would be.

b a strong desire for success

.... 3 He was surprised by the **complexity** of the entertainment industry in America. It was huge and difficult to understand.

c a picture, an idea of what something is like

.... 4 When he was eventually hired to be a character on the TV show *The Drew Carey Show*, he finally felt a sense of job **security**.

d a feeling of being protected

B Academic Phrases 👁

Research tells us that the phrases in bold below are commonly used in academic writing.

ACTIVITY **2.2** Focus on Purpose

Read the paragraph. Then match the phrases in bold next to the purpose, or reason why the writer used them.

People immigrate for many reasons. Some immigrate in order to leave behind a bad situation at home. Others come to a new country **for the sake of** their family. They hope their children will receive a better education or have more opportunities in a new place. Still others come to find better economic opportunities. **In the case of** the Laval family, they moved to France because Mr. Laval felt that he could find better work opportunities than he could at home in Haiti. Living in a new country was stressful at first and required a great deal of adjustment. **Over the course of** several years, however, the family got used to their new life.

PHRASE	PURPOSE
.... 1 for the sake of	a to introduce an example
.... 2 in the case of	b to define a period of time
.... 3 over the course of	c to show the reason for an action

C Writing in the Real World

The author of "An Immigrant's Silent Struggle" uses the narrative to describe an important realization he has gained.

Before you read, answer these questions: What are some common struggles that immigrants often have? What do you think the author means by "silent struggle"?

Now read the article. Think about your answers to the questions above as you read.

ROBERT KOSI TETTE

AN IMMIGRANT'S SILENT STRUGGLE

(ADAPTED)

1 "I want to be just like you," the young man said. He was an onion seller, sitting in the hot tropical sun by the side of the road. He wore an extra-large T-shirt and over-sized jeans that reflected the influence of American pop culture that was everywhere in Africa. I had accepted a seat at his onion stand to take a break before concluding business in Accra that afternoon. Between brisk[1] sales serving customers stuck in traffic, he asked incessant[2] questions about life in America, convinced that having a visa to the United States was like winning the lottery. How could I tell him that I envied his simple innocent life? How could I tell him that I was guilty of creating a false **image** of Africans living abroad?

2 From the outside, I looked the picture of success. I wore a white designer shirt and matching pants that I had bought in a megamall in Detroit, where I worked as an engineer. My clothing suggested that I was a wealthy man, yet the truth was that I could not afford the numerous requests for money from my relatives or even to make gifts of my belongings. When I had left Ghana 10 years ago, uncles and aunts had sacrificed much to raise money for my trip abroad. Now these same uncles and aunts expected me to finance cousins hoping to make the same move to the United States.

3 After two weeks in Ghana, I was in fact broke and eagerly **anticipating** my return to the States. The first time I had left, I was fueled with naïve[3] **ambition**. In fact, until a few years ago I had been planning to return one day and settle back in my home country. This time, though, I was leaving knowing that I was returning to America to face the challenges of living there permanently.

4 America had fulfilled my **ambition**. I had arrived with the equivalent of a high school diploma, and after 10 years, I hold a graduate degree and have a relatively successful professional career. That is not to

[1] brisk: quick and active
[2] incessant: never stopping

[3] naïve: too ready to believe something

say it had been easy. Every inch of progress had been achieved through exhausting battles. My college education had been financed partly through working multiple minimum-wage jobs. Upon graduation, I had gotten a job, but **adjusting** to corporate culture was **initially** very difficult. Then, nervous about job **security**, I went to graduate school part time to give myself an edge in case of job layoffs. And I had spent a small fortune in legal fees and had endured many **stressful** years for **the sake of** becoming a permanent resident in America.

5 Living in America had been like running a marathon, and I had hoped that my trip back home would provide me with some rest and relaxation. But it had not worked out that way. Instead, I felt as though I were drowning in conflict. Part of me wanted to settle permanently in America. But another part of me longed to escape the **complexities** of life there and to return to the uncomplicated life I once knew in Ghana – the life perhaps of the onion seller.

6 Most of us leave home never realizing how much we would change. We also never think about how our experiences might scar us. I suppose my experience is no different from any other immigrant's to America. I am torn between the culture I have entered and the culture I have left behind. I am learning though to accept my new identity and to embrace the blend of the two cultures that exist in me. I have also learned that if I work hard and give something back to loved ones in Ghana, I might turn a life of disenchantment[4] into one that is rich and fulfilling.

[4] disenchantment: no longer feeling the value of something

ACTIVITY 2.3 Check Your Understanding

Answer the questions.

1 Why does the author consider the idea of returning to Ghana?

2 How is the author's trip to Ghana different from what he expected?

3 Have you ever had the experience of feeling "torn between two cultures," as Robert does?

ACTIVITY 2.4 Notice the Features of Narrative

Answer the questions.

1 Look at the last sentence of paragraph 1. What does this line show the reader?

   a The author will present his point of view on U.S. – Africa relations.

   b This piece of writing will tell a personal story.

   c The author is proud that he is a businessman.

2 What do you think is the purpose of the essay?

   a To tell a story about how immigration changes the way you feel about your home country

   b To compare and contrast the economies of Ghana and the United States

   c To persuade readers in Ghana that it is a bad idea to emigrate to the United States

In Section 1 you saw how the writer of the Student Model reflected on his topic. In this section you will analyze the final draft of his narrative essay. You will learn how to structure your ideas for your own essay.

Ⓐ Student Model

Read the writing prompt again and answer the questions.

WRITING PROMPT: Choose a significant event in your life that resulted in a change in your view of the world or taught you a lesson.

1 What is the prompt asking the writer to do?

2 What are some problems a student might have going to school in a new country that he or she did not have at home?

Read the essay twice. The first time, think about your answers to the questions above. The second time, answer the questions in the Analyze Writing Skills boxes. This will help you notice key features of narrative essays.

STUDENT MODEL

How I Became a Mexican American

1   When I was 13 years old, my family – my grandparents, my little sister, and I – moved to the United States from Mexico. I still remember worrying about leaving my lifelong friends behind and having to make new ones in a completely foreign land. My grandparents had made this decision to move, and there was no changing their minds. "Ale, we are moving to make a better life for you and your sister, and you will thank us one day," they explained. I did not believe them. All I could think was that my grandparents, whom I loved and trusted, were doing something that would be the end of happiness as I knew it. I was sure that I would never forgive them. In my teen years, I lacked perspective,[1] above all, the perspective that comes from looking beyond yourself.

2   As it turned out, I had not even come close to fully **anticipating** how difficult my new life in America would be or how lonely and excluded I would feel. Although I tried to present the **image** of being just another student at my new school, I always felt hopelessly different, especially as there were few Spanish-speaking students in my school and I was ashamed of my difficulties learning English. Oddly, what I found to be most **stressful** was when my grandparents would pick my sister and me up after school. They would be so happy to see us and would greet us very loudly in Spanish. I dreaded that

1 Analyze Writing Skills

What does the writer do in the first paragraph? Circle your answer.

a gives the situation for the story

b gives only details about where the story takes place

2 Analyze Writing Skills

In the first paragraph, is the thesis directly stated? Circle your answer.

a yes   b no

3 Analyze Writing Skills

Underline all the adjectives in paragraph 2 that the writer uses to help his reader understand his feelings about his situation. Are they positive or negative feelings?

[1]perspective: the ability to consider things accurately and fairly

moment at the end of the school day, worried about what my American peers,[2] who all went home alone, would think. I wanted to ask my grandparents, "Why did you bring us here if you are going to act and speak like we are still in Mexico?" If I had to **adjust** to my new surroundings, why didn't they? After all, they were the ones who had wanted to come here!

3   Although I managed to keep my mouth shut, these questions bothered me until one day when I came home unexpectedly. My grandmother was looking at old pictures from Mexico. For the first and only time in my life, I saw her sobbing. My grandfather's arms were around her and he patted her hair. I stayed out of sight but overheard her telling my grandfather, "I miss them all so much – Diego, Isa, Hector, all the rest of our family. I miss the whole town; I miss Luz, Mercedes, and all my old friends, the house that you built and that we lived in so many years, my garden …" My grandfather was trying to comfort her. "My love," he told her, "Always remember that we did this so that our grandchildren can have the **security** of a bright future." An overwhelming sense of shame washed over me. "How could I have been so selfish as to be ashamed of them at school and even at home?" I wondered. I had only thought of how the move to the United States had affected me. **In the case of** my grandparents, who had spent such long lives in Mexico, it had been much harder.

4   Suddenly, I gained a new perspective on my situation. I began to understand the **complexity** of my grandparents' lives and the sacrifices they had made and were making for me and my sister and we never knew. Through all their difficulties, they always smiled, made us laugh, and gave us hope about the future. My sister and I had been given a gift from our grandparents. That was it. I decided right then and there to make the most of it. My worries over struggling to speak English like my peers were replaced with an **ambition** to work my hardest to repay my grandparents for what they had done. This hard work paid off more quickly than I had imagined possible in my learning English fluently and feeling more comfortable in my new homeland.

[2]peers: people of the same age, social position, or abilities

(CONTINUED)

---

4 Analyze Writing Skills

a   In which paragraph does the character gain a new understanding?

   3   4

b   Which paragraph describes the event that helps the character gain this understanding?

   3   4

5 Analyze Writing Skills

Good writers vary the length and structure of their sentences to make their writing interesting. Underline the subject of each of the first three sentences of paragraph 4. Do all the sentences begin with the subject?

Yes   No

5   Recently, my grandparents had their fortieth anniversary, and I planned a special surprise party for them. The party was a complete success, and I made sure that our family and our American friends ate the traditional Mexican food and listened to the traditional Mexican music that my grandparents still loved so much. In this and many other ways, I have tried to repay my grandparents **over the course of** the last several years. Sometimes it is only later that we understand we are being given a gift and can see that the gift is much bigger than even the giver could have realized.

6 Analyze Writing Skills

What lesson or message does the writer want to convey from this story? Circle your answer.

a   Understanding and appreciating other people's situations can help us see our own situation in a better, more positive way.

b   If you adjust to a new culture and get to know people from that culture, you can lead a better, happier life.

ACTIVITY **3.1** Check Your Understanding

Answer the questions.

1   How did the writer change? What caused the change, and what positive consequences did it have for the writer?

2   What is the significance of the party scene in the last paragraph?

3   What are some other problems people might have to overcome when they move to a new culture or go to school in a new culture?

ACTIVITY **3.2** Outline the Writer's Ideas

Complete the outline for "How I Became a Mexican American" using the phrases in the box.

grandparents' greeting at school	new opportunities and new perspective
lacked perspective	sacrifices for grandchildren
looking at old pictures and crying	new perspective

ESSAY OUTLINE

I. Introduction ....

Thesis Statement .... ; couldn't see beyond self ....

Body Paragraph 1 II. Hard time adjusting ....

Supporting Idea 1   A. Felt different ....

Detail   1. Felt lonely and left out ....

Detail   2. Felt different from the other students ....

Supporting Idea 2   B. Ashamed ....

Detail   1. Ashamed of problems with English ....

Detail   2. .... felt embarrassing ....

Body Paragraph 2 III. One day came home early ....

Supporting Idea 1   A. Heard grandparents talking about missing Mexico ....

Detail   1. Grandmother .... ; she missed Mexico

Detail   2. Grandfather mentioned ....

Supporting Idea 2   B. Felt ashamed ....

Body Paragraph 3 IV. I gained ....

Supporting Idea 1   A. Understood complexity of their lives and their sacrifice ....

Detail   1. Grandparents never expressed anything but positive thoughts ...

Supporting Idea 2   B. Decided to work hard and made grandparents happy ....

Detail   1. Learned English and felt more comfortable ....

(CONTINUED)

	V. Conclusion
Supporting Idea 1	A. Grandparents' fortieth anniversary party
Detail	1. Traditional Mexican food and music
Detail	2. A way of repaying grandparents
Supporting Idea 2	B. Lesson learned: _____ were grandparents' gifts

B Narrative Essays

A narrative is a story that reveals an important point, message, or theme for the reader. Writers use stories for many purposes: to entertain, to teach, to explain, to evoke empathy and sympathy, and so on. Telling a story is an effective way to engage your readers by appealing to their emotions. The events in a narrative essay usually involve a conflict, such as a disagreement between two people or an obstacle to a goal. These events lead to a climax – the most interesting or significant part of the story.

THE STRUCTURE

A good narrative includes the following:

- an **introductory paragraph** that prepares the reader for the story by describing the setting or the scene and the characters. It also usually presents the **thesis**, which is the point, message, or theme of the story.
- believable **characters** that engage the reader's interest.
- interesting **details** that put the reader in the story, such as sights, sounds, tastes, and other sensations. It may also include dialogue that makes the story come alive.
- a **conflict** or problem to solve.
- a series of **events** that lead to a **climax**. The events are described in a way that draws the reader in and makes the reader want to continue reading.
- a **concluding paragraph** that clarifies the point, message, or theme for the reader.

This is a diagram showing the parts of a narrative.

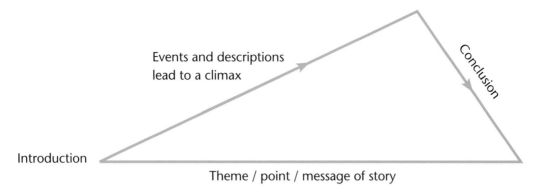

Events and descriptions lead to a climax

Conclusion

Introduction

Theme / point / message of story

3.3 Notice

Work with a partner. Review the information above and complete the statements.

1 Another word for *narrative* is ....

2 The purposes of a narrative include to evoke empathy or sympathy, to explain something, to entertain the reader, and to .... something.

3 The most interesting or significant part of a narrative is the ....

4 A good narrative includes the following components:

- an introductory paragraph

- ....

- believable characters

- interesting .... that put the reader in the story

- a conflict or a problem

- a series of events that leads to a ....

- a concluding paragraph

CHOOSING A GOOD IDEA FOR A STORY

The first step in writing a narrative is choosing a good story idea. The following questions can help writers choose an idea for a story:

1 Will my story communicate the purpose or lesson that I am being asked to write about?

2 Is there enough of a conflict so that the reader is drawn in and wants to see how the problem is resolved?

3 Will this story be interesting to my readers?

4 Are there interesting characters and scenes that I can use to develop my story? Can I create dialogue that helps my readers experience and respond to the situation?

5 Can the story be told in one essay? In other words, are there clear events that have a clear beginning and end over a specific period of time?

ACTIVITY **3.4** Notice

Read the following prompt and story ideas. Answer the writing prompt questions for each idea. Check (✓) the idea that you think would make the best story. Then explain your choice to a partner.

WRITING PROMPT: Think about the first day at a new school or a new job. What obstacles did you overcome? What advice do you have for others facing a new situation?

Story Ideas

a my first job ever, at the supermarket deli counter, and how scared I was when I saw the dangerous meat-slicing machine they wanted me to use. In the end, I decided not to do such a dangerous job.

b the time I brought my insect collection to school on the first day of kindergarten and found out that my teacher was afraid of bugs

c the time I ran into another car on the way to my first day at work, found out that my new manager was the driver of the car I had just hit, and discovered that flexibility and humor can help a person handle even the most difficult situations

d finding out that my best friend cheated on an exam and trying to decide whether to tell the teacher. I never told and I never have forgotten it.

e when I learned that my uncle in Canada would pay for my college education if I agreed to move there for college and then stay afterward and work in his business. It was a decision that made me seriously think about my career.

ACTIVITY **3.5** Apply It to Your Writing

With a partner, ask and answer the writing prompt questions above to evaluate the story idea that you generated for your writing prompt in Section 1 on page 49.

THE INTRODUCTORY PARAGRAPH

The introduction of a narrative essay sets the place and time of the story, or gives details about the main character. The paragraph may include a **thesis statement** that tells the point, message, or theme of the story. The thesis of a narrative essay may also be implied; that is, the writer does not state the thesis directly, but demonstrates it through the evidence in the story. However, a strong thesis statement can help you stay focused as you write and ensure that your essay answers the writing prompt. The student model has a strong thesis statement.

A good introduction includes a strong sense of setting, situation, and purpose for the story. A great introduction does it all with flair by including details and precise and interesting words. These details and words vividly set up the situation and the conflict or problem in a compelling way that illustrates the thesis. For example, if your thesis is "dreams don't always come true and sometimes it's best that they don't," then you need to create the experience of what the dream was, its importance to your characters, and hint at the struggle or frustration that your characters will inevitably deal with. This makes your readers want to continue reading.

3.6 Discuss the Paragraphs

Work with a partner. Which introductory paragraph is better, A or B? Why? Think of more information that you can add, such as details about the setting or the characters, that would improve the other paragraph.

A   I had just graduated from college and it was my first day at my new job. It was my dream job – working as a web designer for my local school district. However, I had no idea that I was about to have a big surprise when I found out who my new boss was. My experience that day taught me that humor and a positive attitude go a long way toward smoothing out difficult situations.

B   I'll never forget that day: It was a warm spring morning and the air was infused with a sense of hope and excitement. I felt this sense of hope throughout my body as I got into my car and set out on the long drive to my new life. After struggling to survive on unemployment for the past year, I had finally found a solution. The offer of a dream job convinced me to move halfway across the country and start a new life. However, one small mistake that day almost robbed me of all of my dreams. As unfortunate as the incident was, I learned an important lesson that day: Dreams don't always come true, and sometimes it's best that they don't.

ACTIVITY **3.7** Apply It to Your Writing

Think about the writing prompt you chose in Section 1. Write some details and incidents that you might use in your introduction. You can change these later.

....

....

....

ACTIVITY **3.8** Thesis Statements

With a partner, read the writing prompt and the introductory paragraph. Then read the three possible thesis statements to complete the paragraph on page 62. Check (✓) the thesis statement that best answers the prompt and expresses the point of the story.

WRITING PROMPT: The American novelist Thomas Wolfe once said, "You can't go home again." This saying became a part of American culture and means that once you grow up and leave home, you will never feel the same again about it. Relate an experience that you or someone you know has had that either supports or contradicts this idea.

INTRODUCTORY PARAGRAPH

As Thomas Wolfe once said, "You can't go home again." The American author was expressing the idea that once you grow up and go out into the world and experience what life has to offer, you will never feel the same again about the place you left. For example, if you move from a small town to a city, when you return home, your town will seem small and inadequate, and the people living there will seem dull and unsophisticated. You'll feel like a stranger in a strange land because you have grown while those who stayed behind never changed.

Thesis Statements

a My decision to stay home and take care of my disabled brother, rather than leave to attend college in another city, taught me the truth of this saying.

b However, an experience that I had returning home after three years of college in a foreign country taught me the opposite of this saying: You *can* go home again.

c However, after backpacking through Asia for three months, I learned that I can make my home anywhere in the world where people are kind, welcoming, and open-minded.

ACTIVITY **3.9** Apply It to Your Writing

Think about the writing prompt you chose in Section 1. Write a possible theme for your narrative. Can you express it as a thesis statement? If so, write a thesis statement for your narrative. Work with a partner and check that your theme and/or thesis statement answers your prompt and expresses the main point of your story.

....

....

....

....

....

BODY PARAGRAPHS

The body paragraphs of a narrative essay include a sequence of well-chosen events; vivid descriptions of characters, feelings, and places; and revealing dialogue that move the action forward and end in a **climax**, a meaningful moment that changes the character.

Although I managed to keep my mouth shut, these questions bothered me until one day when I came home unexpectedly. My grandmother was looking at old pictures from Mexico. For the first and only time in my life, I saw her sobbing. My grandfather's arms were around her and he patted her hair. I stayed out of sight but overheard her telling my grandfather, "I miss them all so much – Diego, Isa, Hector, all the rest of our family. I miss the whole town; I miss Luz, Mercedes, and all my old friends, the house that you built and that we lived in so many years, my garden …" My grandfather was trying to comfort her. "My love," he told her, "Always remember that we did this so that our grandchildren can have the security of a bright future." An overwhelming sense of shame washed over me. "How could I have been so selfish as to be ashamed of them at school and even at home?" I wondered. I had only

> These events are relevant and necessary to the story.

> Instead of reporting speech, the writer uses direct speech to make the story and the characters more real.

> Notice the precise words the writer uses to give us a clear picture of the characters.

thought of how the move to the United States had affected me. In the case of my grandparents, who had spent such long lives in Mexico, it had been much harder.

Suddenly, I gained a new perspective on my situation. I began to understand the complexity of my grandparents' lives and the sacrifices they had made and were making for me and my sister and we never knew. Through all their difficulties, they always smiled, made us laugh, and gave us hope about the future. My sister and I had been given a gift from our grandparents. That was it. I decided right then and there to make the most of it. My worries over struggling to speak English like my peers were replaced with an ambition to work my hardest to repay my grandparents for what they had done. This hard work paid off more quickly than I had imagined possible in my learning English fluently and feeling more comfortable in my new homeland.

> Notice the sentence the writer uses to signal the climax.

Read the two paragraphs from the Student Model.

When using **dialogue,** it is important to follow punctuation rules for direct quotations. These are the MLA (Modern Language Association) rules for punctuating dialogue:

1 Before a quotation, use a comma or a colon.

   The young man said,"I want to be just like you."

2 Question marks and exclamation points go inside the quotation marks if the person being quoted asked a question or exclaimed something. Otherwise, they go outside.

   The interviewer asked all applicants, "What obstacles have you overcome?"

   What did Thomas Wolfe mean by "You can't go home again"?

3 For quotes within quotes, use single quotation marks.

   According to Williams, "When asked why they come here, most immigrants answer 'for economic opportunities.'"

4 For quoted words or phrases with commas and periods, the comma or period goes inside the quotation mark.

   The feeling of not belonging to any culture is sometimes referred to as "anomie."

Read the paragraphs from an essay that a student wrote in response to the same prompt as the Student Model. Complete the tasks.

WRITING PROMPT: Choose a significant event in your life that resulted in a change in your view of the world or taught you a lesson.

1   The first thing my mother said when we arrived in our new country was, "You children have to eat. I'm going out today to find work, and I won't come back until I get a job." She left us with our Aunt Mathilde. Aunt Mathilde was a large, jolly sort of woman. She was always laughing and making jokes. Aunt Mathilde took us to the park that day and let us play for what seemed like hours. Then she took us for a long walk around our new neighborhood. She bought us candy and ice cream all along the way. I do not really like ice cream. She introduced us to all her friends and acquaintances. Finally, it started getting dark. Aunt Mathilde took us home and gave us dinner, all the while remaining very positive and upbeat. It seemed very late to us. Finally, my brother Emile said, "Aunt Mathilde, when is Mama coming back?" Aunt Mathilde finally lost her happy face. "I do not know, children. But I *do* know your mother. If she says she is not coming back until she gets a job, she means it."

2   We had a hard time getting to sleep that night. We were all worried about our mother. Aunt Mathilde put us to bed and sat in a chair next to us in order to comfort us. I'm right here, she said, Do not worry. Your mother will return. We were just starting to fall asleep. It was almost midnight. Suddenly, we heard the front door opening. It was our mother! We ran out of the bedroom and wrapped our arms around her knees. "Mama!" we shouted. "Where were you?", I told you I would not come home until I found a job, she explained. "Well, I found a good job in a restaurant!" It turned out that the restaurant was so busy that day and so in need of our mother that they had asked her to start that very day. Not only did out mother find a good job, but she had also brought us treats from the restaurant. The restaurant was on Smith Street. Our mother worked hard at that job, and she saved a lot of money. In a few short years, we were living in our own house on a tree-shaded street, riding our bikes to one of the best schools in the city.

3   We came from a place where we had no home and could not afford to go to school. Our mother had few skills and spoke little English. When we first came to Canada, we had nothing, only a kind aunt. I think the most important lesson my brothers and I learned when we came here is to never give up. Persistence, even in the face of the most insurmountable obstacles, will always bring rewards.

1 Cross out the sentences that do NOT seem necessary to the story.

2 Circle the words and phrases that help you visualize the characters.

3 Notice the dialogue and the use of punctuation with quotation marks in paragraph 1. Then add three sets of missing quotation marks and correct two other mistakes in punctuation in paragraph 2.

3.11 Identify the Climax

Read the body paragraph below. Underline the sentence that seems like it is the climax. Tell a partner which sentence you chose and why you think it is the climax.

    The mail carrier came by at 1:30 in the afternoon. My mother looked through the mail and pulled out an envelope from the American embassy. Looking at me nervously, she ripped open the envelope. She started to yell as she pulled out the letter approving our visa. We hugged each other for a few minutes. My mother held the envelope tightly in her hand while we hugged. "Well, I guess we should start preparing," she said at last. It was a moment in my life that I will never forget.

ACTIVITY **3.12** Apply It to Your Writing

Think about the writing prompt you chose in Section 1 on page 49. Write one or two sentences describing the climax of your narrative. Show what you have written to a partner. Make sure that it actually feels like a climax to a story.

....

....

....

....

....

THE CONCLUDING PARAGRAPH

The **conclusion** should make it clear that the story is over, and emphasize the theme or message that was stated in the thesis or hinted at in the introduction. A conclusion can make a prediction, or reflect on the lesson that the main character has learned, as the student model essay does. Some examples of language that could be used are:

- *That's how I learned that homesickness is not always a permanent feeling.*
- *Jim realized that, even though more storms might come in the future, next time he would be prepared for them.*
- *After that summer, I always tried to remember that first impressions of people can really change.*

ACTIVITY **3.13** Apply It to Your Writing

Write a conclusion to your narrative following the guidelines above. Make sure it reflects the narrative's theme.

....

....

....

....

In this section you will learn the writing and grammar skills that will help make your writing more sophisticated and accurate.

Ⓐ Writing Skill 1: Parallel Structure

Writers use parallel structure when a sentence has a list of words or phrases that are all the same form and part of speech. This pattern can involve single words, phrases, or clauses and can be used with different grammatical patterns, which are in bold below. If the part of speech and form don't match, this is not considered good writing. Here are some examples of different kinds of parallel structure.

Adjective phrases:

*Immigration can be **not only** <u>very exciting</u> **but also** <u>quite stressful</u>.*

Verb phrases:

*My father knew he had to **either** <u>find work</u> **or** <u>return home</u>.*

He had never <u>spoken English</u>, <u>been to a supermarket</u>, or <u>eaten fast food</u> before he came here.

Clauses:

Albert Einstein emigrated from Germany because <u>he wanted to work in America</u>, <u>he was worried about the war</u>, and <u>his future there was uncertain</u>.

ACTIVITY **4.1** Using Parallel Structure

Read the information. Complete the sentences using parallel structure. You may have to add some words of your own.

1 Supreme Court Justice Sonia Sotomayor's parents were born in Puerto Rico. They came to the United States during World War II. During the war, they got married.

Supreme Court Justice Sonia Sotomayor's parents came to the United States during World War II and ....

2 Sonia Sotomayor is the first Supreme Court Justice of Hispanic heritage. She is also one of the youngest Supreme Court justices.

Sonia Sotomayor is not only the first Supreme Court Justice of Hispanic heritage, but she is also ....

3 Sotomayor graduated from Princeton University. She also received a degree from Yale Law School. She served as editor of the *Yale Law Journal*.

Sotomayor graduated from Princeton University, received a degree from Yale Law School, and ....

4 When Sotomayor first started college, she thought that she did not have the skills to be a good student. She also felt that she did not have enough knowledge to succeed. In addition, she suffered from a lack of confidence.

When Sotomayor first started college, she thought that she did not have enough

...................................., ..., or .... to succeed academically.

5 Sotomayor's biography, *My Beloved World*, does not discuss her political views. It also does not include her judicial philosophy.

Sotomayor's biography does not discuss her .... or

....

6 Sotomayor visits Puerto Rico frequently because she has family there. She also has many fans there. In addition, she also visits Puerto Rico because she is often invited to speak.

Sotomayor visits Puerto Rico frequently because she has family there, she

...................................., and she ....

B Writing Skill 2: Sentence Variety

Writing is better and more sophisticated if the sentences are different from each other. Short sentences in a narrative give a straight-to-the-point feeling. Longer, more complex sentences provide richer feelings and a different kind of flow. By combining these different kinds of sentences, your narrative will sound more natural and be more interesting to read. Here are some techniques for adding variety to the sentences that you write. Notice how they are used in the first paragraph of the Student Model.

<u>When I was 13 years old,</u> my family – my grandparents, my little sister, and I – moved to the United States from Mexico. I still remember worrying about leaving my lifelong friends behind and having to make new ones in a completely foreign land. My grandparents had made this decision to move, <u>and there was no changing their minds.</u> <u>"Ale, we are moving to make a better life for you and your sister, and you will thank us one day," they explained.</u> <u>I did not believe them.</u> All I could think was that my grandparents, <u>whom I loved and trusted,</u> were doing something that would be the end of happiness as I knew it. I was sure that I would never forgive them. <u>In my teen years,</u> I lacked perspective, above all, the perspective that comes from looking beyond yourself.

1 Start with a subordinate clause.

2 Make compound sentences with *and, or, but, so, yet,* and other conjunctions.

3 Vary sentence length.

4 Use relative clauses to combine information.

5 Start with a prepositional phrase.

ACTIVITY **4.2** Providing Sentence Variety

Rewrite the sentences from the paragraph below as directed. Remember to use correct punctuation.

(1) Chinese workers began immigrating to the United States in large numbers after the "Gold Rush" of 1849. (2) Most of them came because they heard that they could work as "prospectors" and mine gold in California. (3) Uncle Lee, my father's great-great-granduncle, was one of tens of thousands of Chinese immigrants who landed in San Francisco in the early 1850s. (4) He settled just north of the city. (5) Gold was not as easy to find as he had expected. (6) Some prospectors did find it. (7) According to my father, life was hard for Uncle Lee and other Chinese immigrants because they were discriminated against and sometimes even attacked by American prospectors. (8) However, thanks to Uncle Lee and others like him, there is a Chinese cultural influence in California, which remains today. (9) For example, in the town of Weaverville, north of San Francisco, Chinese settlers established a Taoist temple. (10) It is still there today.

1 Change sentence 1 so that it begins with a prepositional phrase.

2 Connect sentence 4 to sentence 3 by adding a conjunction to make one sentence.

3 Make sentence 6 a subordinate clause by adding "although" at the beginning. Then rewrite sentence 5 to begin with this clause.

4 Rewrite sentence 7 to make it two separate sentences by removing the word "because."

5 Change sentence 10 into a relative clause that describes the word "temple" in the previous sentence.

C Grammar for Writing: Past Tense Forms

English has several different ways to write and talk about the past. Using past tense forms correctly is important for accuracy in writing academic essays. Because these forms show the order in which two or more events happened, they are especially important in narrative essay writing.

PAST TENSE FORMS	
1 Use the **simple past** to describe actions or events that are completed.	*Albert Einstein **immigrated** to the United States in 1933.*
2 Use the **past progressive** to describe activities or events in progress over a period of time in the past.	*I **was reading** a biography of Einstein all day yesterday.*
3 Use the **past progressive** to describe background activities that were in progress at the same time that a main event occurred. Use the simple past for the main event.	BACKGROUND ACTIVITY *While I **was reading** the biography, my* MAIN EVENT *roommate **answered** the phone.*
4 Use the **past perfect** to describe the first of two events that were completed in the past. Use the simple past for the later event.	FIRST EVENT *I learned that Einstein **had won** the Nobel* SECOND EVENT *Prize in Physics by the time **he came** to the United States.*
5 **Use the past perfect progressive** to focus on an ongoing past action that led up to a point in the past.	*By that time, he **had been living** in Belgium and England for several months.*

Circle the best verb form from the choices given.

1 Einstein graduated from the Federal Polytechnic Institute of Zurich in 1900, and he .... at several European universities after that.

   a worked   b had worked

2 After he .... about equations of special relativity for a while, he developed one of science's best-known equations: $E = mc^2$.

   a had been thinking   b was thinking

3 In 1939, Einstein .... a letter to U.S. President Franklin Roosevelt because he believed that Germany might be developing an atomic bomb.

   a was writing   b wrote

4 In the 1950s, Einstein worked at Princeton University. The Israeli prime minister had offered Einstein the position of president of Israel, but Einstein .... not to accept it.

   a decided   b had decided

5 In 1999, *Time* magazine .... Albert Einstein "the person of the century."

   a had named   b named

6 German physicist Max Planck .... Einstein's work when he began to develop his own groundbreaking work on an idea he called quantum theory.

   a was thinking about   b thought about

Avoiding Common Mistakes

Research tells us that these are the most common mistakes that students make when using past tense verb forms in academic writing.

> **1** **Remember to use *be* in progressive forms.**
>
>   **been**
> Many of them had living in Mexico before moving to the United States.
>
> **2** **Use the simple past form to describe a specific event that finished in the past. Do not use progressive forms.**
>
>   **overhauled**
> Congress ~~was overhauling~~ U.S. immigration law in 1965.
>
> **3** **Do not use the simple present to give a reason for a past event.**
>
>   **considered**
> Many members of Congress rejected the president's idea because they ~~consider~~ it exploitative.
>
> **4** **Do not use the present perfect to describe a completed event that happened before a past event.**
>
>   **had**
> They demolished the monument that ~~has~~ become the city's symbol.

ACTIVITY **4.4** Editing Task

Find and correct seven more mistakes in the following paragraph.

              passed
   In 1882, the U.S. Congress ~~was passing~~ a law called the Chinese Exclusion Act. This law stated that immigrant workers from China were no longer allowed to immigrate to the United States and could not be citizens. Chinese laborers had coming to the United States since the "Gold Rush" more than 40 years before. Rumors of a "mountain of gold" in California started in Hong Kong in 1849, and quickly spread throughout the provinces of China. This brought thousands of Chinese immigrants to America's west coast. These immigrants added an Asian influence to a country that it has not had previously. Still, this influence remained limited because the Chinese Exclusion Act is in effect. In fact, this act was a form of discrimination, since the Chinese were the only ethnic or national group that was not allowed to immigrate. Although the law was supposed to only be temporary, Congress was making it permanent in 1902. They also added new restrictions by stating that each Chinese resident had to register and obtain a certificate of residence. By this time, because so many Chinese Americans were excluded from the mainstream of American life, they have formed "Chinatown" communities where they supported each other. However, things changed during World War II. Many Chinese-American men had fighting in the U.S. military against Japan and helping in the American war effort. The government decided that they had to change their attitude toward Chinese Americans and end the discriminatory law. In 1943, the Exclusion Act was finally being eliminated.

D Avoiding Plagiarism

Sometimes it's not necessary to cite facts and information. It's important to know when you need to cite them and when you don't.

My instructor just returned the essay I wrote about immigration. He said I was missing some citations. I was very careful about citing all facts and statistics, but he said some of the information I didn't cite is rare and unusual. He said those ideas are unique and many people don't know them, so they need citations, too. I'm so confused! How can I tell what kinds of information need citations and what kinds don't? – Mehmet

Dear Mehmet,

Information or facts that most people know are called "common knowledge." You don't need to cite that information. However, if the information is not common knowledge, that is, it is unique or unusual, you do need to cite it. If you're unsure, go ahead and cite your source. It's better to be safe than sorry!

Good luck!

Professor Wright

WHAT IS COMMON KNOWLEDGE?

Here is a simple test to help you decide if something is common knowledge. Ask yourself this question: *Before you started to research your topic, did you already know the fact or information?* If you did, it's probably common knowledge. Also, if the information is easy to find and appears on at least five websites, it's probably common knowledge. Let's look at some examples.

What is common knowledge? *You don't need to cite it.*	What is not common knowledge? *You must cite it.*
• Common scientific or historical facts	• Statistics and data
• Common current topics of discussion	• Scientific theories or philosophical ideas
• Common myths, legends, holidays	• Original opinions or ideas
• Facts common to your major or field	• Studies or research by other people
The first immigrants to the United States came from England.	*According to the 2000 U.S. Census, British immigrant groups are the ninth-largest immigrant group in the United States today.*

ACTIVITY 4.5 Practice

Look at the information below. Check (✓) the information that is common knowledge. This information does not need citations. Discuss your answers with a partner.

☐ 1 The capital of China is Beijing.

☐ 2 Amazon's net income last year was $274 million.

☐ 3 Water freezes at 32°F (0°C).

☐ 4 The World Health Organization reports that there are about 1 billion migrants throughout the world.

☐ 5 The United States is a nation of immigrants.

☐ 6 Research shows that the longer immigrants stay in the United States, the more they assimilate: buy homes, access education, gain citizenship, and become an important part of American society.

ACTIVITY 4.6 Practice

Read this paragraph from a student's essay. Underline the two sentences that should be cited.

Americans come from many different cultures. The United States is a nation of immigrants. Although they came from different countries and backgrounds, they are all part of American society. People came to America for many different reasons, such as political freedom and economic opportunity. Between 1870 and 1930, there were 30 million new immigrants to the U.S. For many immigrants, citizenship has been an important goal. In 2012, over 750,000 people became U.S. citizens, mostly in California, New York, and Florida. Coming to America is still a dream for many around the world, and many people believe the number of immigrants will continue to increase in the coming years.

In this section you will follow the writing process to complete the final draft of your essay.

STEP 1: **BRAINSTORM**

Work with a partner. Follow the steps below to brainstorm more ideas.

1 Before you start, notice how the writer of the Student Model brainstormed. He wrote many ideas, identified two possible climaxes, and thought about two possible themes. Then he went back and crossed some things out.

WRITING PROMPT: Choose a significant event in your life that resulted in a change in your view of the world or taught you a lesson.

What happened?	When?	Feelings and descriptive details
grandparents said we were moving to the U.S. from Mexico	when I was 13	upset, didn't want to leave my friends
arrived in the U.S. and started school	a few months later	felt awful, couldn't speak English, didn't fit in at school
things got worse at school and at home with my grandparents	start of school	embarrassed at school, hated it when my grandparents came to school and spoke Spanish, felt lonely
~~tense times between me and my sister~~	~~first few months of school~~	~~English / school / U.S. all easier for her~~
tenser time with grandparents	first few months of school	feeling angry at them, feeling more like outsider because of them
I came to understand things better, including my grandparents, and started adjusting better (~~climax?~~)	before end of school year	working hard at school and feeling more comfortable, feelings of love for my grandparents, better feelings about the U.S. and Mexico
how this happened: all about my grandparents: day I saw my grandmother cry (climax ✓)	December, around Christmas	feeling shame, this time about being selfish
the party for my grandparents	last year	proud of me, my grandparents, Mexico

Possible theme:

~~People who go to another culture always feel some sadness about what they lose from their own culture.~~

Being able to see how someone feels helps us understand our own lives. ✓

2 Write the ideas that you wrote in Section 1, page 49, in the chart below. Include ideas from the Your Turns throughout the unit. Brainstorm more ideas.

What happened?	When?	Feelings and descriptive details

Theme: ....

When you are finished, circle the three most important events and write them here.

1 ....

2 ....

3 ....

STEP 2: DO RESEARCH: CHOOSING A QUOTATION FOR AN ESSAY

A well-chosen **quotation**, an exact phrase, from a reliable source can help support a thesis, add an interesting perspective, or emphasize a point. However, it is important to use quotations carefully to support and not replace your own ideas.

Guillermo needed a quotation for an essay he was writing for this prompt: *Immigrants often leave a lasting impact on the individuals and communities to which they move. Describe how an immigrant influenced an individual or community in his or her new country.* Read and find out how he did it.

> After I identified the keywords and points in my thesis, I read several sources and found quotations with unique language and support for my thesis. Next, I compared the keywords from each quotation to see which one related best to my main point. Last, I incorporated the quotation into my own writing by using an introductory phrase, the source name, and quotation marks.

Guillermo's Results

Essay Topic: Madeleine Albright – Czech immigrant and former U.S. Secretary of State

Thesis: After fleeing oppression in Europe, Madeleine Albright spent her <u>political career</u> improving <u>foreign relations</u> around <u>the world</u>.

Source	Quotation (keywords)
1 *Time* magazine article, "Madeleine's War" (Isaacson, 1999)	"Some, like Albright, develop <u>an aggressive moralism and idealism</u>, pledging 'never again' <u>to let the world turn a blind eye</u> to atrocities."
2 www.history.state.gov, "Biographies of the Secretaries of State: Madeleine Korbel Albright" (Office of the Historian, n.d.)	"… supported the <u>expansion of free-market</u> democratization and the <u>creation of civil societies</u> in <u>the developing world</u> …"
3 www.greatwomen.org, "Madeleine Korbel Albright" (National Women's Hall of Fame, n.d.)	"… she has created <u>policies and institutions</u> to help <u>guide the world</u> into a new century of <u>peace and prosperity</u>."

Quotation choice: According to the National Women's Hall of Fame, during her time as a public servant, Albright "created policies and institutions to help guide the world into a new century of peace and prosperity" by promoting organizations like NATO ("Madeleine Korbel Albright").

ACTIVITY 5.1 Apply It to Your Writing

YOUR TURN

On a separate sheet of paper, make a chart like the one above and follow the steps Guillermo took to choose a quotation for your essay. Use the quotation in a sentence and be sure to cite the source and the publication year. (If there is no publication date on the website or article, use *n.d.* (no date) for the year.)

Complete the outline below with your ideas from the previous steps.

ESSAY OUTLINE

I. Introduction

Body Paragraph 1   II.

Supporting Idea 1   A.

Detail   1.

Detail   2.

Supporting Idea 2   B.

Detail   1.

Detail   2.

Body Paragraph 2   III.

Supporting Idea 1   A.

Detail   1.

Detail   2.

Supporting Idea 2   B.

Detail   1.

Detail   2.

(CONTINUED)

Body Paragraph 3	IV. ....
Supporting Idea 1	A. ....
Detail	1. ....
Detail	2. ....
Supporting Idea 2	B. ....
Detail	1. ....
Detail	2. ....
	V. Conclusion ....
Ideas for Prediction, Reflection, or Revelation	....

STEP 4: WRITE YOUR FIRST DRAFT

Now it is time to write your first draft. Here are some suggestions on how to get started.

1 Use your outline, notes, and the sentences you wrote in the Your Turns and in Step 3 above.

2 Focus on making your ideas as clear as possible.

3 Remember to add a title.

After you finish, read your essay and check for basic errors.

1 Check that all sentences have subjects and verbs.

2 Go through and check all your verbs. Have you used past tense forms correctly?

3 Check that you have used parallel structure correctly and that there is some variety in your sentence types.

4 If you have a thesis statement, make sure it is clear.

STEP 5: WRITE YOUR FINAL DRAFT

1 After you receive feedback on your first draft, review it carefully. Fix any errors.

2 Make a note of errors that were most frequent (misspellings, wrong verb tense, errors in using commas). Try to avoid them as you write.

3 Review the Academic Vocabulary and Academic Phrases from this unit. Are there any that you can add to your essay?

4 Turn to page 271 and use the Self-Editing Review to check your work one more time.

5 Write your final draft and hand it in.

3 CAUSE AND EFFECT ESSAYS

SOCIOLOGY: EFFECTS OF GEOGRAPHIC MOBILITY

"History in its broadest aspect is a record of man's migrations from one environment to another."

Ellsworth Huntington
(1876–1947)

About the Author:

Ellsworth Huntington was an American geographer and professor.

Work with a partner. Read the quotation about migration. Then answer the questions.

1 Huntington said that history is "a record of man's migrations from one environment to another." What did he mean by a "record"?

2 Give an example of a time in history when people migrated to a new environment. Where did they go and why?

3 Have you ever moved to a new place? If so, how did you change? How did you stay the same?

Ⓐ Connect to Academic Writing

In this unit you will learn skills to help you analyze causes and effects. While some of the writing skills that you will use may be new to you, the skill of identifying causes and effects is not new. In your everyday life you identify causes and effects when you ask questions such as *What effect will my major have on my career options?* and *How will moving to the United States change my life?*

Ⓑ Reflect on the Topic

In this section you will choose a writing prompt and reflect on it. You will develop these ideas throughout the unit and use them to practice skills that are necessary to write your final essay.

The writing prompt below was used for the Student Model essay on pages 86–87. The student reflected on her topic and used a cause-effect graphic organizer to help her remember specific events and details that made the situation clear in her mind. This helped her think of a possible thesis.

WRITING PROMPT 1: Why have so many people moved out of rural communities in recent years? Give at least three reasons.

Causes

| not enough jobs |
| boring for young people |
| not enough educational opportunities |
| |

Effect

Many people are leaving rural communities

My thesis: *A lack of jobs, entertainment, and educational opportunities is causing many young people to move away from rural towns.*

In writing prompt 1, the student reflected on the *causes* of a situation. At other times, you will need to reflect on the *effects* of a situation, as in the writing prompt below.

WRITING PROMPT 2: How has an increased Spanish-speaking population changed Arizona?

Cause

More Spanish speakers in Arizona

Effects

| more jobs advertising for bilingual applicants |
| increased interest in changes in immigration policies |
| |

My thesis: An increase in the number of Spanish speakers in Arizona has resulted in new job openings and business opportunities as well as changes to immigration policies.

 1.1 Notice

Work with a partner. Discuss an additional cause in the first cause-effect graphic organizer and an additional effect in the second one. Share your ideas with the class.

Follow the directions to reflect on your topic.

A Choose a prompt:

- Choose a country. Describe a current trend of migration within the country (e.g., rural areas to urban centers, north to south, east to west). Why has it been happening?

- Choose a country. Describe a current trend of migration to or from the country (e.g., people immigrating there from certain countries, or people moving away to certain countries). How has it affected the immigrants and/or the country itself?

- How has the increasing ease and frequency of international travel affected those who travel and the places they go to?

- A topic approved by your instructor

B Work with a partner and complete the following tasks:

1 Think about your prompt. Decide if you need to write about the causes of something or the effects of something.

2 Choose the cause-effect graphic organizer below that best fits your prompt and complete it. Think of everything that might have happened to cause the situation or all the effects that might result from the situation. Add more boxes if you need them.

3 Write a possible thesis statement.

Causes   **Effect**

Cause   **Effects**

Possible thesis statement:

In this section you will learn academic language that you can use in your cause and effect essay. You will also notice how a professional writer uses the language and features of cause and effect.

Ⓐ Academic Vocabulary

The words below appear throughout the unit. They are from the Academic Word List. Using these words in your writing will make your ideas clearer and your writing more academic.

document (v)	exhibit (v)	reaction (n)	summarize (v)
enhance (v)	mutual (adj)	subsequently (adv)	sustain (v)

ACTIVITY **2.1** Focus on Meaning

Work with a partner. Read the sentences. Decide the meaning of the bold words and circle the correct answer.

1 Many study-abroad programs require students to **document** what they learned overseas in papers and projects after they return home. **Document** means

   a to record the details of something.   b to avoid thinking about something.

2 Some residents of Arizona believe that newer immigrants **enhance** their communities, while others believe immigration is not beneficial to them. **Enhance** means

   a to decrease the quality of something.   b to improve the quality of something.

3 Children who move to a new town often **exhibit** symptoms of psychological problems such as anxiety and difficulty sleeping. **Exhibit** means

   a to talk about something.   b to show something publicly.

4 Expanding internationally offers **mutual** benefits to companies and to their traveling customers. Companies increase revenues, and customers enjoy familiar products and services. **Mutual** means

   a doing something for each other.   b doing two different things.

5 When students move to their new college campus, they often have positive **reactions** when they like things and negative ones when they do not. **Reaction** means

   a statement that one person makes to another.   b feeling in response to something.

6 Many auto workers in Detroit were laid off in the 1980s. **Subsequently**, the city's population decreased as people left to find work elsewhere. **Subsequently** means

   a happening after something.   b never happening.

7 The most recent UN report on urban migration is fascinating but too long for many people to read. However, the first page **summarizes** the key information in the report. **Summarize** means

a to present the most important facts or ideas in a short space.

b to replace older facts or ideas with new information.

8 If a city does not have enough jobs to **sustain** all of its residents who need work, people will begin to leave. **Sustain** means

a to keep something going; to maintain.

b to generate new revenue for.

B Academic Collocations

Collocations are words that are frequently used together. Research tells us that the academic vocabulary in Part A is commonly used in the collocations in bold below.

ACTIVITY 2.2 Focus on Meaning

Read the sentences. Decide the meaning of the phrases in bold and circle the correct answer.

1 One of the results of more Spanish-speaking immigrants in Tucson, Arizona, has been that English-language centers are working with job centers for the **mutual support** of those needing bilingual employees and those seeking jobs. **Mutual support** means

a help that one side gives the other.   b help that both sides give each other.

2 A partnership between ESL centers and job placement services also creates **mutual benefit** for those operations because the partnership makes both of their businesses grow. **Mutual benefit** means

a no change for either side.   b positive results for both sides.

3 It is easy to identify new residents in a city because they **exhibit behavior** similar to tourists who do not know the public transportation system and need maps. **Exhibit behavior** means

a to act a certain way.   b to act in a strange way.

4 A very small portion of students have a **negative reaction** to studying abroad and become too homesick to continue. **Negative reaction** means

a a bad response.   b a good response.

5 The diversity brought to many countries because of increased immigration has **greatly enhanced** the cultural awareness of people around the world, which is valuable in our globalized world. **Greatly enhance** means

a to make something impossible.   b to make something stronger.

C Writing in the Real World

The author of "Moving Is Tough for Kids" uses cause and effect to make her argument clearer and more persuasive.

Before you read, answer these questions: What might make moving tough for kids? What might be easy for them?

Now read the article. Think about your answers to the questions above as you read.

NANCY DARLING   (ADAPTED)

MOVING IS TOUGH FOR KIDS

1   **The bad news.** The *New York Times* recently **summarized** new research on how kids are affected by moving. The study, published in the *Journal of Social and Personality Psychology*, carefully **documents** the fact that frequent moves are tough on kids and disrupt[1] important friendships. The study reports that these effects are most problematic[2] for kids who are introverted[3] and whose personalities tend toward anxiety and inflexibility. The study also goes on to say that adults who moved frequently as kids have fewer high-quality relationships and tend to score lower on well-being and life satisfaction.

2   **The not-so-bad news.** The reports warns, however, that these findings should be treated with caution because often families that move a lot may be doing so because of already existing problems, such as a divorce or a job loss. In addition, the moves may be taking place during a time when children are already making difficult transitions. They may be going through puberty[4] or moving from primary education to secondary school, which can be a particularly difficult period. So the difficult **behaviors exhibited** by kids (and adults) who move may be **greatly enhanced** by factors that are not directly related to moving.

3   **A touchy subject.**[5] The subject of moving is a touchy one for my family. We know a lot about it because during the first 25 years of my marriage, we moved 10 times. Yes, that's right, 10 times! My oldest son moved five times before college (a very touchy subject) and my youngest has moved three. We were always the ones who moved. I don't remember my kids ever being the ones left behind. Now, however, things have changed. I have become tenured,[6] and we are the ones who are staying. It was my son's best friend who moved away.

---

[1]disrupt: prevent something from continuing as usual
[2]problematic: causing difficulty, or hard to deal with
[3]introverted: shy, quiet, and unable to make friends easily
[4]puberty: the stage of life when a child develops physically into an adult

[5]a touchy subject: a subject that must be dealt with carefully
[6]become tenured: receive a job for life, usually as a teacher or university professor

4 **The child left behind.** After his best friend moved, my son went through a very difficult time. Children react very differently from adults when things don't go well. For kids, **negative reactions** can include inattentiveness, hyperactivity, and acting out – yelling, hitting, and generally being difficult to control. Fortunately, my son did not hit those depths, but he did have trouble sleeping, his attention was poor, and he was sad a lot of the time. This, of course, hit his friend as well, who was perhaps even more seriously upset and, being extroverted, was even more prone to acting out.

5 **A different generation.** Fortunately, it is much easier for children today to **sustain** a distant relationship. Technology has changed things a lot. When I was a kid and my best friend moved, we wrote weekly letters, but never made a phone call. It was 7 cents a minute and that was a lot of money. Now the kids use the unlimited phone minutes on their cell phones to call each other. My son and his friend have been video chatting regularly on the Internet. And just seeing each other's faces – and the messiness of our familiar family room and his messy new bedroom – provides them with **mutual support** and comfort. And the kids today have video games that can be played online and that tend to promote communication since the kids inevitably talk around and through a game as they play.

6 **Getting involved.** When we were kids and moved to a new town, my parents would immediately settle themselves in, join organizations, and take on leadership roles. I remember my father saying that one of the reasons that families moving through our community had such a hard time is that they kept their distance and didn't get involved in the community. Often, these families came to town not knowing if they would be there for one year, three years, or a lifetime. As a result, they never really committed to staying; they never made friends; they never set down roots. My father would say – and I agree with him – that although it can be painful to have to tear up roots and leave, it is still better to go through that pain than never to become part of a community.

 **2.3** Check Your Understanding

Answer the questions.

1 What are some of the effects of moving on children?

2 Was the effect of moving mostly positive or mostly negative for the author's son? How convincing is this evidence? What kinds of evidence would be better?

3 How does the author's experience differ from your own? What other effects do you think moving can cause for children?

 **2.4** Notice the Features of Cause and Effect

Answer the questions.

1 Look at the first paragraph. Is this paragraph mostly about the effects of something or the causes of something? What words show you this?

2 Is the second paragraph mostly about the effects of something or the causes of something? What language does the author use to show this?

In Section 1 on page 80 you saw how the writer of the Student Model reflected on her topic. In this section you will analyze the final draft of her cause and effect essay. You will learn how to structure your ideas for your own essay.

Ⓐ Student Model

Read the writing prompt again and answer the questions.

WRITING PROMPT: Why have so many people moved out of rural communities in recent years? Give at least three reasons.

1 What cause and effect relationship will the writer focus on?

2 Will the essay be about the causes of something or the effects of something? Which organization from Section 1 will fit this essay best?

Read the essay twice. The first time, think about your answers to the questions above. The second time, answer the questions in the Analyze Writing Skills boxes. This will help you notice key features of cause and effect essays.

STUDENT
MODEL

Rural Communities Left Behind

1   While many news reports focus on struggling cities like Detroit, there have been few reports about the crisis in many rural communities, which are steadily declining and struggling, too, because of a trend called "outmigration." Outmigration is when people leave one area and move to another. This problem interests me because I have lived in a rural community for three years and have personally experienced seeing friends move away and businesses close. According to William H. Frey of the Brookings Institution, a 2014 Census report showed that as of July 2013 almost two-thirds of rural counties had become smaller. Outmigration happens for many reasons, but some common factors are fewer good job opportunities, lack of amenities,[1] and inaccessible health care.

2   One reason for outmigration is a limited number of decent employment opportunities. There are fewer good jobs and more competition in smaller towns, so it is harder to find a job. Young people are the largest group who are most likely to leave to seek job opportunities (McGranahan, Cromartie, and Wojan). For example, in my town there are not many opportunities for jobs in accounting. Many college students graduate with accounting degrees; **subsequently**, if they want to have a career in accounting, they have to move to a city. In addition, jobs in larger cities usually have a higher salary. In the small town of Macon, Georgia, a paralegal makes around $20,000, but in Savannah the amount is almost double. A lack of economic opportunities is clearly a key factor in outmigration.

[1]amenities: the desirable or useful features of a place

1 Analyze Writing Skills

Does this essay focus on multiple causes or multiple effects?

....

2 Analyze Writing Skills

In paragraph 2, underline all the transition words or phrases that signal reasons or causes.

3   Another reason people leave rural areas is that they often do not have a lot of conveniences, such as entertainment and shops. Young people usually leave areas that do not **exhibit** attractive qualities, such as exciting social and cultural events (McGranahan, Cromartie, and Wojan). In my opinion, this is true because when you are young, you want to learn and know about life, and larger cities have many more things to do and experience. In addition, data in a 2013 USDA report also shows that when people retire they will leave for better services and entertainment ("Population"), which **enhance** their quality of life. These quality of life concerns have played a major role in outmigration from many rural areas.

3 Analyze Writing Skills

In paragraph 3, the writer uses two sources to support her topic sentence. Circle them.

4   A lack of access to health care makes people leave. According to the National Council of State Legislatures (NCSL), 90 percent of physicians work in cities, and over three-quarters of rural counties do not have enough health care professionals to serve the population. This means that families with children will have to travel far to get basic health care and older adults will not get the attention that they need. It seems logical that with fewer health care services, both families and older adults would choose to leave for metropolitan areas.

5   In sum, a shortage of job opportunities, lack of amenities, and difficulty getting health care are compelling causes of outmigration. More attention should be paid to this phenomenon since 20 percent of the population live in these areas and their quality of life is important, too. I will probably move to the city, but I would like one day to return to my town. However, my town may not be able to **sustain** itself until then.

4 Analyze Writing Skills

Look at paragraph 5. What kind of comment does the writer make in the last sentence? Circle your answer.

a   a prediction

b   a recommendation

Works Cited

Frey, William H. "A Population Slowdown for Small Town America." *Brookings.edu.* Brookings Institution, 31 Mar. 2014. Web. 2 Aug. 2014.

McGranahan, David, John Cromartie, and Timothy Wojan. *Nonmetropolitan Outmigration Counties: Some Are Poor, Many Are Prosperous.* ERR 107. U.S. Dept. of Agriculture, Nov. 2010. Web. 11 July 2014.

"Rural Health." *NCSL.* National Conference of State Legislatures, n.d. Web. 2 Aug. 2014.

United States. Dept. of Agriculture. *Population and Migration: Overview,* 3 Apr. 2014. Web. 11 July 2014.

ACTIVITY 3.1 Check Your Understanding

Answer the questions.

1 What is the main idea of this essay?

2 Which paragraphs deal with reasons people leave rural communities?

3 What ideas presented here about rural or urban communities have you experienced?

Complete the outline for "Rural Communities Left Behind" with the ideas in the box.

Lack of access to health care makes people leave
Accounting example
Families with children have to travel far for health care
When people retire, they leave for better services and conveniences
Jobs in larger cities usually have a higher salary
Rural areas often do not have a lot of conveniences

STUDENT MODEL

ESSAY OUTLINE

I. Introduction

Thesis Statement

Outmigration happens for many reasons, but the most important are fewer job

opportunities, lack of amenities, and inaccessible health care.

Body Paragraph 1: Cause 1

II. Limited number of decent employment opportunities

Supporting Idea 1

A. Fewer good jobs and more competition

Detail

1. Young people want good careers (McGranahan)

Detail

2.

Supporting Idea 2

B.

Detail

1. Paralegal example

Body Paragraph 2: Cause 2

III.

Supporting Idea 1

A. Young people leave areas that are not attractive and exciting (McGranahan)

Detail

1. My opinion – young people want to learn and experience new things

Supporting Idea 2

B.

Body Paragraph 3: Cause 3	IV.
Supporting Idea 1	A. 90 percent of physicians work in cities (NCSL)
Detail	1.
Detail	2. Older adults do not get the medical attention that they need
	V. Conclusion

Ⓑ Cause and Effect Essays: Organization

Writers analyze cause and effect relationships to show important reasons why something happened (its causes), or to show how something has changed (its effects). While you may be asked to write a traditional cause and effect essay for a composition class, you will more often use this skill to support an argument.

Read the following outlines that show two ways to organize a cause and effect essay.

Organization A: Many Causes, One Effect

WRITING PROMPT: Why are more people around the world moving from rural to urban areas?

Introduction

Thesis: Rural-to-urban migration results from a lack of job opportunities, difficult farming conditions, and poor health care in rural areas.

Body paragraph 1 (Cause 1): Lack of rural jobs

A Most work is low-paying farm work

B USDA: Rural incomes "substantially lower"

Body paragraph 2 (Cause 2): Farming is difficult

A Major droughts in California and elsewhere

B Farm work harder and riskier than before

Organization B: Many Effects, One Cause

WRITING PROMPT: How has migration from rural to urban areas changed the way people live?

Introduction

Thesis: Urbanization has resulted in overcrowding in many cities, but has also helped people support rural relatives and changed the status of women.

Body paragraph 1 (Effect 1): Overcrowding

A UN: 3 billion people in cities now; will double by 2050

B 863 million live in dirty, crowded slums

Body paragraph 2 (Effect 2): Supporting relatives

A City workers send money to rural relatives

B $250 billion sent home every year

(CONTINUED)

Organization A: Many Causes, One Effect	Organization B: Many Effects, One Cause
Body paragraph 3 (Cause 3): *Poor rural health care*	Body paragraph 3 (Effect 3): *Status of women*
A Fewer hospitals nearby	A *Women in cities have fewer babies*
B Hard to find specialists, e.g., obstetricians	B *Women receive more education in cities*
Conclusion	Conclusion

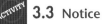 **3.3** Notice

Look at each organizational pattern. Circle *T* if the statements are true or *F* if the statements are false.

Organization A

1 Rural-to-urban migration is presented as a cause in this essay.	T	F
2 The writer discusses more than one effect in this essay.	T	F
3 The writer discusses one cause in each body paragraph.	T	F

Organization B

1 Rural-to-urban migration is presented as a cause.	T	F
2 The body paragraphs in this essay focus on effects.	T	F
3 The writer discusses more than one effect in each body paragraph.	T	F

THE INTRODUCTORY PARAGRAPH IN CAUSE AND EFFECT ESSAYS

Like other introductory paragraphs, a cause and effect introductory paragraph engages readers and prepares them to understand and consider the ideas that the writer will present.

A cause and effect introduction

- mentions the causes or the effects of the situation.
- makes it clear why the topic is important.
- provides background information on the situation.
- states the causes or effects in the thesis statement.

Writers use the language below to indicate causes or effects: The **thesis statement** for a cause and effect essay clearly states whether the writer will focus on causes or effects. Below are examples of good thesis statements that focus on causes. Notice the words in bold that indicate causes.

*There are **three main causes of** illness that can occur when moving to another country: changes in diet, being unprepared for a new climate, and stress.*

*Rural-to-urban migration **results from** a lack of job opportunities, difficult farming conditions, and poor health care in rural areas.*

*Urban areas in many parts of the world are experiencing tremendous population growth **due to** migration and improved health care.*

Language that introduces effects includes: … *consequences of* …., … *leads / has led to* …, … *contributes to* …, … *the effects of* …, *because* … and … *has (positive/negative) effects on.*

Below are examples of good thesis statements that focus on effects. Notice the words in bold that indicate effects.

*Traveling internationally for work **contributes to** personal growth in many ways, including improved communication skills, increased awareness of global politics, and an enhanced ability to get along with diverse groups of people.*

*Changing demographics in France **has had positive effects on** the country's fashion, food, and popular music.*

Some thesis statements do not use the language listed above to introduce causes or effects, yet they clearly show cause and effect relationships through the words in bold. Here are two examples:

*Studies have shown that when children live abroad while growing up, they **tend to have** better grades, experience faster emotional growth, and have an increased tolerance for "newness."*

*Moving to unfamiliar surroundings often **makes** people stressed, disoriented, and isolated.*

ACTIVITY 3.4 Notice

Look at the Student Model on pages 86–87. Circle the words that help you know why the issue is important. Underline the thesis. Which words in the thesis tell you whether the focus is on causes or effects?

ACTIVITY 3.5 Complete the Introduction

Read the prompts for cause and effect essays. Then write a thesis statement.

WRITING PROMPT 1: What are three reasons that people might choose to leave their home country and start a life in a new one?

Thesis statement: *The three reasons that people might choose to leave their home country and start a life in a new one are learn to be independent, explore the world, and change a way of life.*

WRITING PROMPT 2: Many people agree that moving is stressful. What are the positive or negative effects of moving to a new home?

Thesis statement: *Moving to a new home gives people a new beginning, a new place to make friends, and a new chapter of life.*

ACTIVITY 3.6 Apply It to Your Writing

Think about the ideas you wrote for your own essay in Section 1 on page 81. Write some sentences for background information on your topic. Remember to tell your reader why your topic is important.

....

....

....

....

....

....

BODY PARAGRAPHS

Each **body paragraph** develops a main point, in other words, a single cause or a single effect. The **topic sentence** of a cause or effect body paragraph:

- states the cause or effect idea.

- connects the idea to the thesis statement.

A good cause or effect topic sentence uses connecting words such as *one*, *another*, and synonyms of the cause or effect to connect it the thesis statement:

- **One** [significant/important/…] effect/cause of … is …

- **Another** effect/cause of … is …

- **One/Another** reason why …

Read the example below. Notice that the topic sentence repeats the key words of *outmigration* and *reason* and paraphrases the effect *fewer good job opportunities* in the thesis statement.

Thesis statement: *Outmigration happens for many reasons, but some common factors are (fewer good job opportunities,) lack of amenities, and inaccessible health care.*

*Topic sentence, body paragraph 1: **One** reason **for** outmigration **is** a (limited number of decent employment opportunities.)*

Each body paragraph contains **supporting ideas** and **details** that make the ideas clear and interesting to the reader. Read the example below. Notice how the detail gives an interesting personal example that explains the idea that young people "prefer exciting social and cultural events**."**

SUPPORTING IDEA
Young people usually leave areas that do not exhibit attractive qualities, such as exciting social and
DETAIL (PERSONAL EXAMPLE)
cultural events (McGranahan, Cromartie, and Wojan). In my opinion, this is true because when you

are young, you want to learn and know about life, and larger cities have many more things to do

and experience.

Below in the chart are words and phrases that writers often use to explain cause and effect relationships:

WORDS AND PHRASES TO SHOW CAUSE AND EFFECT	
because	***Because*** *they have just moved on to campus, many freshmen get lost easily.*
because of	*Freshmen get lost easily on campus* ***because of*** *their recent move to campus.*
since	*Freshmen get lost easily on campus* ***since*** *they have just moved to the university.*
due to	*Freshmen get lost easily on campus* ***due to*** *the fact that they have just moved to campus.*
as a result	*Freshmen have just moved to campus and,* ***as a result****, get lost easily.*
as a consequence/ consequently	*Freshmen have just moved to the university and,* ***consequently****, get lost easily on campus.*
therefore	*Freshmen have just moved to campus and,* ***therefore****, get lost easily.*
so	*Freshmen have just moved to campus,* ***so*** *they get lost easily.*
so that	*Freshmen are given maps to the campus* ***so that*** *they will not get lost easily.*
for this reason	*Freshmen have just moved to campus, and* ***for this reason****, they can get lost easily.*

ACTIVITY 3.7 Practice Writing Ideas

Read the writing prompt below. Then complete the first body paragraph by writing the missing topic sentence.

WRITING PROMPT: What are three reasons that people might choose to leave their home country and start a life in a new one?

....

....

The desire to improve one's economic circumstances is very strong. When job prospects in one's home country are limited, people tend to move to places where they think they can provide a better life for themselves and their families. The search for improved job prospects is the major reason people immigrate, according to the United Nations Population Fund. The UNFPA points out that many countries that previously had large populations moving away for work, such as Argentina, Ireland, and South Korea, are now experiencing their own influx of immigrants looking for better prospects ("Migration"). This trend illustrates one of the most significant reasons that people move from their home country.

ACTIVITY 3.8 Practice Writing Ideas

Read the thesis statement and first body paragraph topic sentence for a cause and effect essay on moving. Complete the body paragraph with your own ideas.

Thesis: Moving is considered to be one of the top causes of stress because it's expensive, it's disorienting, and it can cause feelings of isolation.

One stressful effect of moving is that people encounter many unexpected expenses.

....

....

....

....

ACTIVITY 3.9 Connect Causes and Effects

Circle the best answers to complete the cause and effect sentences.

1 Redevelopment of failing cities in the United States has brought populations back to run-down and abandoned urban centers. People come back due to ....

  a   the lower cost of living in these areas

  b   the lower cost of living in rural areas

2 Urban development has been considered a negative thing in many developing nations because

  ....

  a   it improves the living conditions of everyone, including the poor

  b   it requires funding that might be better used to provide basic needs such as food and health care

3 Researching new homes in an unfamiliar city can be challenging. Therefore, ...

   a many experts suggest consulting a real estate agent

   b it's a good idea to research new homes on your own

4 Studies show that one of the most important parts of preparing children for a move is finding ways to continue their existing friendships so that ....

   a they will not experience loneliness

   b they will be able to make new friends

5 People tend to .... Consequently, housing is abundant in many rural areas with closed factories.

   a remain in rural areas to be near their families

   b move away from areas lacking in economic opportunities

ACTIVITY **3.10** Apply It to Your Writing

Use the cause and effect expressions in the chart on page 93 to write three cause and effect sentences about the writing prompt you chose in Section 1 on page 81.

....

....

....

....

....

....

....

THE CONCLUDING PARAGRAPH

A concluding paragraph for a cause and effect essay summarizes the thesis and ends with a final comment. This comment can be an observation, prediction, or recommendation.

Read the concluding paragraph below from the Student Model. Notice that the first sentence of the conclusion restates the thesis and the last sentence gives a prediction.

In sum, a shortage of job opportunities, lack of amenities, and difficulty getting health care are compelling causes of outmigration. More attention should be paid to this phenomenon since 20 percent of the population live in these areas and their quality of life is important, too. I will probably move to the city, but I would like one day to return to my town. However, my town may not be able to sustain itself until then.

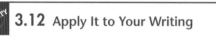 **3.11** Write Final Comments

Complete the concluding paragraph with a final comment.

   In conclusion, moving can be very traumatic for children because it can cause an increased susceptibility to illness, low self-esteem, and depression. However, the parents' attitude and the way in which they handle a move with their children can make all the difference in the world.

....

....

....

....

3.12 Apply It to Your Writing

Think about the ideas you wrote for your own essay in Section I. What might your final comment be? Write some ideas below.

....

....

....

....

....

....

....

In this section you will learn the writing and grammar skills that will help make your writing more sophisticated and accurate.

Ⓐ Writing Skill 1: Paraphrasing

Paraphrasing is an essential skill in U.S. academic culture, and you must practice it in different subjects and with different kinds of essays. Paraphrasing means putting someone else's ideas in your own words, changing the order and the language without changing the original meaning. (You must also cite the source of these ideas.) Paraphrasing is important because it gives a consistent voice to your paper and shows that you understand your subject. Here are some useful strategies for creating a good paraphrase.

STRATEGIES FOR PARAPHRASING

Original Quotation from Robert Huesca:
"When I studied in Mexico City in 1980, telephone access was neither easy nor inexpensive nor of good quality. Attempts to call home were infrequent, costly, and often unsuccessful, which led to feelings of isolation and vulnerability."

1 Use synonyms or antonyms for key words (nouns, verbs, adjectives, etc.).	*Huesca says that <u>phone calls</u> from Mexico City in 1980 were <u>expensive</u> and <u>of poor quality</u>.*
2 Change the parts of speech of some words (verb to noun, etc.).	*According to Huesca, <u>calling home</u> while abroad used to <u>fail</u> regularly and would leave students <u>isolated and vulnerable</u>.*
3 Break up the ideas and/or combine them differently.	*Huesca points out that students studying abroad often felt lonely because of the difficulty of calling home, which was expensive and often failed.*
4 Connect to your own ideas to integrate the quote into your paper topic.	*Huesca talks about the problems of calling home while studying abroad over 30 years ago, noting the cost and the poor connections, but he does not point out how technology has changed things.*

To successfully paraphrase text, you must:

1 Use at least two of the above strategies to change the text so that it reads like your writing – but make sure you do *not* change the ideas.

2 Include the name of the source. Use phrases like the following to give credit to the source:

According to [author/title], …

[Author] states/claims that …

In [name of article/book], [name of author] states/claims that …

Work with a partner. Read the following quotes. Use the strategies in the chart on page 97 to make good paraphrases.

1 "Kids who are economically distressed and those at the top end of the socioeconomic spectrum are more likely to move than those in the middle." – Nancy Darling, "Moving Is Tough for Kids"

Rich children and poor children are easier to change their social status in the future.

2 "Persons who left rural Pennsylvania moved to counties with generally lower unemployment, more business starts, and higher wages." – Center for Rural Pennsylvania, "The Outs and Ins of Rural Migration"

People who move out from Pennsylvania are easier to make money.

3 "Internal migration within countries is also on the rise, as people move in response to inequitable distribution of resources, services and opportunities, or to escape violence, natural disaster or the increasing number of extreme weather events." – The United Nations Population Fund

People who move out of their countries want to have better life.

4 "We identify two types of cross-cultural contact: a) meetings that occur between two societies when individuals travel from their place of origin to another country for a specific purpose and a limited amount of time […], and b) meetings within multi-cultural societies among its ethnically diverse permanent residents." – Stephen Bochner, "Culture Shock Due to Contact with Unfamiliar Cultures"

There are two connections of cultural exchange; temporary travel and permanent resident.

B Writing Skill 2: Avoiding Fragments, Run-On Sentences, and Comma Splices

Complete sentences are expected in academic writing. Using sentence fragments, run-ons, and comma splices undermines the validity of your writing.

1 A complete sentence in English has a subject and a verb, and it expresses a complete idea:

    SUBJECT   VERB

A significant cause of migration is lack of economic opportunity.

2 When a sentence has two independent clauses, the clauses are joined by a comma and a conjunction or a semi-colon.

    INDEPENDENT CLAUSE 1   INDEPENDENT CLAUSE 2

Freshmen have just moved on to campus, so they get lost easily.

Moving is especially stressful for children; the number of changes is overwhelming for them.

Below in the chart are ways to identify and avoid the common errors that writers make.

HOW TO AVOID FRAGMENTS, RUN-ON SENTENCES, AND COMMA SPLICES

1 A **sentence fragment** is a sentence that does not contain a subject or a verb and does not express a complete idea.

  Missing verb: *Another reason people leave rural counties for metropolitan suburbs and*

            is
  cities ^ *for employment.*

        It i
  Missing a subject: *͜s not easy to find a job in a small town.*
             ^

2 A **run-on sentence** has two or more independent clauses that are joined without a comma or a conjunction.

              , and
  Moving is stressful it can cause physical and emotional problems.
              ^

3 A **comma splice** is similar to a run-on sentence. It is when two or more independent clauses are connected only by a comma. Notice the three ways that you can correct the sentence.

                         and
  a **Add *and*:** *There aren't enough services in rural areas, young families are moving out.*
                      ^

                            . Y
  b **Add a period:** *There aren't enough services in rural areas, young families are moving out.*
                          ^

                              ;
  c **Add a semicolon:** *There aren't enough services in rural areas, young families are moving out.*
                           ^

4.2 Correct Mistakes

The following sentences are fragments or run-ons, or have comma splices. Rewrite the sentences correctly.

1 Moving from one city to another.

SF Moving from one city to another, is difficult

2 Tourism has helped the global economy it has harmed the environment.

but/yet/however

Run-on sentence

3 Everyone who comes to the United States must have a visa, people who work in the U.S. must get a special kind of visa and must be supported by a company in a particular field.

And

Comma splice

4 It has always been challenging for immigrant job applicants to be treated equally they are viewed as less important than citizens.

. And

Run-on sentence

5 Many believe moving to a warm location like Florida is easy for everyone recent research shows that changing climates can cause depression and anxiety.

. But / however / yet

. however,

ⓒ Grammar for Writing: Present Perfect and Present Perfect Progressive

In general, we use the **present perfect** to emphasize a time in the past up to now. The time period may or may not be completed, but in both cases, there is a connection to the present. We use the **present perfect progressive** to describe an action that started in the past and to emphasize that it is still going on.

PRESENT PERFECT AND PRESENT PERFECT PROGRESSIVE

1 The present perfect or the present perfect progressive can be used to talk about habitual actions that began in the past and continue in the present, especially with verbs like *get, go, increase, live, study,* and *work.* The meaning is the same.

In the United States, it is rare to encounter people who **have lived** *in the same place their entire lives.*

In the United States, it is rare to encounter people who **have been living** *in the same place their entire lives.*

2 The present perfect is for completed actions, and the present perfect progressive is for actions still in progress.

*Immigrants who **have adjusted** to their new country often find it difficult to return home.*

*The refugees **have been adjusting** to a new culture and hope to feel more comfortable here in the future.*

3 The present perfect progressive is better for actions that are temporary.

*People **have lived** in this city for hundreds of years.*

*Since the storm, many residents **have been living** with relatives while their homes are being repaired.*

4 Use the present perfect to express *how much/many*. Use the present perfect progressive to express *how long*.

*More than 10,000 people **have moved** to the city in the last year.* (more than 10,000 = how many)

*People **have been moving** out of the country for several years now.* (for several years = how long)

5 The present perfect progressive cannot be used with *be* and other stative verbs.

*Geographic mobility **has been** on the rise in the United States for several decades.* (NOT has been being on the rise)

ACTIVITY 4.3 Practice

Complete the paragraph with the present prefect or present perfect progressive forms of the verbs in parentheses. Sometimes both forms are correct.

Some rural communities .... (experience) new growth over the last
(1)
several years because they offer natural beauty and amenities to residents. Part of this change

has come about because dozens of new job opportunities .... (develop)
(2)
in areas like customer service and tourism. Some residents believe these changes are good,

while others .... (increase) their advocacy work against the influx of
(3)
certain kinds of businesses. For example, in one small resort town in Wyoming, residents

.... (protest) the recent attempts of a large chain retailer to gain permits
(4)
to build a new store. The permit has not yet been granted by the town council, and the people

believe they can stop this unwanted growth. The debate .... (be) a
(5)
difficult one, but it is a common topic for similar communities. What all residents agree on in

these growing, rural communities is that they .... (live) in changing
(6)
communities for years and that they should be in charge of how their communities change.

Avoiding Common Mistakes

Research tells us that these are the most common mistakes that students make when using the present perfect and present perfect progressive in academic writing.

> **1 Use the present perfect for an action that is completed. Do not use the present perfect progressive.**
>
>   **have finished**
> Now that workers ~~have been finishing~~ the new airport runway, international flights can land there.
>
> **2 Use *been* when forming the present perfect progressive.**
>
>   **have been asking**
> Interns ~~have asking~~ for more low-cost housing in large cities in the United States for many years.
>
> **3 Use *has* with singular third-person subjects. Use *have* with all other subjects.**
>
>   **has**
> Professor Dixon ~~have~~ spent years studying the effects of frequent moves on the children of military families.

ACTIVITY 4.4 Editing Task

Find and correct five more mistakes in the following paragraph.

    Culture shock is common when moving to a new country, but many people experience cultural difficulties when moving between regions within large countries like the United States. A new study released by Progress University examines how moving to New England (a group of states in the northeastern United States) from many other parts of America comes with challenges. Dr. Rudolph Abrams has **been** studying 25 families that are new to New England for the last five years, gathering data on community and school integration and measuring mood. His completed study shows that most of these 25 families has reported missing favorite foods not available in local grocery stores. Others have been describing the initial difficulty they experienced getting to know people in workplaces, schools, and community groups. However, those families now report significant improvement in their local relationships and increased satisfaction with the move to New England. Other data shared from the study include trouble with accented English. In one example response quoted by the researchers, a father of two said that he "has working with a man whose accent [he] could not understand. Assuming the man was a new immigrant, [he] asked what country he grew up in and was embarrassed to be told America – and Maine" (Abrams et al. 6). The same man reported that he had never lived outside Alabama and never traveled outside the region until moving north for his new job (7). Dr. Abrams and his colleagues have already been spending more than five years studying these subjects and will expand the research to other families in the future. All said, this work so far has presented concrete evidence for something that has coming up in conversations about national migration for a long time.

D Avoiding Plagiarism

Paraphrasing is a useful skill to avoid plagiarizing, but it must be done carefully.

I wanted to use the ideas in this quotation in my paper: "According to the World Health Organization (WHO), in 2005, approximately 1.6 billion adults (age 15+) worldwide were overweight, at least 400 million of whom were obese." I paraphrased it in this way: "In 2005, there were over 1 billion adults over the age of 15 around the world who were overweight, and approximately one-third of those people were obese." My instructor said I plagiarized, but I thought I didn't! What am I doing wrong? I thought I understood paraphrasing. – Olga

Dear Olga,

You've made a good attempt in your paraphrase. You've changed some key words, which is a good start. One thing I notice is that some of your paraphrase isn't quite accurate. For example, one-third of 1.6 billion isn't 400 million. Accuracy in paraphrasing is very important. Always go back and make sure your details mean the same as the original. It is also important to change the structure of the sentences, not just a few words. Finally, and very importantly, you forgot to cite your source. Remember that original research, data, and statistics are not common knowledge. Always tell where this information is from, even when you paraphrase.

Good luck!

Professor Wright

STEPS TO WRITING A GOOD PARAPHRASE

1 Read the material carefully for meaning.
   - Take notes on key ideas. Don't copy whole sentences.
   - Include the source in your notes.
   - Talk to someone about the ideas and details, so you are sure you understand them.
2 Write your paraphrase from memory, or use your notes to help you.
3 Compare your work with the original.
   - Be sure your information is correct and accurate.
   - Be sure you have used your own words: synonyms, sentence structure, word forms.
   - Be sure you cite the original source, both in the text and on your Works Cited page.

4.5 Practice

Read the quotation and the three paraphrases. Discuss with a partner. What is the error in each paraphrase?

"In 2012, 13.7 percent of householders living with their own children moved."

Source: David Ihrke, U.S. Census Bureau website

1 According to David Ihrke, in 2012, 13.7% of houses with children moved (U.S. Census Bureau).

2 According to the David Ihrke, 13.7% of children moved (U.S. Census Bureau).

3 Nearly 14% of parents with children at home moved in 2012.

[handwritten annotations: "Olga" above "in 2012", "house" above "houses", "13.7" below item 3]

4.6 Applying the Strategies

Read the quotation in Activity 4.5. Follow the steps to writing a good paraphrase. Write a paraphrase of the quote.

According to David Ihrke, 13.7% of house owners who have been living with their own kids moved.

5 WRITE YOUR ESSAY

In this section you will follow the writing process to complete the final draft of your essay.

STEP 1: BRAINSTORM
Work with a partner. Follow the steps below to brainstorm more ideas.

1 Before you start, notice how the writer of the Student Model brainstormed. She wrote many ideas. Then she crossed out the causes she thought were not important enough to use in her essay.

WRITING PROMPT: Why have so many people moved out of rural communities in recent years? Give at least three reasons.

Causes   **Effect**

Causes	Effect
not enough jobs	
~~boring for young people~~	
~~not enough educational opportunities~~	Many people are leaving rural communities
~~marriage and friendship prospects limited~~	
~~things are too expensive~~	
lack of access to health care	
want services / amenities of city	

2 Write the ideas that you wrote in Section 1, page 81, in one of the cause-effect graphic organizers below. Include ideas from the Your Turns throughout the unit. Brainstorm more ideas.

Causes   **Effect**

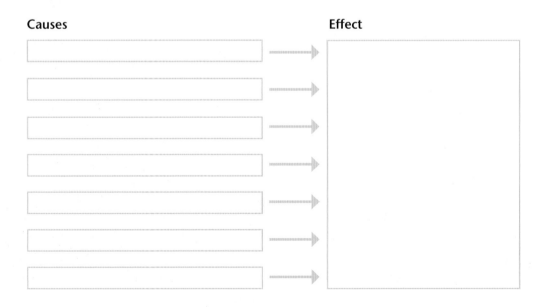

Cause	Effects

When you are finished, circle the three most important causes or effects and write them here. Think about how you will support each one.

1 ....

2 ....

3 ....

STEP 2: DO RESEARCH: CHOOSING A TEXT TO PARAPHRASE FOR SUPPORT IN AN ESSAY

Selecting appropriate texts from credible sources is an important part of doing research. Some credible sources are educational institutions, government agencies, and respected news organizations. You choose texts to paraphrase based on the importance of their **evidence**, like details, explanations, or examples, and how that evidence supports the main ideas in the body paragraphs of your essay.

Sue needed to choose a text to paraphrase for support in an essay response to this prompt: *The populations of most countries are becoming less rural and more urban. What are some reasons for this trend?* Read and find out how she did it.

After identifying the main points in my thesis, I read several sources and identified texts with main ideas related to my thesis. Next, I compared the evidence in the texts to see which one provided the best support for my main ideas. Last, I paraphrased the text into my own words and added a citation for the source.

Sue's Results

Thesis: Primary causes of the rapid urbanization of sub-Saharan Africa are <u>changes in the environment</u>, <u>increased economic opportunities</u>, and <u>population growth</u>.

Focus of research: <u>population growth</u> due to rapid urbanization

Source	Text	How it supports my point
1 <u>Time</u>, "Urban Planet: How Growing Cities Will Wreck the Environment Unless We Build Them Right" (Bryan Walsh, 2012)	"… the wave of urbanization <u>isn't just about the migration of people into urban environments, but about the environments themselves becoming bigger to accommodate all those people.</u>"	shows direct link between population growth & larger cities (more people = more space)
2 http://www.afdb.org/, "Urbanization of Africa" (Mthuli Ncube, 2012)	"In the developing world, <u>Africa has experienced the highest urban growth during the last two decades at 3.5% per year</u> and this rate of growth is expected to hold into 2050."	statistic; general reference to African population growth, but no cause/effect given

Paraphrase of chosen text: Sizes of cities are growing in two phases: first, more people move into the cities, and then the city space must grow to fit all of the new people (Walsh).

ACTIVITY 5.1 Apply It to Your Writing

Follow the steps Sue took to choose a text to paraphrase for support in your essay.

STEP 3: MAKE AN OUTLINE

Complete the outline below with your ideas from the previous steps.

ESSAY OUTLINE

I. Introduction

Hook Idea

Background Ideas

Thesis Statement

Body Paragraph 1: Cause/Effect 1

II.

Supporting Idea 1

A.

Detail

1.

Detail

2.

Supporting Idea 2

B.

Detail

1.

Detail

2.

Body Paragraph 2: Cause/Effect 2

III.

Supporting Idea 1

A.

Detail

1.

Detail

2.

Supporting Idea 2

B.

Detail

1.

Detail

2.

(CONTINUED)

Body Paragraph 3: Cause/Effect 3	IV. _____
Supporting Idea 1	A. _____
Detail	1. _____
Detail	2. _____
Supporting Idea 2	B. _____
Detail	1. _____
Detail	2. _____
	V. Conclusion _____
Ideas for a Final Comment	_____

STEP 4: WRITE YOUR FIRST DRAFT

Now it is time to write your first draft. Here are some suggestions on how to get started.

1 Use your outline, notes, and the sentences you wrote in the Your Turns and in Step 3 above.

2 Focus on making your ideas as clear as possible.

3 Remember to add a title.

After you finish, read your essay and check for basic errors.

1 Check that all sentences are complete sentences.

2 Go through and look at every comma. Is it correct? Should it be a period?

3 Check that you have cited quotes and paraphrases.

4 Make sure your thesis statement and topic sentences are clear.

STEP 5: WRITE YOUR FINAL DRAFT

1 After you receive feedback on your first draft, review it carefully. Fix any errors.

2 Make a note of errors that were most frequent (misspellings, wrong verb tense, errors in using commas). Try to avoid them as you write.

3 Review the Academic Vocabulary and Academic Collocations from this unit. Are there any that you can add to your essay?

4 Turn to page 272 and use the Self-Editing Review to check your work one more time.

5 Write your final draft and hand it in.

4 COMPARISON AND CONTRAST ESSAYS

ANTHROPOLOGY: FOOD AND CULTURE

> *"Tell me what you eat, and I'll tell you who you are."*
>
> Jean Anthelme Brillat-Savarin (1755–1826)

About the Author:

Jean Anthelme Brillat-Savarin was a French politician and lawyer who also became famous for writing about food. This is one of his most famous sayings.

Work with a partner. Read the quotation about food. Then answer the questions.

1 What do you think the quotation means? Paraphrase the idea in your own words.

2 Is there something that you like to eat or drink which reveals something about your personality? What is it?

3 What are some examples of the *cuisine* (style of cooking) of your home country? What do these dishes show about the culture?

A Connect to Academic Writing

In this unit you will learn skills to help you compare and contrast ideas. While some of the writing skills that you will use may be new to you, the skill of comparing ideas is not new. In your everyday life you use the skill of comparison to tell someone how a movie is different from the book it's based on, or talk about how you and one of your siblings are similar and how you are different.

B Reflect on the Topic

In this section you will choose a writing prompt and reflect on it. You will develop these ideas throughout the unit and use them to practice skills that are necessary to write your essay.

The writing prompt below was used for the Student Model essay on pages 118–120. The student reflected on his topic and used a Venn diagram to see similarities and differences. This helped him think of a possible thesis.

STUDENT MODEL

WRITING PROMPT: In U.S. grocery stores, consumers can buy both natural foods and foods with artificial ingredients. Some say that only natural foods are healthy, while others say that foods with artificial ingredients are cheaper, but still healthy. In your view, is one better than the other?

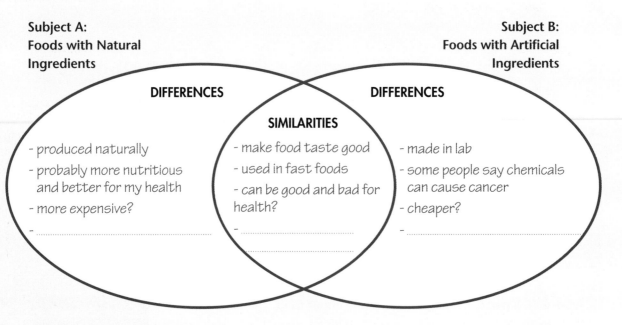

Subject A:
Foods with Natural Ingredients

Subject B:
Foods with Artificial Ingredients

DIFFERENCES

DIFFERENCES

SIMILARITIES

- produced naturally
- probably more nutritious and better for my health
- more expensive?

- make food taste good
- used in fast foods
- can be good and bad for health?

- made in lab
- some people say chemicals can cause cancer
- cheaper?

My thesis: *In my view, although foods with natural ingredients can be more expensive, their health benefits make them a better choice than foods with artificial ingredients.*

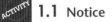 **1.1** Notice

Work with a partner. Discuss one more similarity and one more difference. Which type of food do you usually prefer? Why? Share your ideas with the class.

Follow the directions to reflect on your topic.

A Choose a prompt:

- Compare holiday practices and traditions related to food and eating in two cultures (e.g., Thanksgiving in the U.S. and Lunar New Year in China). What do these traditions tell us about the cultures they come from?

- Choose a country. How do eating habits today differ from eating habits 50 years ago? How do these changes reflect general cultural changes?

- There is a debate that eating locally sourced food (food that has been produced near the place where it is eaten) is better for the environment than eating food that is imported, in other words, food that is transported by truck, train, or plane from far away places. Compare the two kinds of food from a consumer's point of view. Are there more advantages or disadvantages for them?

- A topic approved by your instructor

B Work with a partner and complete the following tasks:

1 Think about your prompt. Decide what you will focus on in your essay.

2 Complete the Venn diagram below. Think of everything you know about both subjects.

3 Write a possible thesis statement.

Subject A: ....   **Subject B:** ....

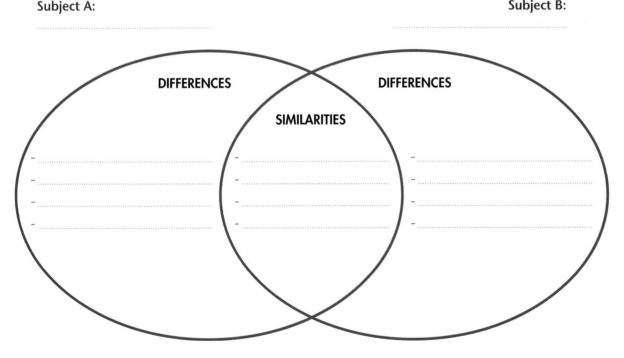

DIFFERENCES   DIFFERENCES

SIMILARITIES

Possible thesis statement:

....

In this section you will learn academic language that you can use in your comparison and contrast essay. You will also notice how a professional writer uses the language and features of comparison and contrast.

Ⓐ Academic Vocabulary

The words below appear throughout the unit. Many are from the Academic Word List. Using these words in your writing will make your ideas clearer and your writing more academic.

alter (v)	concentrated (adj)	consequence (n)	restrict (v)
commodity (n)	condition (n)	dramatically (adv)	virtually (adv)

ACTIVITY **2.1** Focus on Meaning

Work with a partner. Match the words to their meanings. Write the letters.

A

.... 1 Early voyages to the New World had great effects on life in Europe. One **consequence** was the introduction of new foods such as the tomato.

a almost, but not exactly

.... 2 Today, tomatoes grow throughout the world, but their cultivation is particularly **concentrated** in China, the world's top producer of the fruit.

b something that can be bought or sold

.... 3 Chili peppers are found in **virtually** every cuisine in the world. Almost every culture in the world enjoys this New World vegetable.

c result

.... 4 Tobacco, a product used by Native Americans for smoking, was an unknown **commodity** in Europe until Columbus's voyages.

d existing in a particular place in a large quantity

1 European and Native American cultures were **dramatically** different. There were hardly any similarities between the two cultures.

2 In many parts of the New World, growing **conditions** such as climate and soil quality were similar to those in Europe.

3 The European diet was **altered** by Columbus's voyage to the Americas. Changes included the addition of foods such as the tomato and the potato.

4 California **restricts** the importation of certain fruits. People cannot bring them into the state because they might contain pests.

a changed

b very noticeably

c limits

d the state that something is in

B Academic Phrases

Research tells us that the phrases in bold below are commonly used in academic writing.

ACTIVITY 2.2 Focus on Purpose

Read the paragraph. Then match the phrases in bold to the purpose, or reason why, the writer used them.

Overeating during special occasions is another cultural habit that has lost its significance and may no longer be beneficial for society. In ancient times the habit of overeating on special occasions was a way to celebrate life. Food was scarce in certain seasons, and people had to work hard to get it. Thus, people ate a lot during holidays to nourish themselves. **In the same way,** they used food to celebrate their survival. This habit did not affect people's health because they normally ate little and they were physically very active. These days, the habit of overeating during holidays is the cause of health problems. People **are likely to** gain weight during holidays because they eat but they do not exercise very much. **It is important to note,** too, that modern agricultural techniques have made food more affordable at all times during the year. As a result, people rarely go without food. In sum, the habit of eating a great deal of food during the holidays may not be the best option for most people.

PHRASE	PURPOSE
C 1 are likely to	a to bring a reader's attention to something important about the topic
a 2 it is important to note _- significant -_	b to show a similarity between ideas
b 3 in the same way	c to show a noticeable tendency

The author of "The Cost of a Global Food Chain" uses features of comparison and contrast to strengthen his argument.

Before you read, answer this question: What kind of "cost" do you think the title is referring to?

Now read the article. Think about your answer to the question above as you read.

ROBERT GOTTLIEB   (ADAPTED)

THE COST OF A
GLOBAL FOOD CHAIN

1   Check out the garlic the next time you're in the supermarket. In another era it likely would have been grown in Gilroy, California, a town that used to be known as the garlic capital of the world. But today, chances are that your garlic has traveled across oceans and continents to get to your kitchen.

2   Most garlic nowadays comes from China. Since 2003, the amount of garlic imported from China has nearly tripled, whereas the amount grown in California has dropped by nearly half. This means that instead of traveling several hundred miles to get to you, your garlic is probably traveling many thousands of miles.

3   Similarly, the ships that carry the garlic from China utilize highly toxic[1] bunker fuel that is **likely to** have come from distant countries like Venezuela, a leading supplier of oil. The big container ships take on the fuel in South America, then travel across the Pacific, where they or other ships pick up the garlic in China and then sail back across the ocean to the ports of Los Angeles and Long Beach. There, it is loaded on trains or trucks, which in turn create additional diesel pollution. The environmental impacts are global, and they are particularly **concentrated** in each of the destination points, whether in China or the United States, where ships, trains, trucks, and warehouses are located.

4   So why have we shifted to purchasing Chinese garlic? Even with all the transportation costs, it is still cheaper to import garlic from China than to buy garlic grown locally. However, there are hidden costs. The farmer in Gilroy is forced to charge less for garlic and has less money in his pocket to spend on American goods. Moreover, the Chinese garlic doesn't have the same taste or texture as that of locally produced garlic. Finally, the trade deficit[2] with China gets bigger, American unemployment grows, and our connection to the food we eat is undermined.[3]

5   The increasing globalization of food **commodities** isn't just a concern in the United States. For example, Frito-Lay,

[1]toxic: poisonous

[2]trade deficit: the amount by which the value of a country's imports is greater than its exports
[3]undermined: made weaker

a division of PepsiCo, has successfully introduced potato chips, a quintessential[4] American product, into China. It has done so, in part, by adhering to Chinese restrictions on what can be introduced into China. The Chinese won't allow crops produced elsewhere to be imported, so Frito-Lay now grows potatoes in China. "PepsiCo is not a farming company. But to build a market, we had to take extra steps like this," the operations director for PepsiCo's China venture told the *Wall Street Journal*.

6 With potato chip products like Frito-Lay's green tea potato chips joining other fast food products that now flood Chinese stores, the diets of people in China are changing **dramatically**. One **consequence**: Nearly a quarter of the population is overweight or obese,[5] **conditions** that were **virtually** unheard of a generation ago. The Chinese are not as obese as the Americans are yet, but they're on their way.

[4]quintessential: being the most typical example of something
[5]obese: weighing too much in a way that is unhealthy

7 Food has become a global product. That has meant we can sip Chilean wine with our French cheese. **In the same way** it has meant nothing is ever out of season: We can buy peaches in January and Brussels sprouts in August. But at what cost?

8 We hear a lot about the benefits of global trade, which has made the food we eat cheaper. But **it is important to note** that moving food thousands of miles from farm to market increases pollution, **alters** traditional diets, and hurts local farmers.

9 One thing, though, is abundantly clear: Food is intricately[6] bound up with culture, and when we lose our connection to locally grown food, we also lose a piece of our culture. It's time to begin reconnecting with what we eat.

[6]intricately: arranged in a complicated way

 2.3 Check Your Understanding

Answer the questions.

1 What is the impact on the environment that the big Chinese ships have?

2 How has the globalization of food affected culture, according to the author? Do you agree?

3 Have you ever bought food in a store and noticed that it came from somewhere far away? What was it?

 2.4 Notice the Writing

Answer the questions.

1 Look at the first two paragraphs. What two things are compared?

2 Which word in the second paragraph indicates that ideas are being contrasted?

3 Which word in the third paragraph indicates that ideas are being compared because they are similar?

In Section 1 on page 112 you saw how the writer of the Student Model reflected on his topic. In this section you will analyze the final draft of his comparison and contrast essay. You will learn how to structure your ideas for your own essay.

Ⓐ Student Model

Read the writing prompt again and answer the questions.

WRITING PROMPT: In U.S. grocery stores, consumers can buy both natural foods and foods with artificial ingredients. Some say that only natural foods are healthy, while others say that foods with artificial ingredients are cheaper, but still healthy. In your view is one better than the other?

1 What is the prompt asking the writer to compare?

2 What are some similarities and differences that you think the writer will mention?

Read the essay twice. The first time, think about your answers to the questions above. The second time, answer the questions in the Analyze Writing Skills boxes. This will help you notice key features of comparison and contrast.

✓ outline

STUDENT MODEL

The Naturally Inferior Choice

1   When I moved to the United States and first saw the labels "natural" and "artificial" on food packages, I was surprised. In Kenya, food companies did not use these labels, but in the United States, they are found on many foods. I used to assume that natural foods were better because they come from nature, and artificial foods were inferior because they are developed in laboratories. However, when comparing their definitions, prices, and impact on the environment, it soon becomes clear that artificial foods are not always the inferior choice.

One is better than the other

2   One advantage of artificial foods is that they have a clearer definition than natural foods do. Therefore, consumers know what they are eating. In the United States, for example, the term "artificial" is **restricted** to just one meaning. Legally, "artificial" refers to any food, flavor, or color that uses man-made chemicals. For example, when scientists want to make a **concentrated** orange flavor, they create chemicals that match the flavor chemicals in a real orange (Spector). In contrast, natural foods do not have a legal definition. That is because the U.S. Food and Drug Administration, the body regulating food labeling, does not want to define them (Jones). As a **consequence**, "natural" can mean **virtually** anything that food companies want it to mean. Many U.S. companies write "natural" on food packaging just to make their products sound healthy. However, saying that a food has "natural sugar" does not make

---

1 Analyze Writing Skills

Underline the subjects in paragraph 1 that the writer is comparing.

2 Analyze Writing Skills

Underline the thesis statement in paragraph 1. What three points or reasons will the writer use to compare the two subjects? Circle them.

3 Analyze Writing Skills

Underline the point that the writer will discuss in paragraph 2. Which subject does the writer discuss first: artificial or natural foods?

it any healthier. It still has sugar. When we compare their definitions, "natural" is less straightforward[1] than "artificial."

3   In addition, foods with artificial ingredients benefit consumers more. They usually have lower prices than foods with a "natural" label because they are made in a laboratory. Scientists make new flavors by combining chemicals they store in the lab. If they need a new chemical, they can make it by themselves right there. In contrast, natural ingredients must be grown on a farm, processed, and then transported to the lab. They are more expensive to produce because farmers, truck drivers, and distribution companies charge for all of these services. Food companies need to make up for all of the extra expenses, so foods with natural ingredients cost **dramatically** more at the grocery store (Spector). Furthermore, natural foods have become a valuable **commodity** in the United States (Ferdman). Consumer demand for them is high, so food companies charge more just because of the label.

4   Finally, in comparison to natural foods, artificial food products have some important advantages for the environment. Since artificial foods are man-made, the process of manufacturing them does not involve farmland or the cultivation of crops. In contrast, the environmental **conditions** required for natural ingredients are more demanding.[2] For example, **it is important to note** that putting real fruit in a product means that people must first develop the land to grow it. They may have to cut down existing trees to make room for new crops. In addition, they must water the crops regularly to keep them alive. All of these requirements have a more dramatic impact on the planet.

5   In summary, artificial foods are superior to natural foods in certain ways. The "natural" label can be used by U.S. companies to charge more for food that might not truly be healthier, whereas "artificial" has a more transparent[3] definition. Using artificial ingredients saves consumers money and also reduces the amount of land and water needed to grow natural ingredients. The

(CONTINUED)

---

4 Analyze Writing Skills

Underline the point that the writer will discuss in paragraph 3. Double underline the supporting idea that the writer discusses for each subject.

5 Analyze Writing Skills

Underline the phrase in paragraph 3 that shows you the writer is introducing a contrast between the two subjects.

6 Analyze Writing Skills

Underline the sentences in paragraph 4 that provide details for the supporting idea for the second subject.

differences between artificial and natural foods are much more complex than I had first assumed. I no longer believe that natural is always better, and I have **altered** my shopping habits as a result. Now when I go grocery shopping in the United States, there are many artificial foods in my cart.

7 Analyze Writing Skills

Underline the sentences in paragraph 5 that restate the main ideas. Draw a box around the sentences that are a comment by the writer.

Works Cited

Ferdman, Roberto A. "The Word 'Natural' Helps Sell $40 Billion Worth of Food in the US Every Year – and the Label Means Nothing." *Washington Post*. Washington Post, 24 June 2014. Web. 11 Nov. 2014.

Jones, Ashby. "Is Your Dinner 'All Natural'?" *WSJ Video*. Wall Street Journal Digital Network, 20 Sept. 2011. Web. Transcript. 11 Nov. 2014.

Spector, Dina. "The Surprising Truth About How Many Chemicals Are in Everything We Eat." *Business Insider*. Business Insider, 4 Feb. 2014. Web. 11 Nov. 2014.

ACTIVITY 3.1 Check Your Understanding

Answer the questions.

1 What is the purpose for contrasting the two subjects?

2 Which point in the writer's thesis do you think is the strongest? Why?

3 Do you agree or disagree with the writer's point of view? Why or why not?

ACTIVITY 3.2 Outline the Writer's Ideas

Complete the outline for "The Naturally Inferior Choice" using the phrases in the box.

benefits to consumers	high demand so price is higher
environmental advantage of artificial foods	impact on the environment
expensive to grow	refers to foods with man-made chemicals
FDA doesn't want to define them	requires land

ESSAY OUTLINE

I. Introduction

Thesis Statement

However, when comparing their definitions, prices, and impact on the environment, it soon

becomes clear artificial foods are not always the inferior choice.

Body Paragraph 1: Point of Comparison

II. Definition

Subject A

A. Artificial foods have clearer definition

Detail

1. Restricted to one meaning

Detail

2.

Subject B

B. Natural foods no legal definition

Detail

1.

Detail

2. Can refer to whatever companies want it to mean

Body Paragraph 2: Point of Comparison

III.

Subject A

A. Artificial foods benefit consumers more

Detail

1. Lower prices – made in a lab

Subject B

B. Natural foods more expensive

Detail

1.

Detail

2.

(CONTINUED)

homework

Body Paragraph 3: Point of Comparison	IV. ....
Subject A	A. ....
Detail	1. Manufacturing does not require farmland or crops ....
Subject B	B. Natural foods more demanding of environment ....
Detail	1. ....
Detail	2. Must cut down trees for land ....
Detail	3. Use a lot of water ....
	V. Conclusion ....
Restatement of Thesis	A. ....
Comment	B. ....

B Comparison and Contrast Essays

In comparison and contrast essays, writers compare subjects to help reveal important differences and/or similarities between two subjects and arrive at an insight. The ability to compare and contrast subjects is a valuable skill in many types of writing, such as argumentative and cause and effect.

As with other academic essays, the introduction has a **hook, background information**, and a **thesis**. The thesis usually contains the **points of comparison**. Points of comparison are the features or characteristics that the writer will use to compare the two subjects.

Comparison and contrast essays also include a conclusion that restates the thesis and ends with an observation or something important that the writer learned by comparing the two subjects.

Two common ways to structure this type of essay are **point-by-point organization** and **block organization**.

Point-by-point organization works especially well when your subjects share similarities and differences for each point and you want to highlight the distinctions. The following chart shows the structure of a point-by-point essay.

POINT-BY-POINT ORGANIZATION

Introductory paragraph

Body paragraph 1: Point 1: Definition

    Subject A: Artificial foods – clear definition

        Detail

        Detail

    Subject B: Natural foods – no legal definition

        Detail

        Detail

Body paragraph 2: Point 2: Benefits to consumers

    Subject A: Artificial foods – cheaper

        Detail

        Detail

    Subject B: Natural foods – more expensive

        Detail

        Detail

Body paragraph 3: Point 3: Advantages to the environment

    Subject A: Artificial foods – little impact

        Detail

        Detail

    Subject B: Natural foods – more impact

        Detail

        Detail

Concluding paragraph

Another way to write a comparison and contrast essay, **block organization,** is to compare two or more subjects by presenting Subject A and then comparing Subject B to Subject A. The chart on page 124 shows the basic structure using the subjects of the Student Model.

BLOCK ORGANIZATION

Introductory paragraph

Body paragraph 1: Subject A: Artificial foods

 Point 1: Definition – Clear definition

 Point 2: Benefits to consumers – Cheaper; good for consumers

 Point 3: Impact on environment – Little impact on environment

Body paragraph 2: Subject B in comparison to A: Natural foods in comparison to artificial foods

 Point 1: Definition – Not as clearly defined

 Point 2: Benefits to consumers – More expensive

 Point 3: Impact on environment – Much more impact on environment

Concluding paragraph

In this unit, you will learn to structure your essay in the point-by-point format.

 **3.3** Notice

Look at the outline of the Student Model on pages 121–122. Which organizational structure did the writer of the essay use: point-by-point or block organization? Why do you think he chose that organization?

 **3.4** Notice

Read each sentence. Circle *T* if it is true and *F* if it is false.

1 In the block organization, artificial foods and natural foods are mentioned in both body paragraphs. T F

2 In the block organization, in the second body paragraph the writer will always use the comparative to talk about Subject B. T F

3 Both the point-by-point and block organization have the same number of paragraphs. T F

4 Both structures have an introduction and a conclusion. T F

BODY PARAGRAPHS

The **body paragraphs** of a comparison and contrast essay show how the two subjects compare to each other. Each body paragraph in a point-by-point essay discusses one **point of comparison**. **Points of comparison** are the features and characteristics that the writer uses to compare the two subjects. Writers choose the strongest, most interesting, or most striking points that will support their thesis. In each paragraph you will analyze each subject in a parallel manner. In the essay, writers include the same **points of comparison** for their subjects.

Below is a chart showing points of comparison for a writing prompt.

WRITING PROMPT: Compare the food and drink that is common in South Korea today with that which was common there 100 years ago. How do these changes reflect cultural changes?

POINTS OF COMPARISON	100 YEARS AGO	TODAY
1 drinks	tea – traditional tea – cheap and available	coffee very popular readily available status symbol
2 beef	rare expensive – mainly for upper classes more fish-based society	readily available served in many popular restaurants
3 Western-style fast food	nonexistent only local foods	very popular both international and national food chains

ACTIVITY 3.5 Practice

Complete the outline for one of the body paragraphs of an essay based on the writing prompt and information on page 125.

Body Paragraph 1: Point 1 ....

Subject A: ....

Detail ....

Detail ....

Subject B: ....

Detail ....

Detail ....

Detail ....

ACTIVITY 3.6 Apply It to Your Writing

Read the ideas in your Venn diagram on page 113. Choose one point of comparison and complete the chart below. On a separate sheet of paper, create the outline of a body paragraph with the ideas. You can use these ideas when you write your essay in Section 5.

POINT OF COMPARISON	100 YEARS AGO	TODAY
1	....	....

INTRODUCTORY PARAGRAPH

The introductory paragraph includes the same features that you learned about in Unit 1. However, the **thesis statement** has to communicate to your reader what the essay will focus on: similarities, differences, or both.

The thesis statement may include the points of comparison. So, the thesis statement for the writing prompt on page 125 could be written two ways:

With points of comparison: *Several aspects of common Korean food and drink are very different today from 100 years ago, such as the <u>popularity of coffee</u>, <u>beef</u>, and <u>Western-style fast food</u>.*

Without points of comparison: *While some of the common food and drinks consumed in South Korea are the same as they were 100 years ago, there are some key differences.*

 3.7 Notice

Read each sentence. Circle *T* if it is true and *F* if it is false.

1 The points of comparison are the characteristics you will compare. T F

2 For the writing prompt on page 125, the points of comparison are the popularity of coffee, beef, and Western-style fast food. T F

3 Thesis statements in a comparison and contrast essay never mention the points of comparison. T F

The thesis statements below give you some helpful words and phrases to use in writing yours.

FOCUS ON DIFFERENCES

*There are **some fundamental differences** between the eating habits of the Chinese and Americans.*

***Although** Chinese and Italian cuisines have certain features in common, they **differ** in terms of available ingredients and eating utensils, and in the rules and rituals of eating,*

*However, **when comparing** their definitions, prices, and impact on the environment, **it** soon **becomes clear that** artificial foods are not always the inferior choice.*

FOCUS ON SIMILARITIES

*The cuisines of Peru and Japan **may appear very different**, but they actually share some **striking/ interesting similarities**.*

***While** Chinese and Italian cuisines **differ** in some ways, **they are similar** in terms of their emphasis on noodles, their flavor preferences, and their cooking methods.*

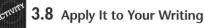 **3.8** Apply It to Your Writing

Think about your prompt and the ideas in your Venn diagram in Section 1. Write a thesis statement. This is just for practice. Then share your thesis statement with a partner. Does the statement make it clear whether the essay will focus on similarities or differences?

Work with a partner. Read the writing prompt and the introductory paragraph. Then read the topic sentence for each paragraph. Discuss the points of comparison with your partner. Then finish each body paragraph.

WRITING PROMPT: Compare two food trends or habits. What, in your opinion, do they reveal about the people who follow them?

THE SPEED OF FOOD

A current debate concerning food is how fast it is. This topic does not make sense to some people, but it makes others become absolutely enraged. On one side of the debate are the fast food people. These consumers prefer food that is quickly and easily prepared and inexpensive. These people would rather order take-out food, such as pizza and hamburgers, or prepare microwaveable packaged foods. Food for them has to fit into their lifestyle and not take up too much space, but it must be tasty. On the other side of the debate are the slow food people. These people are proponents of the slow food movement, which advocates that food should be healthy, fresh, and slowly cooked. Taking the time to prepare and cook food is very satisfying to these consumers and an essential part of their lifestyle. Although there are some similarities between these groups, they are clearly different in their lifestyles, concern for their health, and their tastes in food.

Fast food and slow food eaters have very different enjoyments and routines. ....

....

....

....

Another difference is how concerned they are about their health. ....

....

....

....

Finally, they have entirely different tastes in food. ....

....

....

....

....

 **3.10** Apply It to Your Writing

Work with a partner. Think about the writing prompt you chose in Section 1.
Choose one point of comparison and discuss what the supporting points are. Write two
or three sentences that compare Subject A with Subject B. Share your ideas with your
partner.

....

....

....

....

....

CONCLUDING PARAGRAPH

In the concluding paragraph, writers signal that they have come to the end of an essay. It
often begins with a transition phrase such as *In summary*, *In conclusion*, or *To sum up*. In this
paragraph, the writer restates the thesis and ends with a final comment.

 3.11 Notice

Look at the Student Model on pages 118–120. Circle the summary phrase. What final
comment does the writer make about the topic? Underline those sentences.

3.12 Apply It to Your Writing

Think about the ideas you wrote for your own essay in Section I. What might
your final comment be? Write some ideas below.

....

....

....

....

....

In this section you will learn the writing and grammar skills that will help make your writing more sophisticated and accurate.

Ⓐ Writing Skill 1: Words and Phrases That Show Similarities and Differences

The words and phrases below that show similarity or difference are very common in comparison writing.

WORDS AND PHRASES THAT SHOW SIMILARITIES AND DIFFERENCES

- To show similarities, you can use *similarly, likewise, similar to, like*, and *both*.

  Chinese cuisine is very popular outside of China. **Similarly/Likewise**, *Italian cuisine is a favorite of many people outside of Italy.*

  Similar to/Like *Chinese cuisine, Italian cuisine is popular around the world.*

  Both *Chinese cuisine and Italian cuisine are well loved in numerous countries.*

- To show differences, you can use *on the other hand, in contrast,* or *however, unlike,* and *while* or *whereas*.

  Fast food restaurants focus on price and convenience. **On the other hand/In contrast/However**, *the slow food movement focuses on health and education about how food is grown and cooked.*

  Unlike *fast food, slow food focuses on health and education.*

  While/Whereas *fast food restaurants focus on price and convenience, the slow food movement focuses on health and education.*

- Use *although* and *even though* to show a difference that is unexpected or surprising.

  Although/Even though *technology enables us to transport food across large distances, if good-quality food is abused during transport it can arrive spoiled.*

ACTIVITY **4.1** Combine Ideas

Connect or combine the two sentences using the words in parentheses.

1 French cooking uses a lot of butter. Chinese cooking does not. (on the other hand)

  French cooking uses a lot of butter. On the other hand, Chinese cooking does not.

2 Information is now exchanged very easily between countries because of globalization. Food is now exchanged very easily between countries because of globalization. (similar to)

3 Rice actually originated in Asia. Rice is a common ingredient in Mexican cuisine. (even though)

4 Fast food from big international chains is considered cheap in the United States. In Russia, it is much less affordable. (however)

....

....

5 Indian restaurants typically do not serve beef. Argentinian restaurants are known for their many ways of preparing beef. (in contrast)

....

....

6 Haggis, a traditional Scottish dish, is cooked in a sheep's stomach. Drob, a Romanian dish served at Easter, is cooked in a sheep's stomach. (both)

....

....

 4.2 Apply It to Your Writing

Think about the writing prompt you chose in Section 1 on page 113. Write four sentences using some of the words and phrases above.

....

....

....

....

....

....

B Writing Skill 2: Coherence

Coherence in writing means that the sentences and paragraphs flow well, and that ideas are connected clearly in a way that is easy for the reader to follow. Here are some of the techniques writers use to create coherence.

TRANSITION WORDS AND PHRASES

- To add information, use *also, in addition, moreover, furthermore.*

  Globalization has made it easier for different countries to exchange information.
  Also,/In addition,/Moreover,/Furthermore, *it has resulted in an increased exchange of aspects of culture such as cuisine.*

- To shift focus to a new topic, use *with respect to, with regard to, regarding.*

  With respect to/With regard to/Regarding *American-style fast food, this can now be seen all over the globe.*

- To show the order of a process, use *first, next, followed by, finally.*

  First, *a local company applies for a license to open a local chain restaurant.* **Next,** *it receives approval,* **followed by** *any specific requirements.* **Finally,** *it opens the restaurant.*

- To summarize or conclude, use *in conclusion, in summary, in sum.*

  In conclusion,/In summary,/In sum, *food is an aspect of culture that has been rapidly internationalized in the era of globalization.*

ACTIVITY 4.3 Combine Ideas

Complete the paragraph with the transition words and phrases in the box. Sometimes more than one answer is possible.

first	in addition	next	with regard to
furthermore	in sum	regarding	with respect to

    An examination of Chinese versus Chinese-American food reveals some surprising facts. Chinese food that is popular in the United States today has been adapted from the Cantonese cuisine of China's southeast. It is not so similar, however, to the traditional food of that region. For one thing, the way it is cooked in the United States is much richer. _____ (1) , the American version tends to be sweeter. _____ (2) to this, several "Chinese" dishes popular in the United States did not even originate in China. _____ (3) chop suey, it was actually invented in America in the nineteenth century. _____ (4) General Tso's chicken, Jennifer Lee, author of *The Fortune Cookie Chronicles,* went to the hometown of General Tsung-t'ang Tso, the nineteenth-century military leader, and asked several of the general's ancestors about this dish. They were not aware of it at all. The changes Chinese cooking underwent in the United States are part of a historical pattern. When people emigrate from China to other countries, one of two things generally happens: _____ (5) , Chinese cuisine influences the mainstream cooking style. _____ (6) , Chinese cuisine adapts to local tastes and ingredients. _____ (7) consumers' desire for "authenticity," it is no longer an important element. Essentially, all of this happens because Chinese cooking is not just a set of dishes, but also a philosophy that serves local tastes and ingredients. So, _____ (8) , when you look at the history of Chinese cuisine, you see a history of adaptiveness.

OTHER WAYS TO CREATE COHERENCE

Writers also create coherence with demonstratives, pronouns, and the use of articles.

1 Use demonstratives *this/that/these/ those* + noun to refer to specific ideas from previous sentences.	*Many U.S. cities have a large number of ethnic restaurants. **These** restaurants provide opportunities for local residents to try new dishes.*
2 Use demonstratives *this/that/these/ those* with certain nouns to label a previous idea. These nouns include *argument, belief, effect, experience, fact, opinion, process, setting, situation, study.*	*Many diners today prefer food that comes from local sources. **This fact** is affecting the way restaurants design their menus.*
3 Use pronouns (*he, she, it, they*) to refer to specific nouns in previous sentences.	*Food writer Jennifer Lee was curious about **the dish**. She discovered that **it** was actually invented in the United States.*
4 Use indefinite articles (*a/an*) the first time something is mentioned, and the definite article (*the*) after that.	*A plantain is a fruit similar to a banana but firmer and starchier. **The** plantain is a staple of cuisines throughout Latin America and the Caribbean, and is often fried.*

ACTIVITY **4.4** Editing Task

Use the ways to create cohesion above to complete the second sentence in the following sets of sentences.

1 *Consuming Passions: The Anthropology of Eating* is a survey of eating habits in different cultures. Written in the 1980s, ... continues to be an excellent resource for students of culinary anthropology.

2 Many Europeans believe that GMO foods are dangerous. .... is starting to become popular in the United States as well.

3 Many experts feel that there are too many commercial food products that contain unnecessary sugar. .... include items that we don't usually think of as being sweet, such as vegetables and bread.

4 Unconscious eating is a common cause of obesity. .... occurs when people do not pay attention to the act of eating, such as when they are watching TV.

5 Za'atar is a mixture of spices used in Lebanese cuisine. .... mixture includes oregano, thyme, and sesame seeds.

6 Peter Farb writes that chili peppers do not just flavor foods. .... also contain vitamin C and other nutrients.

C Grammar for Writing: Appositives

An appositive is a noun phrase that renames or gives additional information about the person, place, or thing that it refers to. They are common in academic writing and usually provide extra information. Follow the rules below in using appositives:

APPOSITIVES	
1 Use appositives to give a definition, description, or title of a noun or proper noun. Appositives are always separated by commas, dashes, or parentheses. They can come before or after the noun they modify.	Some people think that the acai, *which is a dark purple Brazilian berry*, is a kind of "superfood." *A sweet rice cake,* nian gao is commonly eaten for good luck during New Year in China. Potato chips were successfully introduced in China by Frito-Lay, *a division of PepsiCo.*
2 Use appositives to refer to tables and figures. References to tables and figures are usually in parentheses.	On the following page is a map of the original Silk Road *(see fig. 1)*.
3 Use appositives to explain abbreviations and acronyms (words formed from the first letters or parts of other words).	GMOs – *genetically modified organisms* – do not occur naturally; they have been manipulated by scientists.

ACTIVITY 4.5 Write About Ideas

Combine the sentences using an appositive. Follow the additional instructions.

1 Frito-Lay sells potato chips in China. Frito-Lay is a division of PepsiCo. (appositive at the beginning)

....

....

2 An example of a popular Lebanese dish is baba ghanuj. Baba ghanuj is a kind of eggplant salad. (appositive at the end)

....

....

3 Christopher Columbus was sent by the king and queen of Spain to see if he could reach Asia by sailing west. He was an Italian explorer. (appositive at the beginning)

....

....

4 An early example of the globalization of food was the trading of spices along the Silk Road. The Silk Road was a group of routes that linked China with Central Asia and Europe. (appositive at the end)

....

....

5 One kind of cheese which can only be made in Italy is Parmigiano-Reggiano. Parmigiano-Reggiano is a kind of hard cheese. (appositive at end)

....

....

Avoiding Common Mistakes 👁

Research tells us that these are the most common mistakes that students make when using appositives in academic writing.

1. **Remember to use an article for an appositive when necessary.**

   Alice Waters is the owner of Chez Panisse, a *California restaurant famous for its organic ingredients.*
   ^

2. **Don't use a relative pronoun in an appositive.**

   Big Food, ~~which~~ *the food production industry in the United States, resists movement toward sustainable practices.*

3. **Always use a comma, a dash, or parentheses with an appositive when it provides extra information.**

   Americans, a people not often acclaimed for their culinary traditions, are experiencing a
   watershed moment in their attitudes toward the food they eat.
                                                    ^

ACTIVITY 4.6 Editing Task

Find and correct four more mistakes in the following paragraph.

   Because of the United States' special history of immigration, American food has been
                                                                          a
influenced by cuisines from all over the world. A melting pot, large pot used to melt multiple
                                                             ^
ingredients together over heat, has often been used as a symbol of American society and

culture. It's true that some food considered "American" did not originate here. Hamburgers

and hot dogs, very common American sandwiches were brought by German immigrants.

Sometimes, food brought by immigrants adapts to American life just as the immigrants do.

Chop suey, dish of mixed meat and vegetables in a thick sauce, is served at Chinese restaurants

in the United States but was not eaten in China. Mayonnaise, that a very common American

condiment, actually comes from Europe. These are just a few examples of culinary adaptation

in the United States.

D Avoiding Plagiarism

Choosing credible sources takes practice. Some sources seem useful, but they may not be accurate.

My instructor always says that we should use credible sources. I'm not sure what she means. There are so many websites, and I want to make sure that I choose the right ones. Can you help me? What is a credible source? – Magda

Dear Magda,

Credible sources are trustworthy. The information from these sources comes from research. An example is an educational institution, such as Harvard. There are specific criteria that all credible sources have and you can ask yourself questions to determine whether a source meets this criteria and should be used for your essay.

There are great sources out there. Use what you learn to make sure that you choose the right ones!

Yours truly,

Professor Wright

CRITERIA FOR EVALUATING A SOURCE

To identify a reliable source, you should be able to answer "yes" to these questions.

1 Is the information up-to-date?

The information should be current and reflect current ideas, especially in subjects that change quickly, like technology.

2 Can you identify the author?

You should be able to find the author's name. The author should be an expert or have credentials in his or her field. You should be able to find other articles written by the author on your topic or other articles that cite the author.

3 Is the information fact-based or research-based?

The author should cite his or her own sources and show both sides of an argument. The author's point should be supported with facts and research, not just opinion. Avoid blogs or other personal websites.

4 If you use a website, is it from a respected organization: an educational institution, government office, or respected news organization?

Look for sites that end in .org, .edu, or .gov. Commercial sites that end in .com may not be reliable. Be careful with sites that have a lot of advertising.

Check (✓) the three best sources for a research project on American food habits today. Discuss your answers with a partner.

1 a 1999 article about American supermarkets

2 a 2015 book about the effects of fast food on the American public by a professor from Stanford University

3 a blog about a writer's eating habits posted on March 12, 2014

4 a website that sells cooking products

5 a 2016 article about the importance of breakfast from the *New York Times*

6 a recent government report on obesity

7 an article on diet tips from this month's fashion magazine

8 a 2014 article on food and culture with no author

In this section you will follow the writing process to complete the final draft of your essay.

STEP 1: BRAINSTORM

Work with a partner. Follow the steps below to brainstorm more ideas.

1 Before you start, notice how the writer of the Student Model brainstormed. He wrote many
ideas. Then he chose three points of comparison he thought were the strongest.

STUDENT
MODEL

WRITING PROMPT: In U.S. grocery stores, consumers can buy both natural foods and foods
with artificial ingredients. Some say that only natural foods are healthy, while others say that
foods with artificial ingredients are cheaper, but still healthy. In your view, is one better than
the other?

Subject A:
Foods with Natural
Ingredients

Subject B:
Foods with Artificial
Ingredients

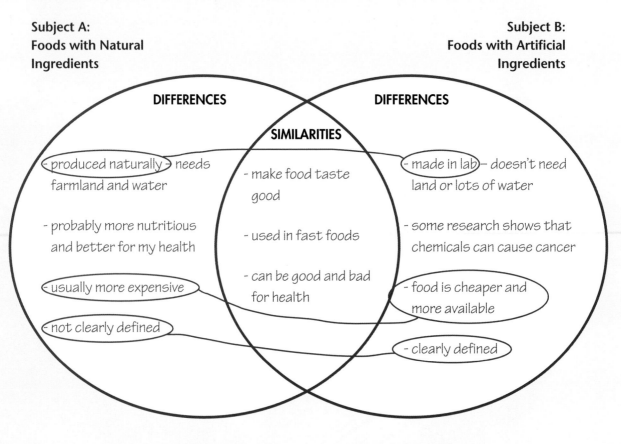

DIFFERENCES

DIFFERENCES

SIMILARITIES

- produced naturally ─ needs
farmland and water

- probably more nutritious
and better for my health

- usually more expensive

- not clearly defined

- make food taste
good

- used in fast foods

- can be good and bad
for health

- made in lab ─ doesn't need
land or lots of water

- some research shows that
chemicals can cause cancer

- food is cheaper and
more available

- clearly defined

2 Write the ideas that you wrote in Section 1, page 113, in the Venn diagram below. Include

Subject A: ....

Subject B: ....

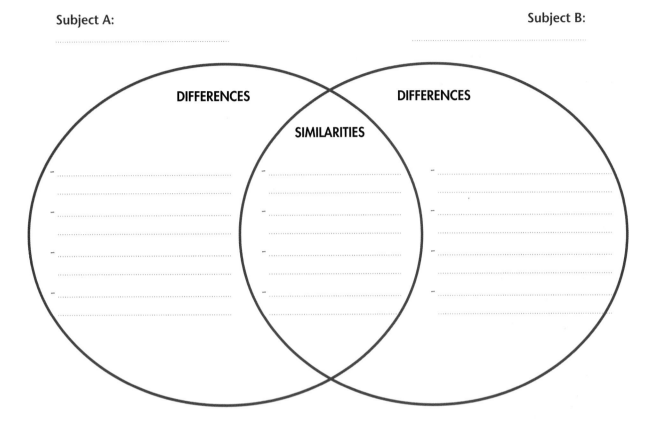

ideas from the Your Turns throughout the unit. Brainstorm more ideas.

When you are finished, circle the three strongest points of comparison and write them here.

1 ....

2 ....

3 ....

STEP 2: DO RESEARCH: EVALUATING INTERNET SOURCES

When doing research, it is important to use information only from sources that are credible. The information should be **current, accurate,** and **complete.** In addition, the writer or organization that is the source of the information should have a reputation for **fairness** and **objectivity.** These things are even more important when you are doing research on the Internet.

Inez needed to evaluate the credibility of her Internet sources for this prompt: *Historical events often bring countries together in unexpected ways. Choose two cultures with historical connections and explore similarities in their modern cuisine that reflect these ties.* Read and find out how she did it.

First, I considered if the publication date is up to date for my topic. After that, I verified the author's background and website's reputation through an Internet search. Then I read and analyzed details from the information to decide if they are relevant to my thesis. Last, I identified the purpose of the information – to inform, to entertain, or to persuade the audience – to make sure it was appropriate for my essay.

Inez's Results

Topic: French and Vietnamese cuisine	
Source: "Vietnam, the Best of Its Art and Culture" from www.theculturetrip.com	
Publication date	2014: Recently written so it provides a modern view. Also discusses the history between France and Vietnam (1849–1954).
Background and reputation	In "About Us" section: The editors are culture experts; website was a finalist for a UK website award in 2013.
Relevance	Details about Vietnamese foods – coffee, soups, sandwiches, pâté – comparing them to French foods.
Purpose	To inform. The information about the food and colonial history between these countries provides evidence for my comparison essay.

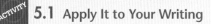

5.1 Apply It to Your Writing

Follow the steps Inez took to evaluate the credibility of Internet sources for your essay. Complete a chart like the one above for your main sources.

STEP 3: MAKE AN OUTLINE

Complete the outline below with your ideas from the previous steps.

ESSAY OUTLINE

I. Introduction

Thesis Statement	
Body Paragraph 1: Point of Comparison 1	II.
Subject A	A.
Detail	1.
Detail	2.
Subject B	B.
Detail	1.
Detail	2.
Body Paragraph 2: Point of Comparison 2	III.
Subject A	A.
Detail	1.
Detail	2.
Subject B	B.
Detail	1.
Detail	2.

(CONTINUED)

Body Paragraph 3: Point of Comparison 3	IV. ....
Subject A	A. ....
Detail	1. ....
Detail	2. ....
Subject B	B. ....
Detail	1. ....
Detail	2. ....
	V. Conclusion ....

STEP 4: WRITE YOUR FIRST DRAFT

Now it is time to write your first draft. Here are some suggestions on how to get started.

1 Use your outline, notes, and the sentences you wrote in the Your Turns and in Step 3 on page 141.

2 Reread the sentences that you wrote using the writing skills and grammar that you learned in Section 4. Try to use them in your essay.

3 Remember to add a title.

After you finish, read your essay and check for basic errors.

1 Check that all sentences are complete sentences.

2 Go through and look at every comma. Is it correct? Should it be a period?

3 Check that you have cited quotes and paraphrases.

4 Make sure your thesis statement and topic sentences are clear.

STEP 5: WRITE YOUR FINAL DRAFT

1 After you receive feedback on your first draft, review it carefully. Fix any errors.

2 Make a note of errors that were most frequent (misspellings, wrong verb tense, errors in using commas). Try to avoid them as you write.

3 Review the Academic Vocabulary and Academic Phrases from this unit. Are there any that you can add to your essay?

4 Turn to page 273 and use the Self-Editing Review to check your work one more time.

5 Write your final draft and hand it in.

5 PROBLEM–SOLUTION ESSAYS

PUBLIC HEALTH: MEDIA

> "He who has health, has hope; and he who has hope, has everything."
>
> Thomas Carlyle
> (1795–1881)

About the Author:

Thomas Carlyle was a Scottish writer and historian known for his social commentary about the Victorian era in Great Britain.

Work with a partner. Read the quotation about health. Then answer the questions.

1 What did the author compare good health to? Why?

2 Carlyle stated, "He who has hope, has everything." What does having "everything" mean to you?

3 What recent advancements in modern medicine have given people hope for a longer, healthier life?

Ⓐ Connect to Academic Writing

In this unit you will learn skills to help you analyze problems and solutions. While some of the writing skills that you will use may be new to you, the skill of solving problems is not new. In your everyday life you solve problems when you ask questions such as *What can I do to catch up when I miss class?* and *What can I do to make sure I get a good job in a tight job market?*

Ⓑ Reflect on the Topic

In this section you will choose a writing prompt and reflect on it. You will develop these ideas throughout the unit and use them to practice skills that are necessary to write your essay.

The writing prompt below was used for the Student Model essay on pages 150–152. The student reflected on her topic and used a chart to identify different solutions. This helped her think of a possible thesis.

WRITING PROMPT: Some families find themselves in a situation where a family member has a disease for which treatment is very expensive. Often these families find themselves in debt from the medical bills. What are some solutions that would help families pay the costs?

Problem: because health care is expensive, some families are going into debt	Possible solution 1: raise money online
	Possible solution 2: use cheaper, nontraditional treatment options
	Possible solution 3: organize a fund-raising event
	Possible solution: ....
	Possible solution: ....

My thesis: *Americans with high medical bills could raise money online.*

 1.1 Notice

All of the solutions above might help someone deal with high medical costs. What other solutions might also be possible? Compare ideas with a partner. Which solution do you think is best, and why?

1.2 Apply It to Your Writing

Follow the directions to reflect on your topic.

A Choose a prompt:

- Now that international travel is very easy, the spread of infectious diseases such as Ebola is expanding. What are some possible solutions for controlling epidemics and outbreaks (diseases quickly spreading around the world)? Consider ways to use technology to identify and warn the public in order to stop or slow down outbreaks.

- When patients are diagnosed with diseases they know nothing about, they tend to feel frightened and helpless. What are some ways to deal with this problem? How can patients in this situation find the information and support they need?

- Many mental health experts are concerned that excessive Internet use can lead to health issues, such as depression and anxiety. What are some ways to avoid these consequences?

- A topic approved by your instructor

B Work with a partner and complete the following tasks:

1 Think about your prompt. Decide what you will focus on in your essay.

2 Complete the chart below. Start by thinking about why this is a problem before you try to solve it. Add more boxes if you need them.

3 Write a possible thesis statement.

Problem:	Possible solution 1:
	Possible solution 2:
	Possible solution 3:

Possible thesis statement:

In this section you will learn academic language that you can use in your problem–solution essay. You will also notice how a professional writer uses the language and features of problem–solution writing.

Ⓐ Academic Vocabulary

The words below appear throughout the unit. Many are from the Academic Word List. Using these words in your writing will make your ideas clearer and your writing more academic.

anxiety (n)	demonstrate (v)	logical (adj)	tendency (n)
apparent (adj)	irrational (adj)	probability (n)	trigger (v)

ACTIVITY **2.1** Focus on Meaning

Work with a partner. Match the words to their meanings. Write the letters.

A

.... 1 Allergy symptoms have many causes and, according to one study, can even be **triggered** by reading news reports about increased pollen counts.

a reasonable and based on good judgment

.... 2 One pattern that researchers have noticed is that people who read about an illness online have a **tendency** to believe they may suffer from the same disease.

b to cause something to start

.... 3 Because Internet searches are cheaper and more convenient than a doctor's visit, looking up symptoms online is a **logical** first step for many patients.

c how likely it is that something will happen

.... 4 The **probability** of finding reliable health information on the Internet is often not good because there is so much inaccurate information online.

d a way of acting or thinking that someone does repeatedly

B

.... 1 Many people have an **irrational** need to diagnose themselves with web-based information, even though they know they lack medical training.	a an uncomfortable feeling of worry
.... 2 The evidence in the study helped doctors **demonstrate** the need for online communication with patients between appointments.	b not based on clear thinking; not reasonable
.... 3 More evidence is needed to prove that the **apparent** link between Internet use and depression is real.	c seeming to be true
.... 4 Patients who diagnose themselves online often suffer **anxiety** when a website incorrectly tells them they have a serious disease.	d to show that something is true; prove

ⓑ Academic Collocations 👁

Collocations are words that are frequently used together. Research tells us that the academic vocabulary in Part A is commonly used in the collocations in bold below.

ACTIVITY **2.2** Focus on Meaning

Read the paragraph. Then match the phrases in bold next to the purpose, or reason why, the writer used them.

Recent research on cyberbullying, posting hurtful comments on the Internet, reveals that cyberbullying is a real problem with mental health consequences. The data **clearly demonstrate** that cyberbullying has a connection to reports of low self-esteem and depression in teenagers. Before the Internet became the primary social space for young people, teenagers could get away from their bullies when they left school. Now, because young people continue to interact on the Internet after school, they have a **high probability** of meeting those same bullies and new ones online. This is one of the reasons why cyberbullying is such a serious problem. One recent study of teenage girls indicated that they have an **irrational tendency** to reach out to those bullying them online and try to form friendships, even though this does not seem to make sense. The **logical conclusion** of this activity, as the study showed, is that the bullying will only get worse, which means the problem gets worse. The girls also reported feeling worse about themselves after this interaction, but they continued the connections in various social media. **Basic logic** would say that the girls should stop doing this because it makes them feel bad about themselves, but they also reported being afraid of more bullying if they broke the connection all together. The complexity of this problem comes from these interrelated factors that make any solution very difficult.

Collocation	Purpose
.... 1 clearly demonstrate	a to show that there is a good chance of something occurring
.... 2 high probability	
.... 3 irrational tendency	b to introduce an obvious result
.... 4 logical conclusion	c to emphasize common sense
.... 5 basic logic	d to introduce something that has been proven
	e to emphasize a strange habit

C Writing in the Real World

The author of "The Psychology Behind Cyberchondria" analyzes a problem and possible solutions to strengthen her argument.

Before you read, answer these questions: Have you ever read an article online that made you believe you had an illness you did not have? How can people solve this problem?

Now read the article. Think about your answers to the questions above as you read.

THE PSYCHOLOGY BEHIND CYBERCHONDRIA (ADAPTED)

BRITT PETERSON

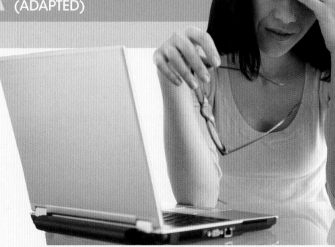

1   It's a familiar story. You're not feeling very well, so you rush to a website such as WebMD or MedicineNet to find out what might be wrong with you. When you leave the sites, you're convinced that your headache and nausea indicate that you must have brain cancer. This kind of hypochondria[1] that comes from reading medical websites has been called "cyberchondria." It is now increasingly common for people to visit the Internet instead of the doctor's office. According to a 2009 Pew poll, 61 percent of Americans use the Internet for medical information, and other recent studies have shown wide levels of increased **anxiety triggered** by this habit.

2   But why should simply reading online about, say, Hodgkin's lymphoma[2] convince us that we too have the disease? A study in the April 2012 issue of *Psychological Science* suggests that an **irrational tendency** is at work in the brains of cyberchondriacs. The study looks at what happens when people read a list of symptoms.[3] If the first few symptoms on the list are common ones that a person might actually have, such as headache, nausea, and fatigue, the cyberchondriac will jump to the conclusion that he or she must have all of the other symptoms on the list, too. According to the study, gamblers may have a similar **tendency**. When they get a number of good rolls of the dice, for example, they believe – irrationally – that they have "hit a hot streak" and their good luck will continue.

3   To test this theory, researchers devised an experiment. They started by inventing a fictional type of thyroid[4] cancer. They then created three different lists of the same six symptoms. One list grouped the milder and more common symptoms (fatigue, shortness of breath) together at the top of

[1]hypochondria: a condition in which a person worries about their health more than is normal although they are not really ill
[2]Hodgkin's lymphoma: cancer of the lymphatic system, the part of the body that helps fight infection and disease
[3]symptoms: physical feelings or problems which show that a person has a particular illness
[4]thyroid: an organ in the neck that produces a substance that helps the body grow and develop

the list. The more severe and rare symptoms (pain in the throat or neck, lump in the throat or neck) were listed together at the bottom. The second list presented the more severe symptoms together first, followed by the milder ones. In the third list all the symptoms were mixed up. Healthy individuals were given one of the three lists. They were asked to check off their symptoms, and then asked how likely they were to have the cancer compared to the average American. Both groups that read the lists of mild symptoms separated from severe symptoms were far more likely to believe themselves at risk for this fictional cancer than the group with the symptoms mixed up.

4 According to Virginia Kwan, a psychologist at Arizona State University and lead author on the study, the results **clearly demonstrate** that the human brain unconsciously looks for and finds patterns. Unfortunately, it appears that the brain is often too quick to assume that there is a pattern and this frequently leads us to ignore **basic logic** and to imagine **probabilities** that don't exist. Like gamblers who say they have hit a hot streak, Kwan says that cyberchondriacs believe they have "hot symptoms." In other words, when they read that they have the first couple of symptoms on a list, they think they must have the rest of the symptoms, and they must have the disease.

5 Kwan hopes that sites like WebMD will use her results to help decrease **anxiety** among their customers. They could do this by not listing a lot of common symptoms together. On the other hand, Kwan points out that heightened **anxiety** isn't always a bad thing. For example, during an outbreak of a serious disease in a community, she says, "It may be good to group the common symptoms together [in that situation] so that people pay more attention." In any case, next time your neck aches and WebMD suggests you may have viral meningitis, don't panic. Just remember that diagnosis[5] is best left to a medical professional.

[5]diagnosis: when a doctor says what is wrong when someone is sick

---

 2.3 Check Your Understanding

Answer the questions.

1 Why does the author think that cyberchondria is a problem? Which of these reasons do you think are the strongest? What are some other reasons why it might be a problem?

2 What were the results of Kwan's study, and why does she think the different groups reacted differently? Do you agree with her interpretation of the results?

3 Do you think the solution to cyberchondria suggested in this article is a good one? Why or why not?

2.4 Notice the Writing

Answer the questions.

1 In which paragraph(s) does the author describe why cyberchondria is a problem? In which paragraph(s) does the author propose a solution to the problem? Circle the words that helped you find this.

2 What kinds of evidence does the author use to show why cyberchondria is a problem? Underline specific words and phrases.

In Section 1 you saw how the writer of the Student Model reflected on her topic. In this section you will analyze the final draft of her problem–solution essay. You will learn how to structure your ideas for your own essay.

Ⓐ Student Model

Read the writing prompt again and answer the questions.

WRITING PROMPT: Some families find themselves in a situation where a family member has a disease for which treatment is very expensive. Often these families find themselves in debt from the medical bills. What are some solutions that would help families pay the costs?

1 What is the central problem the writer must propose a solution to?

2 Will the writer need to provide background on the problem and the solution?

3 What are some solutions the writer might propose?

Read the essay twice. The first time, think about your answers to the questions above. The second time, answer the questions in the Analyze Writing Skills boxes. This will help you notice key features of problem–solution essays.

STUDENT MODEL

Social Media, Consumers, and Health Care

1   What is the number-one cause of serious financial problems for people in the United States today? The answer is medical bills. Recovering from a serious illness or accident is not only physically challenging, it is also expensive. I found this surprising when I moved here from Thailand. Back home, the government has established a universal health care system that covers almost all medical expenses. In the United States, however, even people with health insurance must pay many of the charges for their care. Since surgeries, treatments, and medications often cost thousands of dollars, medical bills can force people into debt and even bankruptcy. Unfortunately, this problem has not been solved by the government yet. However, there is now a creative solution: crowdfunding, or raising money on the Internet. Crowdfunding is a practical and effective way for Americans struggling with medical costs to get help.

2   Recent research **clearly demonstrates** that financial difficulty related to medical expenses is common. According to a study by the National Bureau of Economic Research, 75 percent of American adults would have trouble producing $2,000 in a medical emergency (Childers). What if they needed more? For example, the average cancer patient must pay about $8,500 each year for health care (Childers). Exorbitant[1] costs are one problem; another is

---

[1]exorbitant: much too large (a price or demand)

1 Analyze Writing Skills

How does the writer begin the introduction?

a with an interesting question

b with a quote from an expert

c with a personal anecdote

2 Analyze Writing Skills

How does the writer organize the background information in the introduction?

a explaining steps

b giving definitions

c comparing and contrasting

3 Analyze Writing Skills

Read the thesis statement and underline the problem it mentions. Then, circle the solution it gives.

loss of wages. If a sick family member misses work and loses income as a result, it may be impossible for the family to pay their bills. In fact, over 62 percent of personal bankruptcies are attributed to[2] medical expenses (Himmelstein et al.). Life-threatening health problems cause enough **anxiety** for individuals and the people close to them. It is shocking that they have to suffer financially, too. However, with the rise in the cost of health care and without a universal health care program, this unfortunate situation will persist.[3]

3　　Crowdfunding is an excellent solution because it is easy to get started, and the results are usually good. Fund-raising websites, such as Giveforward.com and GoFundMe.com, offer simple instructions for setting up a web page and sharing it on social media, such as Facebook and Twitter. The page usually explains the reason for raising money and states a goal. Contributors are encouraged to donate as much as they want and to include personal notes. Since crowdfunding sites can reach a large number of people, and many small donations add up, there is a **high probability** that fund-raising goals will be reached. The Kennett family is just one example. When Chip Kennett needed financial support for lung cancer treatment, his family started a web page on Giveforward.com. It **triggered** a huge response, and in just two weeks, 325 of their friends and family members donated almost $57,000 dollars (Mayer). The money eased the family's concerns and raised their spirits, too. "It was inspiring to check the dollar figure and the notes from friends. It provided emotional comfort that was extremely uplifting, " Kennett says.

4　　Whereas some people think fund-raising events attract more donors because of their personal nature, this **apparent** advantage is outweighed by the disadvantages. First, there is a **tendency** to charge a lot of money for tickets. When I received an invitation to a fund-raising concert for a neighbor who was sick, I felt sorry that I could not afford the cost of a seat. However, if I had been asked to decide on an amount and contribute online, I certainly would have. Another drawback is the time and effort required to organize an event. By contrast, it takes only minutes to raise money online. Furthermore, fundraisers only attract local donors. Crowdfunding, on the other hand, reaches a much larger audience, attracting donors from all over the world.

[2]attributed to: said or thought to be the result of something
[3]persist: to continue to exist or to do something past the usual time, even when facing opposition

(CONTINUED) ▶

4　Analyze Writing Skills

Why does the writer include research in paragraph 2?

a　to give solutions for high medical bills

b　to prove that medical expenses are expensive

c　to show why universal health care is a better option

5　Analyze Writing Skills

Circle the sentence in paragraph 3 that introduces the benefits of crowdfunding.

6　Analyze Writing Skills

Why does the writer include the example of the Kennett family in paragraph 3?

a　to give background about the problem

b　to show an example of how the solution works

c　to criticize the U.S. health care system

7　Analyze Writing Skills

In paragraph 4, the writer uses *First*, *Another*, and *Furthermore*. What is the purpose of these transition words?

a　to list the disadvantages

b　to give examples

c　to explain the benefits

5   In short, it is a shame that medical costs are unreasonably high and that seriously ill people need to ask others for help in a country as rich as ours. At present, crowdfunding is the most effective and efficient way to solve this problem. However, this solution should be temporary. The **logical conclusion** is that the government should replace its current system with one that provides care for everyone.

Works Cited

Childers, Linda. "When Medical Bills Pile Up, Can You Crowdfund Your Health Care?" *Forbes*. Forbes, 17 Apr. 2013. Web. 11 Mar. 2014.

Himmelstein, David U., Deborah Thorne, Elizabeth Warren, and Steffie Woolhandler. "Medical Bankruptcy in the United States, 2007: Results of a National Study." *American Journal of Medicine*. 112.8 (2009): n. pag. 5 June 2009. Web. 14 Nov. 2014.

Mayer, Caroline. "A Growing Number of Patients Turn to Crowd-funding Sites to Defray Medical Costs." *Washington Post*. Washington Post, 1 July 2013. Web. 14 Nov. 2014.

> **8 Analyze Writing Skills**
>
> Underline the sentence in the conclusion that restates the problem and solution.

ACTIVITY 3.1 Check Your Understanding

Answer the questions.

1 Why does the writer think that this problem is important? Do you agree with the reasons she gives? Why or why not?

2 Do you think the proposed solution is a good one? Why or why not?

3 What does the writer say about fund-raising events in body paragraph 3? Do you agree? Why or why not?

ACTIVITY 3.2 Outline the Ideas

Complete the outline for "Social Media, Consumers, and Health Care."

ESSAY OUTLINE

I. Introduction ....

Thesis Statement ....
....
....

Body Paragraph 1: The Problem

II. Financial difficulty from medical bills ....

Supporting Idea 1

    A. High medical costs ....

Detail

        1. ....

Detail

        2. ....

Supporting Idea 2

    B. ....

Detail

        1. Families can't afford their bills anymore. ....

Detail

        2. ....

Supporting Idea 3

    C. Anxiety also a related problem ....

Body Paragraph 2: The Best Solution

III. Crowdfunding is easy and effective. ....

Supporting Idea 1

    A. ....

Detail

        1. Web page shared on social media ....

Detail

        2. ....

Supporting Idea 2

    B. The Kennet family ....

Detail

        1. ....

Detail

        2. Raised $57,000 online ....

Detail

        3. ....

(CONTINUED)

Body Paragraph 3: An Alternative Solution	IV. Fund-raising events not as effective
Supporting Idea 1	A. Ticket prices too high for many people
Supporting Idea 2	B.
Supporting Idea 3	C. Only attract local donors
	V. Conclusion

B Problem–Solution Essays

Writers use the structure of a problem–solution essay to analyze a problem for their readers and propose a solution based on the analysis. As part of their proposal, they consider alternative solutions and explain why those solutions are not as effective as the one they are proposing.

There are different ways to structure this type of essay. Below is a typical method of organization.

Introductory paragraph: Introduces the topic and prepares the reader by including

- a **hook**, such as a fact, quotation, or question that makes readers care about the problem.
- **background information** that makes readers understand the importance of the problem.
- a **thesis statement** that gives both the problem and the solution, and makes clear why the solution will work.

Body paragraph 1: Describes the problem in more detail, by stating

- what the problem is.
- who it affects and how it affects them.
- reasons why it is still a problem.

Body paragraph 2: Describes the proposed solution to the problem, by including

- a clear description of the solution.
- reasons, evidence, or examples that show why the solution would work.

Body paragraph 3: Explains why another solution would not work as well by describing

- an alternative solution.
- why some people think it will work.
- reasons and examples to show why this idea will not work as well as the proposed solution.

Concluding paragraph: Brings the essay to a close by

- restating the thesis and the main idea of each body paragraph.
- reminding readers of the importance of the topic.
- ending with a recommendation of something people can do to solve the problem.

In which paragraph(s) would you expect to find the answers to these questions?

1 Why should readers care about this topic? ....

2 Why does this problem need to be solved? ....

3 Has the problem already been solved? Why or why not? ....

4 What is the best way to solve the problem? Why? ....

5 What other solutions have been proposed? Why will they not work as well?

....

6 What can people do about this problem? ....

BODY PARAGRAPH 1

The first important step in writing a problem–solution essay is making sure your reader understands the problem and why it needs to be solved. You can do this in the first body paragraph of your essay. A good paragraph will do all of the things below. Notice the bold words in the examples. These are common phrases used to describe problems and will help make your own writing more effective.

- Explain what the problem is.

  The word cyberbullying ***describes*** *bullying that happens online, for example, by posting hurtful or untrue comments about someone on social media.*

- Describe who the problem affects.

  Cyberbullying ***has become a serious issue*** *around the world, not only for young people on the Internet, but for adults as well.*

- Explain how the problem affects these people.

  It ***is a problem because*** *studies have shown a strong link between cyberbullying and serious, long-term psychological problems for not only the victims but also their friends, colleagues, and family.*

- Explain why the problem needs to be solved.

  The challenge is *to address this problem so that young people and adults can go online without fear of being mistreated.*

- Explain why the problem hasn't been solved yet.

  However, cyberbullying ***has been difficult to stop*** *in the past* ***because*** *people can post hurtful comments anonymously and because many victims are reluctant to report the abuse.*

There are many phrases you can use to introduce problems, including:

X is / describes / refers to …

the problem / challenge is …

the main / key / most important problem is …

a secondary issue / problem is …

while X is a factor, the most urgent issue is …

X is / has become a (serious) problem because …

3.4 Identify Purposes

Below is the first body paragraph from the Student Model. Write the numbers of the sentences in the paragraph next to the blanks beside their purpose. You may write some numbers more than once.

(1) Recent research clearly demonstrates that financial difficulty related to medical expenses is common. (2) According to a study by the National Bureau of Economic Research, 75 percent of American adults would have trouble producing $2,000 in a medical emergency (Childers). What if they needed more? (3) For example, the average cancer patient must pay about $8,500 each year for health care (Childers). Exorbitant costs are one problem; another is loss of wages. (4) If a sick family member misses work and loses income as a result, it may be impossible for the family to pay their bills. (5) In fact, over 62 percent of personal bankruptcies are attributed to medical expenses (Himmelstein et al.). (6) Life-threatening health problems cause enough anxiety for individuals and the people close to them. It is shocking that they have to suffer financially, too. (7) However, with the rise in the cost of health care and without a universal health care program, this unfortunate situation will persist.

Explains what the problem is: ....

Describes who the problem affects and how it affects them: ....

....

Explains why the problem still needs to be solved: ....

3.5 Practice

Read the writing prompt about a problem associated with social media. Write five sentences that explain the problem using the phrases in the box.

is / describes / refers to	a secondary issue / problem is
the problem / challenge is	while … is a factor, the most urgent issue is
the main / key / most important problem is	is / has become a (serious) problem because

WRITING PROMPT: Social media can cause users to become depressed as a result of a feeling of dissatisfaction from comparing their lives to others. What are some solutions to this problem?

1 ....

2 ....

3 ....

4 ....

5 ....

ACTIVITY 3.6 Apply It to Your Writing

Think about the writing prompt you chose in Section 1 on page 145. Use the space below to write sentences that describe your problem. Try to use the phrases on page 156.

BODY PARAGRAPH 2

In the second body paragraph, you will present your solution and why it would work. That means explaining specifically and convincingly how the solution would solve the problem. The elements below will help you do this. Notice the bold words in the examples. These are common phrases used to describe solutions.

- Explain what the solution is.

  One solution to *cyberbullying is to contact the parents or teachers of the bully, or another person who is an authority figure.*

  Completely removing an addict from the Internet to begin recovery ***is a possible solution to the problem****.*

  Bringing bullies and their victims together for therapy ***must be considered as a solution*** *to cyberbullying.*

- Describe how the solution can be implemented.

  The solution to the problem lies in *emailing or calling the parents of a bully or speaking in person to a school official.*

  The problem of *Internet addiction* ***can be solved by*** *providing counseling and psychological treatment in the same way that other addictions are treated.*

  In order to make this solution work*, parents and schools must work together.*

- Give reasons, evidence from research, or examples that show why the solution would work.

  Involving authorities from the offline world ***would solve the problem because*** *they can talk to the bully and closely monitor his or her Internet use.*

  For example*, Gail Andrews, a noted advice columnist for parents, has written that contacting the parents of the girls who cyberbullied her daughter provided a great deal of relief.*

  One study demonstrates *that it is effective to hold a family intervention for Internet addicts so they can hear how their behavior has hurt loved ones.*

3.7 Notice

Read the second body paragraph from the Student Model on pages 150–152. Circle the phrases or words that help show the solution.

3.8 Practice

Use the phrases below to write sentences that explain solutions. Use the example language from this section to help you.

1 (Reliable websites / accurate information / because)

Reliable websites can provide accurate information because they are based on

research and updated regularly.

2 (Intensive addiction counseling / can be a solution / because)

....

....

3 (The problem of / can be solved by / psychological treatment)

....

....

4 (One recent study / in-patient addiction counseling)

....

....

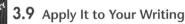 **3.9** Apply It to Your Writing

Think about the writing prompt you chose in Section 1. Write sentences explaining the solution you will propose in your essay and why it will work.

....

....

....

....

....

BODY PARAGRAPH 3

The third body paragraph in a problem–solution essay presents an alternative solution and identifies its weaknesses. In this paragraph, you may sometimes acknowledge that the alternative solution has some strengths, but the main purpose is to explain its disadvantages. This will help make it clear why your solution is better.

A strong paragraph will do all of the things below. Notice the bold words in the examples. These are all common phrases used to acknowledge and refute alternative solutions and will help make your own writing more effective.

- Describe an alternative solution.

  Some people may argue *that the only way to avoid cyberbullying is not to go online at all, or at least not to use social media.*

  It has been argued that *no treatment is needed for these people, as they are not really addicts.*

  It has been suggested that *cyberbullying can be solved with the same methods as face-to-face bullying.*

- Explain why some people think it will work.

  Some may argue that *cyberbullies can only hurt people who are actually online, so by staying offline you will not be hurt.*

  It seems reasonable that *Internet addiction is not as serious a problem as drug addiction.*

  It is generally accepted that *face-to-face bullying includes physical violence that cyberbullying does not.*

- Give reasons, evidence, and examples that show why this solution will not work as well or has disadvantages.

  However, the problem with this solution is *that bullies can still post hurtful or untrue things about someone, even if that person is not on social media. The effect is still the same because people continue the bullying face-to-face as well as online.*

  While some research shows *that Internet addiction may be exaggerated and gives evidence that treatment is not needed,* ***the truth is*** *that the problem requires attention and the addicts need treatment.*

For example, if you do not open your own social media account, bullies could open one in your name and use it to insult and hurt you.

- Explain how your solution works better.

  *Teaching students that cyberbullying is a crime and showing them ways to get help **is a better way** to prevent cyberbullying. This creates an environment that does not allow bullies.*

- Writers use a variety of phrases and expressions to convince the reader of their solution.

  *As these examples show, Internet addiction is **in fact** a real disease and must be treated as one.*

  ***It is clear that** completely avoiding the Internet is the only solution to the problem.*

  *As these studies show, **it is obvious that** this approach is the only way to help children deal with cyberbullying.*

It is also worth noting that sometimes this paragraph appears as body paragraph 2, with your own solution proposed in body paragraph 3.

ACTIVITY 3.10 Identify Purpose

Below is the third body paragraph from the Student Essay. Write the number of each sentence next to its purpose below, using the explanation above to guide you. You may write some numbers more than once.

(1) Whereas some people think fund-raising events attract more donors because of their personal nature, this apparent advantage is outweighed by the disadvantages. (2) First, there is a tendency to charge a lot of money for tickets. (3) When I received an invitation to a fund-raising concert for a neighbor who was sick, I felt sorry that I couldn't afford the cost of a seat. (4) However, if I had been asked to decide on an amount and contribute online, I certainly would have. (5) Another drawback is the time and effort required to organize an event. (6) By contrast, it takes only minutes to raise money online. (7) Furthermore, fundraisers only attract local donors. (8) Crowdfunding, on the other hand, reaches a much larger audience, attracting donors from all over the world.

Describe the alternative solution and why some people think it would work: ....

Give disadvantages of the alternative solution: ....

Give a fact, example, or statistic to show the weakness of the solution: ....

Explain why the writer's solution is better: ....

ACTIVITY 3.11 Apply It to Your Writing

Return to your chart for your essay in Section 1 on page 145. Write sentences that describe another solution and why it will not work well.

....

....

....

....

....

INTRODUCTORY AND CONCLUDING PARAGRAPHS

In the **introductory paragraph**, give background information that makes readers care about the problem and see the need to solve it. Show your readers that this problem could affect them or people they care about. You can do this with facts, specific examples, or a short description of a situation that illustrates the problem.

- Facts:

  *The Family Caregivers Alliance **estimates** that 44 million Americans over 18 provide unpaid care to family members who are seriously ill or not able to care for themselves ("Caregiving").*

- Examples:

  ***For example**, thousands of Americans have sought counseling for Internet addiction in the last decade.*

- Description of a situation:

  ***Joshua H.** suffered from Internet addiction in high school and stopped showing up to class in February. **His parents** did not know this was such a problem.*

The thesis statement should mention the problem and the solution, and make clear why this solution would work.

| SOLUTION | PROBLEM | WHY IT WILL WORK |

<u>Online support groups</u> offer the <u>support caregivers need</u> while also providing <u>the flexibility to allow them to get help when they can</u>.

3.12 Notice

Look at the introductory paragraph below. Underline the sentences that make you care about this problem and the need to solve it.

The Internet has changed the world in so many positive ways. Who would have thought that an addiction to it could harm people and do real damage to their lives? The thousands of Americans who have sought counseling for Internet addiction have realized this. Their loved ones have as well because they have seen family members lose jobs, friends, and lives because they became addicted to the Internet. As online life grows more important to professional and academic lives each year, Internet addiction becomes a more important problem to solve. By treating Internet addiction like a real addiction and providing counseling and treatment, these addicts and their families can get the help that they desperately need to save themselves and their futures.

3.13 Notice

Read the thesis statements below on cyberbullying. Does each statement include the problem, the solution, and a reason why the solution would work? If not, what is missing? Compare your answer with a partner.

1 Cyberbullying is a widespread problem that impacts many young people around the world today. It can be solved by involving parents and school officials.

2 Cyberbullying is a serious problem that needs to be solved by involving school officials and parents because they have the power to change online behavior and its real-world consequences.

3.14 Apply It to Your Writing

Think about the writing prompt you chose in Section 1. Write three sentences that make your readers care about the topic. Compare with a partner. Which of the strategies above did your partner use? Were your partner's sentences effective?

In the **concluding paragraph**, remind readers of the importance of the problem, the need to solve it, and the reasons why your solution will work.

In short, it is a shame that medical costs are unreasonably high and that seriously ill people need to ask others for help in a country as rich as ours. At present crowdfunding is the most effective and efficient way to solve this problem. However, this solution should be temporary. The logical conclusion is that the government should replace its current system with one that provides care for everyone.

The last thing to leave your reader with is a strong comment, recommendation, or call to action in order to motivate the reader to think about the problem further. Read the examples below. The phrases in bold are commonly used for these statements.

***It is necessary to** recognize Internet addiction as a physical and psychological problem that requires the same treatment as drug or alcohol addiction.*

***In order to** help victims of bullies, schools and parents **must** join forces to change behavior on both sides.*

*I sincerely **hope that** the government will soon replace its current system with a better one, but until that time comes, crowdfunding seems to be a viable solution.*

 3.15 Compare

Read the sentences from concluding paragraphs. Work with a partner. Check (✓) the statement that is better at reminding readers about the problem and solution. Think about the strategies described above.

☐ 1 Finding the right health information online is important, and consumers really do need to learn how to do this to save themselves anxiety.

☐ 2 Unless consumers learn to evaluate health information and its sources online properly, they risk worry and anxiety for themselves and trouble for their doctors. It is necessary to learn this Internet skill because deceptive websites will always be out there.

 **3.16** Apply It to Your Writing

Think about the writing prompt you chose in Section 1. Write three recommendations that you might include in your conclusion. Compare with a partner. Which one is the best ending for your paper? Why do you think so?

....

....

....

....

....

4 SHARPEN YOUR SKILLS

In this section you will learn the writing and grammar skills that will help make your writing more sophisticated and accurate.

Ⓐ Writing Skill 1: Introduction to Summarizing

Summarizing means condensing a text or passage into the most important ideas, usually the thesis and the main points. In academic writing you will often use the skill of summary to describe a complicated event or a research study in a concise way that omits the details.

Here are strategies that you can use to summarize a text:

1 Read the text or passage a few times and identify the thesis or the main idea.

2 Find the main supporting points. These could be the main events, causes and effects, steps, results, or other key points. Make note of any important details and examples that will help you explain each point. Only include the most important details and examples.

3 Restate the ideas using synonyms and different sentence structures to avoid plagiarism.

4 Relate the summary to the point that you are making. In other words, be clear on how it supports the point.

5 In your essay, include the author's name and title of the source. State the source in your Works Cited according to the citation style.

Below is a summary of the first two paragraphs of "The Psychology Behind Cyberchondria" on page 148.

Britt Peterson, in her article "The Psychology Behind Cyberchondria," discusses cyberchondria and what makes people believe that they have every disease that they read about on the Internet. One reason for this phenomenon is how people respond to a list of symptoms. If a few items in a row match their symptoms, cyberchondriacs believe that they must have the rest. Therefore, they have the disease.

ACTIVITY **4.1** Practice Summarizing

Look at the notes below. Then read the two summaries of the article. Answer the questions. Compare your ideas with a partner.

Article notes:

Health Times, May 4, 2013

Dr. Sanjay Shah

- Misleading websites and how to find the truth

- Advertisements look like factual, neutral content

- Look in "About," "Terms and Conditions," and "Policies."

A

A recent article in *Health Times* discusses the problems that health consumers can run into when searching for information online about illnesses. The article describes a rise in lobbying groups for pharmaceutical companies hosting websites that seem like they offer unbiased information on certain illnesses but really are designed to support and promote drugs made by client companies. The article includes screenshots from the website, but a pharmaceutical company representative says his company does not do this on its website. The article ends with information about how to decide which websites to trust.

B

In a May 4, 2013, article in *Health Times*, health expert Dr. Sanjay Shah explains how health consumers can become more careful about the websites they use to learn about illnesses and medications. He described the problem with a case study, explaining how one healthcare lobbying group was hosting a website to promote a new drug for dementia. Shah emphasized that the problem is not that the medication is dangerous, but that the website is misleading because it claims this drug is the market leader and best choice. Shah explained how to search a website both in its "About" section as well as in its policies and terms and conditions to understand who is presenting the information. In this way, Shah's article highlights the problem health consumers face when searching online for information.

1 Does each summary:
- give the author's full name and explain who he or she is?
- say where and when the text was published?
- include the important details from the article?
- not include unimportant details?

2 Which summary is better?

ⓑ Writing Skill 2: Acknowledging and Refuting Opposing Solutions

An important part of writing problem–solution essays is acknowledging and refuting an opposing solution. Using this approach convinces your reader that you understand both solutions but that your solution is better than the alternative solution.

Here are strategies you can use to acknowledge and refute a solution:

- Acknowledge what someone says without saying it is correct or true.

  Dr. Marcus Salam argues that *cyberbullying can be solved with some of the same solutions as real-world bullying.*

- Concede a point, then refute it.

  That may be true, but *that problem comes from the anonymous nature of online communication.*

- Acknowledge what someone says, then counter it with your own idea.

  While Dr. Salam claims that parental and school supervision is *the best solution,* ***this does not prevent*** *teenagers from continuing their online bullying and hiding it from parents.*

- Use words that show contrast like these:

  Even though *some parents claim they cannot regulate their children so closely, Dr. Salam says they should try.*

  Although *schools want to help, some state laws prevent them from doing so.*

  Despite *clear evidence about the damage of cyberbullying, not everyone believes this is a problem.*

  Some people claim that real-world bullying has more consequences than cyberbullying; ***nevertheless****, research shows that is not true.*

 **4.2** Practice Acknowledging

Complete the sentences with your own ideas. Each sentence should refute an alternative solution for a problem–solution essay.

1 Although some doctors believe the only way to stop cyberchondria is to tell their patients never to research symptoms online, ...

   ....

2 It may be true that some caregivers prefer face-to-face support groups; nevertheless, ...

   ....

3 It is true that cyberbullying can be stopped by having parents prevent their children from bullying, but ....

   ....

4 While some people argue that doctors save time by connecting to patients on social media, ...

   ....

 **4.3** Apply It to Your Writing

Read the ideas from the Your Turn for Body Paragraph 3 on page 161. Write three sentences explaining why some of those solutions will not work well. Use the examples above to help you. These sentences might become part of your essay.

C Grammar for Writing: *It* Constructions

In academic essays, writers often express their personal viewpoint in a more objective-sounding way by using sentence structures with *it*. These structures include the following:

IT CONSTRUCTIONS	
1 The following constructions are often used in academic writing: a *It* + *be* + adjective + *that* clause b *It* + *be* + adjective + infinitive c *It* + *be* + adjective + *for* + subject + infinitive d *It appears/seems* + *that* clause	*It is* unfortunate *that* many medical websites provide inaccurate information. *It is* now very **common to visit** medical websites instead of doctor's offices. *It is better for* most **people to avoid** researching their illnesses on the Internet. *It seems that* more people are using the Internet for health resources every year.
2 The following modals are common in *it* construction: *may be, might be,* or *could be*	For particularly anxious patients, **it might be** better to avoid medical websites altogether. *It may be* that disclaimers would help people know when they are on a medical website not written by doctors.
3 Another common structure is *it may/might/could be* + adjective + *for* + subject + infinitive.	*It might be better for* parents **to monitor** their children's online behavior. *It could be effective for* doctors **to suggest** reliable websites for patients to go to for medical information.

ACTIVITY 4.4 Write Objectively

Rewrite the sentences with *it* clauses and the words in parentheses to sound more objective. You may need to change some words in the sentence.

1 **I think that** many people rely too heavily on Internet research instead of going to the doctor. (unfortunate) It is unfortunate that many people rely too heavily on Internet research instead of going to the doctor.

2 **I think that** bullies need treatment rather than punishment. (better)
It might be better for bullies to get treatment rather than punishment.

3 **I believe doctors should not** use social media to reach out to patients. (inappropriate)

....

4 **I am pretty sure that** too much time on the Internet can cause health problems like headaches and eye strain. (appear)

....

5 **I know that** many people regularly look up medical information online before they go to the doctor. (likely)

....

6 **I think people** who are addicted to the Internet need psychological treatment. (seems)

....

Avoiding Common Mistakes

Research tells us that these are the most common mistakes that students make when using *it* constructions in academic writing.

1 **Make sure *important* is spelled correctly.**

   It seems ~~import~~ to take responsibility for our own health.
   (above "import": important)

2 **Remember to include *to* in infinitives.**

   It is impossible account for every possibility when a person tries to self-diagnose.
   (above: to)

3 **Don't forget to include *It* before the verb *be* at the start of a sentence.**

   ~~Is~~ difficult for a doctor to argue with a patient who has done a great deal of research online.
   (above: It is)

ACTIVITY **4.5** Editing Task

Find and correct six more mistakes in the following paragraph.

The high number of unreliable health websites is a significant problem, and it is ~~import~~ to use (above: important) only reliable websites when searching the Internet for health-related information. This simple solution will solve this problem for many people. One thing consumers can do is find out who owns or manages a health website, because this information can help users decide if a site is reliable. For example, is possible to provide marketing information on a drug company's website that seems like it is posted by doctors and designed for education, when, in fact, the site was created only to make money for the company. Some people think it is impossible find out who is behind a website and determine its reliability, but it is actually very easy. At the bottom of most sites, users will see a Terms of Use link or a privacy policy. These legal statements usually list a contact person or parent company. It is also import to read any "About" sections that describe the company, website, or its goals. This information can help users decide if the source of the information is reliable. The most useful websites for health information are considered reliable because they are posted by medical organizations and written by those with medical knowledge. It is impossible find out everything about a website or its content, but smart health consumers need to understand what they are reading and why it was published. Is one key way to solve the growing problem of users finding and relying on inaccurate health information online. Therefore, is necessary to educate consumers of online health information to use the steps outlined here to research not just health questions but who is providing the answers and why.

D Avoiding Plagiarism

Time management is a common problem for students. Those who don't plan well may plagiarize when they copy at the last minute.

I need help. Every time I have a paper due, I wait until the last minute and I'm usually disappointed by my grades. I know I should start earlier, but I feel so overwhelmed and nervous that I keep putting it off. What can I do? – Beza

Dear Beza,

This often happens with students. The first step is to manage your time. Plan each step of a project and give yourself a deadline. That will help you get organized. In addition, when you feel nervous or overwhelmed, ask for help. Teachers and librarians are there to help you. They want you to succeed.

Best regards,

Professor Wright

STRATEGIES FOR TIME MANAGEMENT

Sometimes procrastination can lead to plagiarism. Students who run out of time may be tempted to copy because it takes time to understand difficult sources. It also takes time to think about how to present others' ideas. Finally, when students wait until the last minute, they often make errors in their citations or confuse their sources. Here are some time management strategies.

Strategy 1: Get started efficiently

Getting started is often the hardest part of writing an essay. An essay is a major project and it can sometimes feel overwhelming. Sometimes the best way to get started is to divide the project into a list of smaller tasks.

1 Make a list of all the tasks you need to complete to write the essay.
2 Decide how long you need to spend on each task. For example: *brainstorm topic – 1/2 hour, Internet research – 3 hours.*
3 Look at the due date and decide when you need to start.
4 Get started!

Strategy 2: Avoid procrastination

It is easy to procrastinate – to put off doing the things you need to do to complete your essay. If you leave all of your tasks from Strategy 1 until the last minute, you may not have enough time. It is better to plan in advance and do a little bit every day.

1 Look at your list of tasks and decide what needs to be done first.
● 2 Write down a start and finish date (or time) for each task.
3 Cross off each task when you complete it to see your progress.
4 Leave time at the end to review and revise your essay.

Strategy 3: Get support

If you try Strategies 1 and 2 but you are still having trouble managing your time, talk to an instructor, friend, or classmate about it. They can encourage you and remind you to stay on schedule. It is also possible that you are having trouble with your schedule because you need help understanding how to do one of the tasks on your list. Your teacher and others can help you with this – just ask them!

 4.6 Practice

Think about the next essay you have to write for school, or another important assignment or task. Which time management strategies would be useful for you? Work with a partner and discuss your next time management strategy.

In this section you will follow the writing process to complete the final draft of your essay.

STEP 1: BRAINSTORM

Work with a partner. Follow the steps below to brainstorm more ideas.

1 Before you start, notice how the writer of the Student Model brainstormed. She wrote many ideas, and then circled one solution that she thought was the best, as well as one solution that she thought didn't work as well.

STUDENT MODEL

WRITING PROMPT: Some families find themselves in a situation where a family member has a disease for which treatment is very expensive. Often these families find themselves in debt from the medical bills. What are some solutions that would help families pay the costs?

Problem:	Possible solution 1:	Why/how the solution works:
because health care is expensive, some families are going into debt	(raise money online)	- avoid costs of modern medicine - herbal supplements - meditation, yoga, acupuncture
	Possible solution 2:	Why/how the solution works:
	use cheaper, nontraditional treatment options	- avoid costs of modern medicine - herbal supplements - meditation, yoga, acupuncture
	Possible solution 3:	Why/how the solution works:
	(organize a fund-raising event)	- sell tickets to fund-raising events - benefit dinners and concerts - charities donate money to families

2 Write the ideas that you wrote in Section 1, page 145, in the chart below. Include ideas from the Your Turns throughout the unit. Brainstorm more ideas.

Problem:	Possible solution 1:	Why/how the solution works:
	Possible solution 2:	Why/how the solution works:
	Possible solution 3:	Why/how the solution works:

When you are finished, choose two solutions (one you think is best, and one to refute) and write them here.

The best solution: ....

....

A solution that doesn't work as well: ....

....

STEP 2: DO RESEARCH: FINDING UP-TO-DATE INFORMATION

When doing research, using **current information**, from sources published in a time frame relevant to your topic, adds credibility to your writing. In the academic world, information is constantly changing or being updated. If your information is too old, more recent information may be available that changes or even contradicts the older information, thus weakening your position. When choosing sources, searching for **timely**, or up-to-date, sources and verifying the dates in those sources are important steps.

Jean-Bosco needed current information for this prompt: *Caregivers of seriously ill family members may require support to deal with their own emotions and challenges. What type of assistance offers them the best emotional support?* Read and find out how he did it.

When entering my keywords into a search engine, I added a relevant date range (2008–2015) after my keywords to keep the results current. When skimming the sources, I located the publication date or copyright date to verify that the information was timely. Sometimes the date was at the bottom of the page, in the margins, at the top of the article, or in the text of the article, so I had to look carefully for it. Finally, I noted which articles with up-to-date information I would read closely to use for my essay.

Jean-Bosco's Results

Thesis: Caregivers have many support options in the United States, but one of the most cost-effective and comprehensive support systems for caregivers can be found through Internet-based support groups.

Keywords and date range: effectiveness of online support groups caregivers 2008–2015

Source (Web address and/or title)	Source date (Where found)	Read closely? (Y/N: Reason)
www.alz.org, Resource Directory	2014 (copyright, at bottom of web page)	Y: many locations & resources for Alzheimer's & dementia caregivers; will research 1–2
www.lifelinesys.com, "Dealing with Anxiety When Caregiving"	2014 (top of article; link to archive of blogs dated 2013–2014)	Y: current support information on a variety of caregiver topics
"Dementia Caregivers' Responses to 2 Internet-Based Intervention Programs" by Marziali & Garcia	2011 (top of first page of article)	Y: primary research about caregivers by university researchers in Canada; published in a peer-reviewed journal

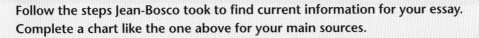

ACTIVITY 5.1 Apply It to Your Writing

YOUR TURN

Follow the steps Jean-Bosco took to find current information for your essay. Complete a chart like the one above for your main sources.

STEP 3: MAKE AN OUTLINE

Complete the outline below with your ideas from the previous steps.

ESSAY OUTLINE

I. Introduction

Thesis
Statement

**Body
Paragraph 1:
Describe the
Problem**

II.

Supporting
Idea 1

A.

Detail

1.

Detail

2.

Supporting
Idea 2

B.

Detail

1.

Detail

2.

**Body
Paragraph 2:
The Best
Solution**

III.

Supporting
Idea 1

A.

Detail

1.

Detail

2.

Supporting
Idea 2

B.

Detail

1.

Detail

2.

**Body Paragraph 3:
A Solution
that Won't Work
as Well**

IV. ....

Supporting
Idea 1

A. ....

Detail

1. ....

Detail

2. ....

Supporting
Idea 2

B. ....

Detail

1. ....

Detail

2. ....

V. Conclusion ....

Ideas for My
Recommendation

....

STEP 4: WRITE YOUR FIRST DRAFT

Now it is time to write your first draft. Here are some suggestions on how to get started.

1 Use your outline, notes, and the sentences you wrote in the Your Turns and in Step 3.

2 Focus on making your ideas as clear as possible.

3 Remember to add a title.

After you finish, read your essay and check for basic errors.

1 Check that all sentences are complete sentences.

2 Go through and look at every comma. Is it correct? Should it be a period?

3 Check that you have cited quotes and paraphrases.

4 Make sure your thesis statement and topic sentences are clear.

STEP 5: WRITE YOUR FINAL DRAFT

1 After you receive feedback on your first draft, review it carefully. Fix any errors.

2 Make a note of errors that were most frequent (misspellings, wrong verb tense, errors in using commas). Try to avoid them as you write.

3 Review the Academic Vocabulary and Academic Collocations from this unit. Are there any that you can add to your essay?

4 Turn to page 274 and use the Self-Editing Review to check your work one more time.

5 Write your final draft and hand it in.

6

SUMMARY–RESPONSE ESSAYS

COMMUNICATIONS: THE INFORMATION AGE

"People today are in danger of drowning in information; but, because they have been taught that information is useful, they are more willing to drown than they need be."

Indries Shah
(1924–1996)

About the Author:

Indries Shah grew up in England and had Scottish, Indian, and Afghan heritage. He published many books on spirituality, psychology, and cultural topics.

Work with a partner. Read the quotation about information overload. Then answer the questions.

too much info.

1 What does the author mean by saying that we are "drowning in information"? Can you think of any examples of "drowning in information" from your own life? *news. computer, Youtube.*

2 How does social media increase the amount of information available to you?

3 Note that Indries Shah died in 1996. What were the causes of "information overload" in his lifetime? Explain.

Ⓐ Connect to Academic Writing

In this unit you will learn skills to help you summarize and respond to texts written by others. While some of the writing skills that you will use may be new to you, others are not. In your everyday life, you use the skills of summarizing and responding to explain and share your opinion of a movie or a new policy at your school or workplace.

Ⓑ Reflect on the Topic

In this section you will read an article and then summarize and respond to its ideas. You will develop your response throughout the unit and practice skills that are necessary to write your essay.

The article mentioned below was used for the Student Model essay on pages 184–185. The student read the source article and used the chart to reflect on the author's ideas about curation. This helped him understand the main idea.

STUDENT MODEL

Source: "Stop Knocking Curation" by Steven Rosenbaum	
The author's ideas:	**My reaction to them:**
1. True content curation filters and contextualizes massive amounts of information in order to make it more meaningful, accessible, and useful for readers.	I think this is the author's opinion, not a fact. People might have different definitions of what "true" curation is and is not.
2. Wine stores are not real curators because they don't offer creative ways to help people understand wines.	What about stores that organize the wines by themes, such as ones that go well with chocolate, etc.? Isn't that curating?
3. The constant overflow of unfiltered content would overwhelm us if there was no one to organize and watch over it.	I completely agree. People simply do not have the time to sort through all the data available on the Internet by themselves.
4. Every day, 50 million photos are uploaded to Facebook.	Didn't know it was so many. Surprising!

  1.1 Notice

Take turns with a partner. Give your personal response to two of the ideas from the source article that the student noted above.

ACTIVITY 1.2 Apply It to Your Writing

Follow the directions to reflect on the ideas for your essay.

A Read the article "Face Time vs. Screen Time: The Technological Impact on Communication" on pages 211–212 (or another article approved by your instructor). As you read, highlight and react to interesting and important points in the article. Some things to look for are:

- the main idea or thesis of the text
- important supporting points and evidence
- ideas that you agree or disagree with
- points that you feel are strong or weak

B Write a possible thesis statement for your response to the article. This should be your own "big idea" in response to the ideas in the article.

Source: face time vs. screen time	
The author's ideas:	**My reaction to them:**
realy on technology to communicate are paying heavy price	more and more people use the internet to communicate
people feel really real	People will know you what you are thinking when you are talking.
nonfacial online communication are made worse in families where parents don't understand	Cannot use the internet to talk with parents.
finding a balance	sometime face time sometime screen time

Possible thesis statement:

....

In this section you will learn academic language that you can use in your summary–response essay. You will also notice how a professional writer uses the language and features of summary and response.

Ⓐ Academic Vocabulary

The words below appear throughout the unit. Many are from the Academic Word List. Using these words in your writing will make your ideas clearer and your writing more academic.

attribute (v)	deviate (v)	establish (v)	inevitably (adv)
constant (adj)	dismiss (v)	exceed (v)	minimize (v)

2.1 Focus on Meaning

Work with a partner. Match the words to their meanings. Write the letters.

A

___b___ 1 Some researchers **attribute** an inability to focus on work to the rise of social media such as Facebook.

___a___ 2 The **constant** use of social media all day long among young people in our society may contribute to a decrease in face-to-face encounters.

___d___ 3 Among young people in developed countries today, those who do not use social media sites are **deviating** from what is now the common way of living.

___c___ 4 The negative effect of social media on our ability to focus on work is significant and should not be **dismissed**.

a nearly continuous or very frequent

b to say that something is the result of something else

c to decide that something is not worth considering

d to change from the usual way

B

___c___ 1 Parents should **establish** time limits for use of social media with their teenagers.

___d___ 2 The amount of time spent looking at social media should not **exceed** the time spent on homework.

___b___ 3 If all of your friends are on Facebook, you will **inevitably** want to check it regularly to see what they are doing.

___a___ 4 In order to **minimize** the distraction of social media so that it doesn't interfere with homework, time limits must be set.

a to reduce something to the smallest possible level or amount

b in a way that is certain to happen

c to set something

d to be greater than; to go beyond a limit

B Academic Phrases

Research tells us that the phrases in bold below are commonly used in academic writing.

ACTIVITY

2.2 Focus on Meaning and Purpose

Read the summary paragraph. Decide the meaning or purpose of the phrases in bold and circle the correct answer.

John Danahy's article "The Origins of the Internet" aims to show the importance that **the idea of** partnership can have in innovation. The article is rather technical and is most relevant to computer science students, but at **the same time** it also appeals to general-interest readers as a tribute to two individuals: engineers Vint Cerf and Bob Kahn, known as the "Fathers of the Internet." Danahy uses their story to support his thesis. First, he details their work in the early 1970s for the U.S. Defense Department. He then recounts their invention of the Transmission Control Protocol (TCP), which enabled military data to be moved around. He explains that **part of the reason** that this was so important was that it was necessary for the creation of the modern Internet used worldwide today. Finally, he emphasizes how closely they continued to work in later years to manage this new creation by forming the Internet Society in 1992. He explains the aims and purpose of this non-profit group, which addresses Internet-related standards, education, and policy.

1 The phrase **the idea of**

  a introduces a concept.

  b gives the thesis of an essay.

2 The writer uses the phrase **at the same time**

  a to show that two things are happening at once.

  b to introduce a different idea or point of view.

3 The writer uses **part of the reason** to mean that

  a this was a less important reason for something.

  b this was one reason for the importance of something.

C Writing in the Real World

The author of "Overcoming Information Overload" uses features of summary and response to make her claims valid and engage her readers.

Before you read, answer these questions: What do you think "information overload" refers to? What are some of the effects of having access to too much information?

Now read the article. Think about your answers to the questions above as you read.

OVERCOMING
INFORMATION OVERLOAD
MARGARITA TARTAKOVSKY

(ADAPTED)

1   As a writer for the web, I'm well acquainted with information overload. One bit of information leads to five facts, which leads to three articles, which leads to an interesting interview that you just must listen to right now, which leads to 10 pages in your browser. But, wait, there's still one more thing to look up, to learn, and to digest.[1] Information is merely a click away. And depending on what you want to find out, there are likely to be at least a dozen, if not hundreds, of blogs on the topic, a similar number of books, and many more articles.

2   This is a good thing, but **at the same time** it can also overburden our brains. Too much information has been shown to **exceed** our brain's capacity to deal with it.

3   According to Lucy Jo Palladino, PhD, a psychologist and author of *Find Your Focus Zone: An Effective New Plan to Defeat Distraction and Overload*, "[i]nformation overload occurs when a person is exposed to more information than the brain can process at one time." The term "information overload" was actually coined[2] in 1970 by Alvin Toffler in his book *Future Shock*. It became a more and more popular phrase as people started using the web and realized that it described how they felt about going online.

4   Palladino **attributes** indecisiveness, bad decisions, and stress to information overload. Palladino says that when you're "overwhelmed by too many choices, your brain mildly freezes and ... you passively wait and see." In other words, you become paralyzed.[3] Alternatively, Palladino reports, you may make a hasty[4] decision because you can't tell the difference between vital facts and trivial[5] ones, and you consider credible[6] and non-credible sources equally. The **constant** demand to make decisions and to process information, Palladino notes, **inevitably** leads to stress and anxiety.

[1]digest: think about and understand
[2]coin: to be the first person to invent a new word

[3]paralyzed: unable to move your body
[4]hasty: very quick
[5]trivial: small and unimportant
[6]credible: believable

Overcoming Information Overload

5 In *Find Your Focus Zone*, Palladino suggests that readers think of incoming information as bags of groceries that you bring into your home. "To put them away, you need time, an amount that's limited to what fits on the counter, and an already clean fridge and organized pantry." These are her tips:

1. **Schedule breaks.** Take a break away from the computer. This gives your brain a rest and helps you regain perspective. Plus, the quiet time can help you make a good decision.

2. **Establish limits.** Because the Internet is available 24/7, you can consume information for hours. Limit how long you scan for information. Filter your sources, focusing only on the high-quality ones.

3. **Keep your virtual and physical spaces clutter-free.** Make sure your computer files and desk are "clear, well-organized, and ready to handle overflow."

The Conundrum of Control

6 In his column on information overload, *Guardian* reporter Oliver Burkeman also focuses on finding ways to **minimize** the stress of overload. Burkeman speculates, however, that it is not the fact that there is so much information that is stressful, but the fact that we feel like we are not in control.

7 Ironically, it's often technology that helps me feel in charge of information and not controlled by it. The programs that I use a lot are Freedom, which blocks the Internet, and OmmWriter, which provides a distraction-free writing space. This helps me to focus on one task at a time. (Deadlines also help.) Another strategy that I use when consuming information is to know exactly what information I need to find and how I am going to find it. Then I refuse to **deviate** from my plan. If I come across anything that is interesting but unrelated, I save it for another time.

8 Regardless of how you decide to approach information overload, don't **dismiss** the importance of regularly disconnecting.

ACTIVITY **2.3** Check Your Understanding

Answer the questions.

1 What is the relationship between information overload and our brain?

2 According to this article, why might too much information cause you to make a hasty decision?

3 The article states that information overload makes it hard to tell the difference between credible sources versus non-credible sources. Do you agree? Have you encountered this problem?

ACTIVITY **2.4** Notice the Writing

Answer the questions.

1 Does Tartakovsky spend more time explaining her ideas or the ideas of others?

2 Read paragraph 4 and notice how Tartakovsky integrates Palladino's ideas. Do all Palladino's ideas that Tartakovsky refers to support her own main idea?

3 Read the last two paragraphs. What is the relationship between Tartakovsky's ideas and the authors that she mentions?

In Section 1 on page 178 you saw how the writer of the Student Model reflected on his topic. In this section you will analyze the final draft of his summary–response essay. You will learn how to structure your ideas for your own essay.

Ⓐ Student Model

A student read the article "Stop Knocking Curation" by Steven Rosenbaum and made notes. Then he wrote a summary–response essay about the article.

Read the introduction to the topic of content curation and then read the article. Next, read the student's essay and answer the questions in the Analyze Writing Skills boxes. This will help you notice key features of summary–response writing.

Curation is the act of finding and organizing information on a topic online, while also providing links to the original content. Companies that benefit from using content curation include the Huffington Post, an insightful online news aggregator and blog, and Reddit, a popular website where contributions from its community members provide for amusing discussions and tales from the world of entertainment, news, and social networking.

ANNOTATED REAL-WORLD ARTICLE

Stop knocking curation (adapted) ——— Steven Rosenbaum

Content curation is not appreciated but it's invaluable

Curation is a growing concept as the enormous volume of mostly identical content has made it nearly impossible for mere mortals to find useful, thoughtful, contextual content on the Web. But its practice is undervalued. In just one example, a 2012 writing in *The Atlantic* called "curate" one of the "words we'd just as soon never write or see or hear spoken again."

I disagree. Information overload **inevitably** drives content consumers to look for human-filtered, journalist-vetted, intellectually related material. This demand for coherence isn't unreasonable; it's essential. And for those who think and write every day, gathering bits of ideas here and there that can be turned into a thoughtful narrative "on a topic" isn't cheating, or being lazy. Far from it. For those who would **dismiss** or **minimize** curating, it is in many ways harder than writing (at least *good* curating is). It's far easier for me to write 500 words from my head than to find themes and sources and tie them into a broader narrative.

AGREE – There's too much info – we need help choosing

Now, my issue with the current state of curation is that there are many people who wrongly attribute misguided meanings to the word. In so doing, they **deviate** from the core concepts that make curation so appealing and relevant.

Not clear – What is "misguided meanings"?

HOW?

Is this what Tartakovsky meant?

Curation started as a term for a practice that was emerging over the past few years to filter the overabundance of data and create quality, thoughtful, human-organized collections. The most urgent need for curation was in Web content. This is because there is far too much data being produced by digital devices, video-enabled mobile phones, auto-tweeting devices, and overzealous Facebook friends. Curators create entirely new editorial works by finding, filtering, and contextualizing. Meaning is produced from within massive amounts of data.

Curation, in its purest form, helps to **establish** a solution to a problem that meets a growing need. But then a bunch of random marketers and sign makers got in the act. Today, things are curated that shouldn't be. For example, a wine store can be known as a "social wine store" (whatever that means) if it claims to provide "curated" craft beer and spirits. As if another wine shop isn't "curated" (heck, they just stock whatever boxed wine they can get their hands on).

Interesting example – why can't wine be curated???

If the word *curation* is allowed to be diluted to simply mean "selected" or "quality collection," then it no longer solves the problem we need it to solve. Content *needs* curation. The **constant** overflow of unfiltered content would overwhelm us if there was no one to objectively organize and watch over it. Wine doesn't pose this problem.

Now I see what he means by "misguided meanings"!

Wow! It's not just me – haha!

YIKES!

Here are a few scary stats: Everyday, 50 million photos are uploaded to Facebook, 864,000 hours of video are uploaded to YouTube, and 294 BILLION emails are sent. That's why you can't read all the mail you get anymore.

Tartakovsky would agree!

This all makes curation an important, even essential, part of journalism. The world is full of meaningless data. Readers are hungry for clarity and understanding. And journalists are trained to find meaning and assemble facts into something that can be rationally and logically understood. They're rewarded with enlightened readers, engaged audiences, and a revitalized role in the new world. In this new world, anyone can be a creator of information. Quality curation is a wonderful thing.

What about the reader's role? Isn't that important?

Summary–Response Essay for "Stop Knocking Curation"

1   In his article "Stop Knocking Curation," Steven Rosenbaum argues that content curation is misunderstood and misused, and asserts that *correct* curation is invaluable[1] for helping us process information on the Internet. Content curation is the collection and organization of information on a topic or theme. One popular example is Pinterest, which allows people to share and collect information on all kinds of topics. While I agree with some of the author's points to an extent, I feel that they could have been clearer, and included the point of view of the reader who is the user of content curation.

2   Rosenbaum makes two points in his article. The first point is that **the idea of** content curation is misunderstood – or misused by people to sell things. He criticizes stores that use the term "curation." According to Rosenbaum, these stores are not really curating because they are just creating collections of the same things. This is different from true content curation. Rosenbaum further states that content curation should be defined as creating "entirely new editorial works by finding, filtering, and contextualizing" information. He goes on to argue that this practice is critical[2] now, as there is so much content on the Internet that it is overwhelming. He includes facts such as "every day, 50 million photos are uploaded to Facebook, 864,000 hours of video are uploaded to YouTube, and 294 billion emails are sent." He asserts that this is too much information to process,[3] and readers need help sorting through it. Content curation provides this help. Rosenbaum ends by saying that curation is a new critical role for journalists.

3   Rosenbaum's article contains interesting points, but I found some of his examples and explanations debatable.[4] He claims that the term "curation" is misused, and gives an example of a wine store that curates wine. Why can't a wine store curate wines? This example made me think of the museum in my neighborhood. Museums have curators who put together collections of paintings that are thematically related. The curators contextualize[5] them by sharing information on who the artist was, when the artist painted, and so on. That can be done for wine collections, too. Curators could bring together

[1]invaluable: very valuable
[2]critical: extremely important
[3]process: to deal with, handle, or manage
[4]debatable: not clear; possibly not true
[5]contextualize: show the environment, surroundings, history, etc. that something exists in

1 Analyze Writing Skills

Circle the title of the original text and its author's name in the introductory paragraph. Circle the information about the article that the writer includes in the first sentence to make sure that the reader understands whose ideas will be discussed.

2 Analyze Writing Skills

Read the thesis statement. Which two weaknesses in the author's article does the essay focus on?

3 Analyze Writing Skills

How does the writer organize his ideas in paragraph 2? Circle your answer.

a He presents the ideas from the most important to the least important.

b He presents the ideas in the same order as they appear in the article.

4 Analyze Writing Skills

Read the sentence starting with "This example made me …." What previous idea does "this example" refer to?

wines related on a theme, maybe because they were all mentioned in a novel, or all taste good with chocolate. They could share information on how the wines were made, or why they are relevant to the theme. I think it is possible to curate a wine store. If Rosenbaum had talked more about why the wine store was not really curated in his opinion, it would have made his point clearer. Reading this part of the article, I felt unconvinced that the label was being used inappropriately.

4   However, another part of the argument is Rosenbaum's very clear second point about the need for content curators, and I agree with it to an extent. The facts and figures about the volume of information are indeed compelling. Many people can relate to the feeling of being overwhelmed by the amount of data coming to us on social media and in our email. We simply do not have time, or the patience, to read or look through all this data on our own. Curation might be the type of "filtering" that Margarita Tartakovsky mentions as a strategy for dealing with all of this information in her article "Overcoming Information Overload." However, Rosenbaum says that content curation is the job of journalists. I find that assertion[6] questionable. It's also important that readers think for themselves and make sure that the content they see isn't just one person's opinion. For example, I go on one particular website for home decorating ideas. I see lots of pictures of the same styles over and over. I know that this site is just one point of view, so I go to other sites, too, for fresh ideas. I think that responsible readers seek out information in addition to the information curated for them so that they can broaden their perspectives. In this way, content curation isn't just a journalist's job – it is everyone's job.

5   In conclusion, Rosenbaum makes some interesting points about what curation is and why we need it. However, there are some weaknesses in his argument because some of his examples of "true" curation are less convincing, and he also does not consider the reader's responsibility. As the amount of information we come across will only increase in the future, I believe the process of content curation will become even more necessary. It would be helpful to know how to do this for ourselves so that we, as readers, can know when content curation is done right, or choose to do it for ourselves.

[6]assertion: something that is said or claimed

---

5 Analyze Writing Skills

In paragraph 3, the writer compares his neighborhood museum to a wine store. What is the purpose of this comparison? Circle your answer.

a   to prove that museums and wine stores give different information

b   to prove that they can both be curators for similar reasons

6 Analyze Writing Skills

Why does the writer mention Tartakovsky in paragraph 4? Circle your answer.

a   to show why Tartakovsky would agree with Rosenbaum

b   to show why Tartakovsky would disagree with Rosenbaum

7 Analyze Writing Skills

In paragraph 4, the writer states, "I find that assertion questionable." What is the effect of saying "questionable" rather than "wrong"? Circle your answer.

a   It sounds less emotional

b   It sounds more direct

8 Analyze Writing Skills

Underline the prediction that the writer makes in paragraph 5.

Answer the questions.

1 According to the writer, which two main points does Rosenbaum make in his article?

2 Why does the writer believe that a wine store can be curated? Do you agree or disagree?

3 The writer suggests that content curation is everyone's job. Do you think Rosenbaum would be convinced by his argument? Why or why not?

3.2 Outline the Writer's Ideas

Complete the outline for "Summary–Response Essay for 'Stop Knocking Curation'" using the phrases in the box.

> √ readers need help sorting through it
> √ curators of wine stores are like museum curators
> √ curation is critical today
> √ stores are collecting – not curating
> curation could be "filtering"
> content curation is everyone's job

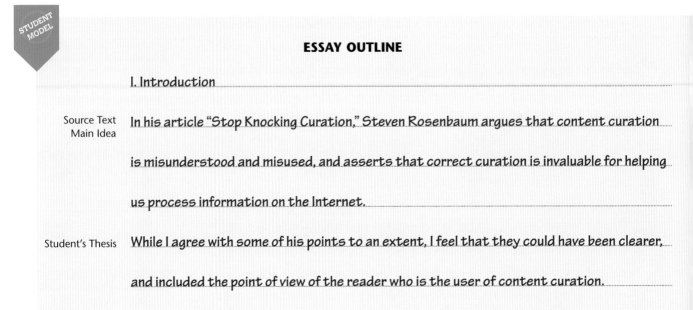

STUDENT MODEL

ESSAY OUTLINE

I. Introduction

Source Text Main Idea In his article "Stop Knocking Curation," Steven Rosenbaum argues that content curation is misunderstood and misused, and asserts that correct curation is invaluable for helping us process information on the Internet.

Student's Thesis While I agree with some of his points to an extent, I feel that they could have been clearer, and included the point of view of the reader who is the user of content curation.

Body Paragraph 1: Summary	II. Rosenbaum makes two points
Point 1	A. Label misunderstood and misused by stores
Detail	*Stores are* 1. collecting not curating
Detail	2. Definition of true content curation
Point 2	B. Curation is critical today
Detail	1. So much content on the Internet
Detail	2. Readers need help sorting through it.
Detail	3. New roles for journalists
Body Paragraph 2: Response	III: Disagree with author's examples
Point 1	A. Wine store example of misuse – unconvincing
Detail	1. Museum curators – paintings on theme
Detail	2. Curators of wine stores are like museum curators
Detail	3. Author should have given more explanation
Body Paragraph 3: Response	IV: Agree that curators necessary – to an extent
Point 1	A. Facts and figures are compelling
Detail	1. No time to read or look through data
Detail	2. Curation could be "filtering"
Point 2	B. Curation is job of journalists – questionable
Detail	1. Readers must think for themselves
Detail	2. Content curation is everyone job.
	V. Conclusion

B Summary–Response Essays

A summary–response essay gives writers the opportunity to express their understanding of another author's ideas and evaluate them in an objective and logical way. Summary–response essays are similar to other academic essays: there is a thesis that the writer supports and develops. The difference is that in this type of essay, writers reflect on an author's ideas.

This type of essay has the following organization:

- An **introduction**, including:
  - the **title and author** of the text you will summarize and respond to
  - background information on the topic
  - the author's main idea
  - a **thesis** that gives your main response to the text
- **Body paragraph 1 summary**: A **summary** of the author's text, including:
  - the author's main idea
  - supporting ideas that illustrate the idea well, such as important examples, evidence, and information from the text
  - a short quotation from the text – but only if necessary
- **Body paragraphs 2–4 response**: Each paragraph responds to a different point in the article that you feel strongly about. A response paragraph includes:
  - a topic sentence that identifies whether you will support, criticize, or illustrate a point the author makes
  - your own critical analysis of the point using examples and supporting details
  - evidence from your own observations or those of other authors
- A **conclusion**, including:
  - a brief summary of the text's main idea
  - a restatement of your thesis
  - a concluding statement, such as a comment, prediction, or call to action

---

ACTIVITY 3.3 Notice

Look again at the summary–response for "Stop Knocking Curation" on pages 186–187 and at the information above. Circle your answers.

1 In which paragraph does the writer mention the title and author of the source text?

    1 2 3 4 5

2 In which paragraph does the writer explain the main ideas of the source text's author?

    1 2 3 4 5

3 In which two paragraphs does the writer give his own responses to the author's ideas?

    1 2 3 4 5

4 In which paragraph does a prediction and call to action appear in the essay?

    1 2 3 4 5

INTRODUCTORY PARAGRAPH

The introductory paragraph presents readers with important background information about the article. Your readers might not have read the article, so you need to give credit to the author and provide enough context to help readers understand the topic and the author's point of view. Include the following information:

- the author's name and the title of the source text)1
- the author's main idea in your own words
- background information about the audience and purpose of the text) 2-4
- a thesis statement that states your response to the main idea(s) of the text

Read the introductory paragraph from the Student Model below and notice how the writer has marked up the text to note the key features included.

> In his article "Stop Knocking Curation," Steven Rosenbaum argues that *— credit to the author and his article*
> content curation is misunderstood and misused, and asserts that *correct* *— a paraphrase of the author's main idea*
> curation is invaluable for helping us process information on the Internet.
> Content curation is the collection and organization of information on a topic *— background information about the article's audience and purpose*
> or theme. One popular example is Pinterest, which allows people to share
> and collect information on all kinds of topics. While I agree with some of
> the author's points to an extent, I feel that they could have been clearer, and *— the writer's thesis statement*
> included the point of view of the reader who is the user of content curation.

ACTIVITY 3.4 Practice

Use the information below to write the first sentence of an introductory paragraph. Use the model above as an example.

<u>Author's name:</u> Margarita Tartakovsky

<u>Name of article:</u> "Overcoming Information Overload"

<u>Main idea:</u> Information overload can cause the brain to work too hard and make people feel stressed, but the secret is to find ways to control it through the decisions we make.

> In his article "Overcoming Information Overload," Margarita Tarcakousky claims that the brain will work too hard and people will feel tough which because too many information getting at the same time. However, we can make a decision to control it, and that is the key to solve it.

SUMMARY PARAGRAPH

A summary paragraph takes key information from a source text and condenses it in writing for the reader. It is structured just like any paragraph in an academic essay: with a topic sentence and supporting information. A summary paragraph includes the following:

- a restatement of the author's main idea or a general introduction of the main idea
- key supporting ideas from the text in your own words
- details from the text such as examples and short quotes that support the main idea

Because the only goal of a summary paragraph is to help readers understand the author's main points, it should not add any personal or unnecessary information. When writing a summary:

- Do not include your own opinions about the author's ideas. Be objective. You will have an opportunity to give your opinion in the body paragraphs that come later in the essay.
- Do not include details from the source that are irrelevant.
- Do not use emotional language. Be neutral and avoid overly strong words.

ACTIVITY 3.5 Notice

Below is the first draft of the summary paragraph written by the writer of the Student Model essay, along with instructor comments. Match the words, phrases, or sentences with the teacher comment that accompanies them.

> *claims that*
>
> ① Rosenbaum's first point is that content curation is misunderstood – or misused by people to sell things. He <u>hates</u> ② stores that use the term "curation." According to Rosenbaum, these stores are not really curating because they are just creating collections of the same things. This is different from true content curation, <u>but I guess stores do it because they just want to make more money.</u> ③ Rosenbaum further states that content curation should be defined as creating "<u>entirely new editorial works by finding, filtering, and contextualizing</u>" ④ information. He goes on to argue that this practice is critical now, as there is so much content on the Internet that it is overwhelming. He includes facts such as <u>every day, 50 million photos are uploaded to Facebook, 864,000 hours of video are uploaded to YouTube, and 294 billion emails are sent.</u> ⑤ He asserts that this is too much information to process, and readers need help sorting through it. Content curation provides this help. Rosenbaum ends by saying that curation is a new critical role for journalists.

_2_ a This word is too emotional – can you use a more neutral word?

_5_ b This is a direct quote from the article – add quotation marks or paraphrase it. " "

_4_ c An important quote to include – good!

_1_ d Please begin with a topic sentence that introduces the paragraph.

_3_ e Delete this – no personal opinions in the summary paragraph.

3.6 Practice Summarizing

Write your own brief summary of Steven Rosenbaum's article "Stop Knocking Curation" on pages 184–185 by following the two steps outlined below.

1 Write a sentence that introduces the author's main idea following this format: *"[Author's name] argues that …"*

Steven Rosenbaum argues that curation is not appreciated but It's a invaluable

2 Find a supporting sentence from the article that supports Rosenbaum's main idea. Write it in your own words using this format:

"In support of this idea, the author states that …"

The Curatorial helped to establish a place to provide solutions and someone needs to take care of it.

3.7 Apply It to Your Writing

Read the ideas that you wrote about your article in Section 1 on page 179 that you thought were important. Choose two and write about them using the language that you have just learned. Compare your sentences with a partner and decide if they have mentioned the main ideas and key points of the source text.

RESPONSE PARAGRAPHS

In body paragraphs 2–4, give your objective responses to, and critique of, the source in terms of the quality of the writing and ideas.

Each paragraph responds to a different point in the article. The topic sentence states the point to be discussed. It can be supported in any of the following ways:

- a reflection on what it means based on your knowledge of the world
- a personal connection to an idea through an example
- question(s) you may have
- connections between an idea and the ideas of another author
- strengths or weaknesses in the author's reasoning

Response paragraphs can focus on the author's main idea, major points, or weaknesses in ideas or examples. Writers often choose to write a different paragraph for each idea. For example, they may write one paragraph for a point they agree with, and another paragraph about a point that they feel is not well supported. Alternatively, they may include several paragraphs that show how their own experiences illustrate different ideas mentioned in the article.

Here are strategies to use in a good response paragraph, along with examples of each from the Student Model essay.

- Include a topic sentence that identifies which idea you are responding to and states your opinion about it.

  Another part of the argument is Rosenbaum's very clear second point about the need for content curators, and I agree with it to an extent.

- State whether or not you agree with an idea in the source text, and explain why.

  He claims that the term "curation" is misused and gives an example of a wine store that curates wine. Why can't a wine store curate wines?

- When you do agree or disagree with something, illustrate your point with an example.

  This example made me think of the museum in my neighborhood. Museums have curators who put together collections of paintings that are thematically related. The curators contextualize them by sharing information on who the artist was, when the artist painted, and so on. That can be done for wine collections, too.

- Evaluate how well the author explains his/her ideas. If you think an idea is faulty, you can express that with phrases like "[author's name] does not provide enough examples to support this idea" or "the article presents this as supporting evidence, but this is not convincing."

  Reading this part of the article, I felt unconvinced that the label was being used inappropriately.

ACTIVITY 3.8 Practice Responding

Read the notes on a source text below. Then read paragraph A and paragraph B, which are responding to the source text. Check (✓) which paragraph uses the four strategies in the chart below.

File   Edit   View   Insert   Tools   ⊖ ▢ ⊗

Author: Lincoln, Anthony

Article title: "FYI: TMI" from the journal *First Monday*

Date: March 2011

Main idea: The large amount of information available to us in the age of technology seems like an advantage, but it has actually caused problems.

Supporting idea 1: Useful information online can easily be "contaminated" (made dirty, or poisoned) with information that might not be fully accurate.

Supporting idea 2: People conduct research thinking that they understand and can handle information overload, but they may not be able to do that.

A

It is undeniable that we are currently in an age of technology. The author believes most people do not understand information overload or how to handle it. He gives some examples in the article of how information overload is negative. The examples are supposed to support his thesis. Sometimes too much information can overwhelm people. A lot of web users follow multiple news websites and blogs, but they may not notice their differences because there are so many choices. Other people are able to handle all the information and make wise choices about which sites offer useful information, and which have "contaminated" information.

B

Lincoln's article is interesting, but he focuses too much on the negative side of all the information we have in "the age of technology." Maybe this is because others who have written on this topic usually highlight the benefits. It is true that information which we get from the web and social media can be less accurate than an original source due to "contamination." However, his examples to support the second problem are not convincing. He claims that we tend not to understand information overload, or know how to handle it. The examples he gives for this are confusing, and I don't agree that they are applicable to everyone, such as serious scholars or web designers.

	A	B
1 The writer has a topic sentence that identifies which idea she is responding to and states her opinion about it.	☐	☐
2 The writer identifies whether she agrees or disagrees with the idea.	☐	☐
3 The writer gives examples to illustrate why she agrees or disagrees.	☐	☐
4 The writer evaluates how well the source text explains its ideas.	☐	☐

 3.9 Discuss

Now decide which paragraph you think does a better job of using the strategies, A or B. Discuss your answer with a partner.

CONCLUDING PARAGRAPH

The concluding paragraph restates the author's main idea and your thesis. It ends with a few final comments that give readers something to think about after they read, such as a predication or a call to action.

Read the concluding paragraph from the Student Model below and notice how the writer includes these features:

RESTATEMENT OF THE AUTHOR'S MAIN IDEA

In conclusion, Rosenbaum makes some interesting points about what curation is and why we

RESTATEMENT OF THE WRITER'S THESIS

need it. However, there are some weaknesses in his argument because some of his examples of "true" curation are less convincing, and he also does not consider the reader's responsibility. As the amount

PREDICTION

of information we come across will only increase in the future, I believe the process of content curation

CALL TO ACTION

will become even more necessary. It would be helpful to know how to do this for ourselves so that we, as readers, can know when content curation is done right, or chose to do it for ourselves.

ACTIVITY 3.10 Notice

Read the sentences from the concluding paragraph for a summary–response essay about Anthony Lincoln's article "FYI: TMI." Number the sentences in the correct order from 1 to 4. Discuss your answers with a partner.

.... a I think that people need to be made aware of how much information they are taking in and how they understand it.

.... b However, the author seems to ignore the benefits that come from being able to access so much information.

.... c Then they will be better prepared to handle it.

.... d All in all, Lincoln makes some interesting observations about how information overload affects people's ability to understand and handle information.

HOW TO ANNOTATE A TEXT FOR A SUMMARY–RESPONSE ESSAY

Good writers read a text a few times and annotate (or "mark up") the text as they read. They note their questions and annotate as they read to help them find and evaluate the ideas and writing of an author.

STEPS FOR ANNOTATING

1 Draw a box around the name of the author and his/her credentials, if provided.

2 Double underline the thesis. Is the thesis clearly stated and is it logical based on the evidence that the author gives? Write your opinion of the thesis in the margin. For example:

agree   *disagree – not enough evidence*   *unclear*   *strong thesis*

3 Find the main supporting ideas that the author uses to support his/her thesis and underline them. You will use this information in your summary paragraph.

4a Notice the facts, examples, and other ideas the writer uses to make each idea clear and convincing. Do they clearly support the thesis? Are they logical? Are they convincing? Circle the important ones and note in the margins your opinions of them. Say how well the writer conveys the supporting ideas and what you think of each one. Did he or she miss something? Note that as well. For example:

confusing   *don't see connection to thesis*   *great example!*
Really?   *Interesting!*

Why does the author say this? Not logical   *Yes! Agree!*

Missing: friends' influence – sometimes that's more important than family's

You will use these notes to create your response paragraph.

4b Find connections between your experiences and the ideas to help support your opinion and write them in the margins. Also, note connections to other texts you have read that would support your opinion.

Reminds me of high school experience   *Rosenbaum would agree!*

4c Think about the support again. Has the author omitted, or not included, ideas that you think are important or better support the thesis? Do you have questions about the ideas? Note them in the margins.

Doesn't discuss pressure among girls, only boys   *What about school policy on this?*

ACTIVITY 3.11 Practice

Reread "Overcoming Information Overload" on pages 182–183 and annotate the text. Then compare your annotations with a partner. Did you and your partner have similar or different reactions to the author's ideas? Explain.

In this section you will learn the writing and grammar skills that will help make your writing more sophisticated and accurate.

Ⓐ Writing Skill 1: Language for Summarizing

In academic writing, writers often use the following phrases when summarizing the ideas in other texts.

- Use *according to* and *in the article … X states that …* to introduce the author, the text, and the main ideas.

  According to Hoak, time and money limitations have weakened the effectiveness of TV news.

  In the article "Have 24-Hour TV News Channels Had Their Day?" the authors **state that** the need to broadcast continuously causes mistakes in reporting.

- Use the expressions below to talk about additional points made in the text.

  Michael Hoak also points out that channels often have to "kill time" on the air.

  The author further states that the Internet and social media have replaced TV news.

  Hoak **goes on to say that** this loss will have negative effects in the future.

ACTIVITY **4.1** Practice With the Vocabulary

Use the best choice of the two phrases in the boxes to complete these sentences.

According to Margarita Tartakovsky,	In the article "Overcoming Information Overload,"

1 .... Margarita Tartakovsky provides useful advice.

2 .... there are strategies that we can use when our brain is overburdened, which she lists in the article.

As Tartakovsky points out in her article,	The author states that

3 .... she is not sure she agrees with Oliver Burkeman's conclusion about technology's influence.

4 .... some software programs can help us to organize all the information we have to make us less overwhelmed.

In the article "Overcoming Information Overload,"	The author further states that

5 .... the author, Margarita Tartakovsky, claims that the huge amount of information we receive today has been shown to exceed our brain's capacity to deal with it.

6 .... we must not dismiss the importance of "disconnecting" as a result of this.

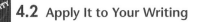

Write three sentences about your own source article using the expressions you learned on page 198.

....

....

....

....

Ⓑ Writing Skill 2: Neutral and Unbiased Language

In many academic writing tasks you will be expected to use language that is neutral and unbiased. Using neutral, unbiased language makes your writing as objective and impersonal as possible. It also helps you avoid offending your readers.

One specific example of this is language that minimizes unnecessary emotion in academic writing.

In the chart below, use the words on the right instead of the ones on the left.

INSTEAD OF THESE EMOTIONAL WORDS ...	USE THESE MORE NEUTRAL WORDS ...
hate	dislike, have an issue with
adore	admire, appreciate
wrong	questionable, misguided
ridiculous	debatable, problematic, not convincing
crazy	illogical, unsupportable
stupid	naïve, ill-considered

Another example is language that avoids specifying a group of people unnecessarily. For instance, in academic writing it is often best to use gender-neutral language.

In the chart below are some examples of gender-neutral language.

INSTEAD OF THESE SPECIFIC GENDER WORDS ...	USE THESE GENDER-NEUTRAL WORDS ...
he, she	they
his, her	their, his or her
mankind	humankind
men (meaning "humans")	people
businessman	businessperson
chairman	chair
policeman	police officer

Circle the words in each sentence that are biased or not neutral. Then rewrite the sentence so that it is neutral.

1 Professors at this university generally (hate) Wikipedia and say that students must never use it, but I think that is a (ridiculous) policy.

Professors at this university generally dislike Wikipedia and say that students must never use it but I think that is a problematic policy.

2 The (chairman) of the new company is (crazy.)

The chair of the new company is illogical.

3 (Policemen) in Chicago arrested a student for illegal downloading. They seem to think this will stop illegal downloading throughout the city, which is (stupid.)

Police officer in Chicago arrested a student fur illegal downloading. They seem to think this will stop illegal downloading throughout the city, which is ill-considered.

C Writing Skill 3: Avoid Overuse of Key Words

As you saw in Unit 4, coherence in writing means that the flow of ideas from sentence to sentence and paragraph to paragraph is logical and clear. Overusing key words can make your writing repetitive and harder to understand.

STRATEGIES TO AVOID OVERUSING KEY WORDS	
1 Use *this* with the following nouns to refer to ideas in previous sentences. *achievement, approach, aspect, concept, development, experience, fact, factor, feature, finding, idea, issue, phenomenon, reason, topic*	*Some people feel that <u>24-hour television news is no longer needed</u>. **This idea** is the thesis of the article by Michael Hoak.* *The Internet <u>allows us to share information, technology, and creativity with anyone regardless of geography</u>. **This feature** has been one of the primary revolutions of the information age.*
2 Use synonyms of words or phrases to refer to ideas in previous sentences.	*Because the Internet is always available, experts suggest <u>establishing</u> limits on your use. By deliberately **setting** a time limit on your surfing, you can waste less time.* *Social media keeps people <u>connected</u> with one another. Families and friends are **linked** now in a way that they were not 30 years ago.*
3 Use pronouns to refer back to nouns and noun phrases instead of repeating the same nouns.	*<u>The Internet</u> has changed the relationship between national governments. **It** has allowed them to share information as never before.*
4 Reduce a long noun phrase to one or two words when you refer to it again.	*The <u>U.S. National Security Agency's data collection program</u> became controversial when more details of its operations were made public. **The program** seemed like an invasion of privacy to many people.*

Rewrite the sentences below to avoid repeating the nouns. Use the strategies on page 201.

1 Tim Berners-Lee's creation of the World Wide Web is regarded as one of the most important innovations of the twentieth century. Tim Berners-Lee's creation of the World Wide Web has changed the way most people in the world get their information.

....

....

2 Indries Shah felt that people today have access to too much information, and that people today are in danger of drowning in information.

....

....

3 There is an enormous amount of information on the web right now. The amount of time required to read all of the information on the web exceeds the time any of us have. Also, the supply of information exceeds the demand.

....

....

4 The invention of Transmission Control Protocol (TCP) allowed the movement of data on the Internet. The invention of Transmission Control Protocol was the result of research by Vint Cerf and Bob Kahn.

....

....

Ⓓ Grammar for Writing: Noun Clauses

A noun clause has a subject and a verb but acts like a noun in a sentence. Noun clauses often begin with *wh-* words (*who, what, where, when, which,* and *how*). They can also begin with *if* or *whether* to show an alternative (or a *yes/no*) choice. They are often used with these verbs: *agree, disagree, know, remember, see, understand,* and *wonder.*

NOUN CLAUSE
How students *can know which information is reliable is something that they will learn in this class.*

NOUN CLAUSE
Our department assistant is wondering **which** *website is the most trustworthy one for travel advice.*

NOUN CLAUSE
Dr. Steinberg agreed that it is not clear **if** *patients should use this website.*

NOUN CLAUSE
Whether *the news posted on his Twitter feed is trustworthy or not is the issue which is unclear.*

Work with a group. Return to the article by Margarita Tartakovsky on pages 182–183. Then complete the sentences below with a noun clause from the article.

1 Depending on ...., there are likely to be at least a dozen, if not hundreds, of blogs on the topic. (paragraph 1)

2 The term "information overload" became a more and more popular phrase as people started using the web and realized that it described .... (paragraph 3)

3 "To put them away, you need time, an amount that's limited to ...., and an already clean fridge and organized pantry." (paragraph 5)

4 Because the Internet is available 24/7, you can consume information for hours. Limit .... (paragraph 5, point 2)

5 Another strategy that I use when consuming information is to know exactly .... and .... (paragraph 7)

6 Regardless of ...., don't dismiss the importance of regularly connecting. (paragraph 8)

Avoiding Common Mistakes 👁

Research tells us that these are the most common mistakes that students make when using noun clauses in academic writing.

> 1 With *wh-* word noun clauses, use statement word order (subject + verb), not question word order. Do not put an auxiliary or modal verb before the subject.
>
> *We want to understand why* ~~*is the source*~~ **the source is** *less credible.*
>
> *We need to be able to trust our news sources to give us correct information when* ~~*do*~~ *we need it.*
>
> 2 When a noun clause is the subject of a sentence, use a singular verb after it. Don't use the plural verb form. This is true even when the verb is followed by a plural noun.
>
> *What they heard about the sites* ~~*were*~~ **was** *not true.*
>
> *What the Internet needs now* ~~*are*~~ **is** *more people who can curate content effectively.*

Find and correct five more mistakes in the following paragraph.

    Paul Baker's article brought up many ideas about social media sites that I had not considered
before. Whether or not a person can be addicted to these sites ~~are~~ ^{is} something that I have
wondered myself. What does the author say about Facebook is especially relevant to me.
I often find myself checking Facebook several times per hour. The article is very persuasive
about the dangers of overusing social media. It has forced me to consider why do I need to
check Facebook so often. What have I noticed is that I often see comments and photos which
describe and show my friends doing fun things. Very often, these plans and activities look
more fun than what I am doing. This causes me to wonder if knowing about other people's
activities makes me dissatisfied with my life. It's not actually necessary for me to know what is
everyone doing all the time. In addition, what I see on Facebook about other people's lives give
an inaccurate picture. My friends' days are probably just as ordinary and unremarkable as my
own. Baker says, "Sometimes, it's as simple as taking a 'Facebreak.'" That's a good suggestion,
well stated. I do think I need to reduce the amount of time I spend looking at Facebook and
comparing my life to the lives of others. The article has therefore provided me with some
valuable advice.

E Avoiding Plagiarism

It is helpful to take notes when you do research, but keeping track of your sources can be a problem.

I worked hard on the essay I wrote about Bill Gates. I read a lot of articles and took a lot of notes. I thought my paper was good, but my instructor said I plagiarized some information! I guess I mixed my notes with the word-for-word ideas from sources. I didn't mean to plagiarize! I'm really sorry. How can I be better at taking notes? – Ruby

Dear Ruby,

Good note taking does not have to be difficult, but you do need a system to organize your notes. Notes can come from many places, for example, your own ideas, common knowledge, or other sources. If you organize your notes from the beginning, you'll know which ideas are yours and which ones need to be cited. You'll also know which notes are quotations and which ones are paraphrases. The important thing is to have a simple system that you can use for <u>all</u> your notes.

Good luck!

Professor Wright

CREATING A NOTE-TAKING SYSTEM

In order to avoid plagiarizing, you always need to quote your sources. It is important to be able to distinguish between your sources, quoted material, and your ideas in your notes. Organizing your notes from the beginning makes it easier to locate your sources and correctly cite them in your writing.

Here are some suggestions for creating an effective note-taking system.

1 **Take notes** in a notebook, on index cards, or in a document on the computer. Keep notes together. Use a separate page in your notebook, a separate index card, or a new page in a word document for each source. Write all the source information at the top: authors, titles, dates, medium, page.

2 When you write down the **exact words** from a source, write the words in big quotation marks ("..."). Write the word *quote* after the quotation. Highlight all quotations in the same color, for example, in blue.

3 When you **paraphrase** someone's words or ideas, write the word *paraphrase* next to the information you paraphrase. Highlight all paraphrases in the same color, for example, in yellow.

4.7 Practice

Work with a partner. Read the original source text below. Then read the notes from Ruby's notebook. Use the ideas in the system on page 205 to organize Ruby's notes.

Text from Original Source　　　⊖ ▢ ⊗

| Home | Articles | About | Register | Sign up |

When we surveyed undergraduates last spring in a large-scale survey, 8 in 10 of our 8,353 respondents reported having overwhelming difficulty even starting research assignments and determining the nature and scope of what was expected of them.

Nearly half of the students in our survey sample experienced nagging uncertainty about how to conclude and assess the quality of their research efforts. They struggled with the same frustrating open-endedness whether they were researching something for a college course or in their personal lives.

File　Edit　View　Insert　Tools　　　⊖ ▢ ⊗

Ruby's Notes

Source: "College Students Eager to Learn but Need Help Negotiating Information Overload." Alison J. Head and Michael B. Eisenberg. June 3, 2011.

http://seattletimes.com/html/opinion/2015227485_guest05head.html

- Authors did survey. 8,353 people

- 8 of 10 respondents had a hard time starting their research project.

- They had a hard time determining the nature and scope of what was expected of them.

- Half of students → not sure how to finish or evaluate their research. Nagging uncertainty.

- Frustrating open-endedness. Both for classes and in private

- My opinion: I agree with the survey. I am insecure about assi...

 4.8 Practice

Work with a partner. Discuss the ways you organize notes. D... you use quotation marks? Discuss ways you could organize y... next assignments.

[Handwritten note:]

1. Highlight the author and name of article
2. Circle topics and underline main ideas of paragraphs.
3. Underline the thesis- paraphrase the thesis in the margins
4. Number Main Ideas.
5. Bullet point supporting details; examples, evidence the author uses to support her ideas
6. Find connections between ideas.

In this section you will follow the writing process to complete the final draft of your essay.

STEP 1: **ANNOTATE**

Here are the steps for annotating that you read in Section 3. Using these steps as a guide, annotate "Face Time vs. Screen Time: The Technological Impact on Communication" on pages 211–212.

Steps for Annotating

1 Draw a box around the name of the author and his/her credentials, if provided.

2 Double underline the thesis. Is the thesis clearly stated and is it logical based on the evidence that the author gives? Write your opinion of the thesis in the margin. For example:

agree   *disagree – not enough evidence*   *unclear*   *strong thesis*

3 Find the main supporting ideas that the author uses to support his/her thesis and underline them. You will use this information in your summary paragraph.

4a Notice the facts, examples, and other ideas the writer uses to make each idea clear and convincing. Do they clearly support the thesis? Are they logical? Are they convincing? Circle the important ones and note in the margins your opinions of them. Say how well the writer conveys the supporting ideas and what you think of each one. Did he or she miss something? Note that as well. For example:

confusing   *don't see connection to thesis*   *great example!*
Really?   *Interesting!*

Why does the author say this? Not logical   *Yes! Agree!*

Missing: friends' influence – sometimes that's more important than family's

You will use these notes to create your response paragraph.

4b Find connections between your experiences and the ideas to help support your opinion and write them in the margins. Also, note connections to other texts you have read that would support your opinion.

Reminds me of high school experience   *Rosenbaum would agree!*

4c Think about the support again. Has the author omitted, or not included, ideas that you think are important or better support the thesis? Do you have questions about the ideas? Note them in the margins.

Doesn't discuss pressure among girls, only boys   *What about school policy on this?*

STEP 2: DO RESEARCH: TAKING CLEAR NOTES TO AVOID CITATION MISTAKES

Taking organized notes on your reading helps you in many ways. First, identifying the relevant ideas of the reading can help you organize your ideas for your essay. Second, writing down exact quotes you might use helps you remember which quotes to include in your essay. Third, by recording the **citation information** – such as the article title, author's name, source title, web address, and the article's publication date – you have all the information you will need to cite and reference the article in your essay.

Abubaker needed to take notes on an article he was reading for this writing prompt: *Write a summary and response to an article that discusses the benefits and/or dangers of the 24-hour news cycle.* Read and find out how he did it.

> In my notebook, I wrote down all of the citation information about the article: title, author, source, web address, publication date, and the date I looked up the website. While reading, I paraphrased the relevant information from the article that I wanted to use in my summary–response. I also made sure to write down which paragraph and page the information was in so that I could find it again later when I needed to cite it and create my references.

Abubaker's Results

Citation Information

Title: "Has 24-Hour News Killed Print Media?"
Author: Wyn Grant
Source: University of Warwick Knowledge Centre
Web: http://www2.warwick.ac.uk/knowledge
Publication date: June 2012
Date I looked it up/retrieved it: April 14

Notes and Paraphrases	Paragraph/Page
– "print journalism . . . is under threat from a variety of economic and cultural forces" (quote)	paragraph 1
– Because the network has to use all the time, they will report on nonsense issues or constantly report on one major issue.	paragraphs 2–3
– 24-hour news challenges democracy; leaders are forced to give a fast solution to complicated problems and issues.	paragraphs 6–7

ACTIVITY 5.1 **Apply It to Your Writing**

Follow the steps Abubaker took to take notes for your summary–response essay. Complete a chart like the one above.

STEP 3: MAKE AN OUTLINE

Complete the outline below with your ideas from the previous steps. Include ideas that you wrote in the Your Turns throughout the unit.

ESSAY OUTLINE

I. Introduction

Source Text Main Idea

Thesis Statement

Body Paragraph 1: Summary

II.

Point 1   A.

Detail   1.

Detail   2.

Point 2   B.

Detail   1.

Detail   2.

Body Paragraph 2: Response

III.

Point 1   A.

Detail   1.

Detail   2.

Point 2   B.

Detail   1.

Detail   2.

(CONTINUED)

Body Paragraph 3: Response	IV. ....
Point 1	A. ....
Detail	1. ....
Detail	2. ....
Point 2	B. ....
Detail	1. ....
Detail	2. ....
	V. Conclusion ....

STEP 4: WRITE YOUR FIRST DRAFT

Now it is time to write your first draft. Here are some suggestions on how to get started.

1 Use your outline, notes, and the sentences you wrote in the Your Turns and in Step 3 on page 209.

2 Focus on making your ideas as clear as possible.

3 Remember to add a title.

After you finish, read your essay and check for basic errors:

1 Check that all sentences have subjects and verbs.

2 Go through and look at every comma. Is it correct? Should it be a period?

3 Check that you have used noun clauses correctly.

4 Make sure your thesis statement and topic sentences are clear.

STEP 5: WRITE YOUR FINAL DRAFT

1 After you receive feedback on your first draft, review it carefully. Fix any errors.

2 Make a note of errors that were most frequent (misspellings, wrong verb tense, errors in using commas). Try to avoid them as you write.

3 Review the Academic Vocabulary and Phrases from this unit. Are there any that you can add to your essay?

4 Turn to page 275 and use the Self-Editing Review to check your work one more time.

5 Write your final draft and hand it in.

Face time vs. screen time:
The technological impact on communication (adapted)

By Chandra Johnson

Marc Brackett, director of Yale University's Center for Emotional Intelligence, realized the importance of having the skills to understand and manage his feelings after being bullied as a kid. Today, Brackett uses a specially developed app and classroom curriculum to help people use technology to better articulate, understand, and control their emotions.

That ability to understand emotions is more important than ever since the advent of the Internet, social media, and texting. When Brackett was growing up, there was no Facebook for **venting**,[1] no emoji catalog to illustrate his feelings, and no online community to listen. But in an age with more methods than ever to talk online, researchers are now studying how technology is changing the way people communicate.

What they're finding is that people communicate more often with family and friends because of technology, but the quality of that communication is likely weaker. Particularly, kids who spend more time online than with others can struggle to understand emotions, have trouble creating strong relationships, or can become more dependent on others. "These kids aren't connecting emotionally," declares parenting expert and pediatric nurse Denise Daniels. She explains that emails and texts make poor substitutes for the **emotive**[2] qualities of face-to-face interaction. Brackett sees this as a lack of balance, where there is not enough interpersonal connection. As he says, "Kids want to be hugged and touched; they don't want to be texted. There's a basic need to fill that social bond." So, does a friendly emoji replace a hug or even a phone call? Probably not, finds psychologist Jim Taylor. Even worse, Taylor feels that all the time spent communicating through technology is preventing kids from developing even basic communication skills.

Smile vs. :)

People who increasingly rely on technology to communicate are paying a heavy price, asserts Dr. Kate Roberts, a Boston-based school psychologist. She sees families texting rather than communicating face-to-face and correlates this with diminishing verbal skills and emotional intelligence. Moreover, we are losing actual physical interaction and the benefits it provides. Roberts mentions, "We're down on the interaction time. Right now, at Boston College, there's a course on how to ask a person out on a date. It's like we've lost the skill of **courtship**[3] and the ability to make that connection."

Technology and the ways we use it to communicate are literally changing us biologically. For children, the overuse of technology to communicate affects neurotransmitters – chemicals in the brain that relay information between nerves. A developing child is born with pathways that expand based on stimulation like a parent's voice, music, touch, and eventually play. But for

[1]**venting:** expressing thoughts and feelings forcefully, especially negative ones
[2]**emotive:** appealing to or expressing emotion
[3]**courtship:** the activities that occur when people are developing a romantic relationship that could lead to marriage, or the period of time when such activities occur

(CONTINUED)

children who spend too much time alone and interacting through a screen, Daniels claims that the neural pathways of their brains change, affecting concentration, self-esteem, and their ability to have as deeply personal relationships. As a result, Daniels has found that these children do not develop the sympathetic and empathetic skills they need.

Emotional attachment

The disconnection – or sense of feeling separate from others – that people feel is very real, Roberts warns, because people who are not using face-to-face contact for personal issues do not have their need for intimacy filled. She claims that using Twitter and Facebook is not necessarily as effective in arriving at a resolution to a conflict as dealing directly with the person or people face-to-face. Emoticons are also ineffective in expressing emotions, though they're an attempt to signify them. Taylor adds that voice inflection, body language, facial expressions, and the chemicals released during face-to-face interactions are all fundamental to establishing human relationships. And they're all missing with most forms of modern technology.

Language barrier

Taylor says that emotional problems with nonfacial online communication are made worse in families where parents do not understand the language of digital communication. Conversations do not result in deeper understanding or intimacy. "Because parents are not speaking digital, the dinner table talk can suddenly be like someone speaking Spanish to someone who doesn't," Taylor explains. Also, Dr. Roberts and Toronto-based linguist Heather Lotherington both express concern that people prefer using technology to interact without realizing how they are losing meaningful ties to important people in their lives, such as their parents, children, and spouses.

Finding a balance

Experts agree that the problem is not technology itself, but with the way we are using it. It is essential for us to find a good balance that works to limit our technology use in favor of more personal interactions. Roberts claims that it is human nature to avoid things and make uncomfortable situations easier on ourselves, so we often use technology instead of direct forms of communication. "Place a value on one-to-one interaction," Taylor suggests. A great way for people to start doing this is to make it a requirement that everyone unplugs or shuts off their electronic devices during things like family time and meals.

7 ARGUMENTATIVE ESSAYS

SOCIOLOGY: SOCIAL INTERACTION

> "Social media is the ultimate equalizer. It gives a voice and a platform to anyone willing to engage."
>
> Amy Jo Martin (1969–)

About the Author:

Amy Jo Martin is an American social media expert and entrepreneur.

Work with a partner. Read the quotation about social media. Then answer the questions.

1 Martin calls social media "the ultimate equalizer." In your opinion, does social media make people more equal? How does social media give people a "voice"?

2 Do you believe interaction on social media is as meaningful as face-to-face interaction? Why or why not?

A Connect to Academic Writing

In this unit you will learn skills to help you make arguments to support your ideas. While some of the writing skills that you will use may be new to you, others are not. In your everyday life, you already use many of the same skills when you discuss questions such as *What kind of car is best for our family?* and *What is the best way to spend a free afternoon?*

B Reflect on the Topic

In this section you will choose a writing prompt and reflect on it. You will develop these ideas throughout the unit and use them to practice skills that are necessary to write your essay.

The writing prompt below was used for the Student Model essay on pages 220–222. The student reflected on her topic and decided to write about girls in girls-only classrooms. She used a chart to help her think of reasons why girls should or should not learn in girls-only classrooms. This helped her think of a possible thesis.

STUDENT MODEL

WRITING PROMPT: Single-sex education is a controversial topic in the United States. In your opinion, is it beneficial for students – either girls or boys – to learn in a single-sex classroom?

Yes / Positive	No / Negative
• environment less distracting when separated	• competition between girls and boys is useful
• builds confidence in girls	• does not treat girls and boys equally
• do better in school	• reinforces stereotypes
• girls learn differently	• does not prepare girls for the real world
•	• ....
•	• ....

My thesis: *I think that girls should learn in girls-only classrooms because they learn differently and girls-only classes help them do better in school.*

 1.1 Notice

Work with a partner. Discuss two more reasons for each column of the chart. Then, for each column, choose the reason that you think is the strongest.

Follow the directions to reflect on your topic.

A Choose a prompt:

- Some research shows that social networking sites have a negative impact on young people. Do you agree? Why or why not?

- Peers can have an influence on the behavior of a child. This influence can be negative or positive. Is peer pressure mostly beneficial? Why or why not?

- People have different opinions about what kind of school community is best for students. Is it positive or negative for young people to go to school with students who come from similar social backgrounds?

- A topic approved by your instructor

B Work with a partner and complete the following tasks:

1 Think about your prompt. Decide what you will focus on in your essay.

2 Complete the chart below. Think of as many reasons as you can to support each side of the topic. Add more rows if you need them.

3 Write a possible thesis statement.

Yes / Positive	No / Negative
• Many info on Apps	• Info are not always correct
• Apps are more easier to find the info	• too many useless info
• Don't have to buy book.	• Some info are advertising
• Save time , Ex search	• hard to focus on time

Possible thesis statement: ....

....

In this section you will learn academic language that you can use in your argumentative essay. You will also notice how a professional writer uses the language and features of argumentation.

Ⓐ Academic Vocabulary

The words below appear throughout the unit. They are from the Academic Word List. Using these words in your writing will make your ideas clearer and your writing more academic.

capacity (n)	constraint (n)	evidence (n)	selective (adj)
conclusion (n)	equate (v)	perception (n)	stable (adj)

 2.1 Focus on Meaning

Work with a partner. Match the words to their meanings. Write the letters.

A

_d_ 1 He is a very **stable** person. He doesn't get angry easily, nor does he make quick decisions.

_a_ 2 Time zones are one important **constraint** people must deal with when trying to stay in touch with family far away.

_b_ 3 Having expensive technology is often **equated** with being wealthy, but many poor people own smartphones as well.

_c_ 4 Online relationships often cause people to come to the wrong **conclusion** about someone and misjudge who they are and what they believe.

a something that limits what you do

b to be similar to

c an opinion based on information

d not likely to change or end

B

_c_ 1 Young people do not always understand how **selective** they should be about who they choose to "friend" on the Internet.

_d_ 2 It is a common **perception** among young people that if you know someone through social media, they are your friend, but this is often proven false.

_b_ 3 Some people believe that women have a natural **capacity** for dealing with children because of how cultures view motherhood and fatherhood.

_a_ 4 Survey results, medical statistics, and other **evidence** in the report show the dangers of social media for children.

a fact or idea that helps prove something true

b ability to do or understand something

c careful in choosing

d an opinion based on appearances, often an opinion many people have

B Academic Collocations 👁

Collocations are words that are frequently used together. Research tells us that the academic vocabulary in Part A is commonly used in the collocations in bold below.

ACTIVITY 2.2 Focus on Meaning

Read the sentences. Decide the meaning of the phrases in bold and circle the correct answer.

1 Among high school students, there is a **popular perception** that joining many school clubs will make their college applications stronger, but some people say that being very active in one club is better. **Popular perception** means

   a the way most people see something.

   b an uncommon belief.

2 Being in a **stable relationship** can help people stay sane during stressful situations because they know that they can depend on a partner for support. **Stable relationship** means

   a a difficult relationship that ends quickly.

   b a relationship that lasts a long time.

3 The study by the Work and Family Research Center at Boston University presented **strong evidence** that mothers in the workplace were less likely to get promoted than fathers. It documented this trend in companies all over America for ten years. **Strong evidence** means

   a many facts that support many different conclusions.

   b facts obviously leading to a single conclusion.

4 Researchers **drew a conclusion** from several studies that all showed the same facts: cyberbullying has the same effects as real world bullying on young people. **Draw a conclusion** means

   a to decide on a single idea based on evidence.

   b to sketch out an idea based on a guess.

5 It seems obvious that principals **have the capacity** to change the behavior of their students, but they do not always realize that their impact spreads beyond the classroom. **Have the capacity** means

   a to be unable to do something.

   b to be able to do something.

C Writing in the Real World

The author of "Dunbar's Number" uses features of argumentation to make the article's ideas stronger.

Before you read, answer these questions: How many friends can a person really have? Why do you think so?

Now read the article. Think about your answers to the questions above as you read.

Dunbar's Number

DAWN BRANLEY (ADAPTED)

1 In 1992, Robin Dunbar concluded that the maximum number of friends one individual can have is 150. This is now referred to as Dunbar's Number.

2 You might be wondering how there can be a maximum limit. Surely we can have as many friends as we wish? Well, Dunbar was talking about real friendships, that is, **stable** social relationships, not mere acquaintances.[1] On average, he says, we have 5 best friends, 15 good friends, 50 close friends and/or family, and a total of 150 friends.

3 According to Dunbar, the processing **capacity** of our brain's neocortex[2] places a biological **constraint** on the number of **stable** friendships we can maintain.

So what about Dunbar's Number and social media?

4 Many social media users have over 150 friends on their social networking accounts.

What does this mean in relation to Dunbar's Number and his **conclusion** that we cannot cognitively[3] manage more than 150 friends?

5 As I see it, there are two possible explanations:

- Social media "friends" are not really friends in the traditional sense.[4] Therefore Dunbar's Number still applies.

- Social media aids our management of relationships in a manner that frees us from our previous limitations. Therefore Dunbar's Number does not apply[5] in the online environment.

6 Goncalves, Perra, and Vespignani (2011) found **evidence** to suggest that Dunbar's Number still applies in the online world. They found that even though individuals may have more than 150 connections on their social media accounts, they still showed signs of limiting social interaction to around 150 people.

[1]acquaintance: a person you know but do not know well
[2]neocortex: a part of the brain responsible for feeling and thinking

[3]cognitively: in a way related to thinking and reasoning
[4]in the traditional sense: in the way we normally think of something
[5]does not apply: is not true, relevant, or important

7 In 2009, *The Economist* asked Facebook to find out the average number of friends per user; their answer was 120. This number may surprise you because there is a **popular perception** that many users have many more than this. It's true that some do, but it is interesting to note that the average falls close to Dunbar's Number.

8 This all suggests that the cognitive limits to the number of friendships that we can manage still applies even when we use social media to maintain friendships. What seems to be happening is that the term "friend" is not being used on social media in its commonly accepted sense, and that an online friend does not necessarily **equate** to a true friendship.

> People who are members of online social networks are not so much "networking" as they are "broadcasting" their lives to an outer tier of acquaintances who aren't necessarily inside the Dunbar circle. (Rainie, qtd. in *The Economist*, 2009)

Social media with Dunbar's Number in mind

9 Interestingly this has been recognized by one social media platform. Path is an application designed to work as an online journal,[6] which you share with your close friends and loved ones. It was developed in 2010 by a designer who used to work at Facebook. In contrast to many social media sites, Path limits the number of friends a user can have to 150. This is no coincidence since Path was inspired by Dunbar's Number and built with it in mind.

What do you think?

10 What are your thoughts? How many social media friends do you have, and how many of these do you perceive as being true friendships? Do you believe you can maintain more than 150 close social connections? In my case, I have fewer than 150 Facebook friends. This has not been a conscious decision based on Dunbar's Number. My Facebook friends are fewer than some users because I choose to be very **selective**. I only add people who I want to communicate with on a fairly regular basis.

11 Personally, I think 150 people sounds like a lot of connections if we are talking about fairly close connections. All of this brings me to the **conclusion** that the term "friend" on social media is not a very useful or appropriate one. Perhaps the term "followers" as used on Twitter or "connections" as used on LinkedIn are more accurate than Facebook's "friends" when it comes to defining our social media relationships.

[6]journal: a diary

ACTIVITY 2.3 Check Your Understanding

Answer the questions.

1 What is Dunbar's Number?

2 What is the central problem surrounding friends and social media that the author addresses?

3 Do you agree with the author's claims about the possible number of friendships? Why or why not?

ACTIVITY 2.4 Notice the Writing

Answer the questions.

1 Look at paragraphs 6 and 7. Circle the evidence used by the author.

2 Look at paragraph 11. Underline the words that show the author's stance on this topic.

In Section 1 you saw how the writer of the Student Model reflected on her topic. In this section you will analyze the final draft of her argumentative essay. You will learn how to structure your ideas for your own essay.

Ⓐ Student Model

Read the writing prompt again and answer the questions.

WRITING PROMPT: Single-sex education is a controversial topic in the United States. In your opinion, is it beneficial for students – either girls or boys – to learn in a single-sex classroom?

1 What issue is the prompt asking the writer to have an opinion about?

2 What reasons could the writer give in support of boys or girls learning in single-sex classrooms? What reasons could she give against them?

Read the essay twice. The first time, think about your answers to the questions above. The second time, answer the questions in the Analyze Writing Skills boxes. This will help you notice key features of argumentative essays.

STUDENT MODEL

Why Girls Should Learn Alone

1   Can learning in girls-only classrooms help girls be more successful? I believe it can. In contrast to coed[1] classes, single-sex education means that only students of one gender will be in a class together. In some countries, all schools are single-sex. In other countries, such as the United States, students can choose a single-sex school only if there is one close by. The number of single-sex schools is rising in the United States, but educators disagree on the benefits of them. Proponents[2] say that girls-only classes remove the social pressures that girls feel. Opponents say that they make girls less competitive and act stereotypically. In my opinion, girls should learn in girls-only classes because they become more self-confident and perform better in math and science.

2   First of all, girls in girls-only classes develop a confidence in themselves that stays with them. When I was younger, I attended a girls-only high school in Ecuador. Without boys in class, we were less shy. We felt free to express ourselves and take risks. Personally, I started to participate in class more, and the more I did, the more confident I became. This is true of many of my friends, too, and this confidence remained after we graduated. There is also **strong evidence** of the effect of girls-only education on confidence in a 2014 report by Linda Sax and her colleagues at the Higher Education

1 Analyze Writing Skills

a Underline the sentences in paragraph 1 that give background information on the issue.

b Circle the sentence that states the writer's opinion about the topic. Is she for or against single-sex classrooms?

2 Analyze Writing Skills

In paragraph 2, which kind of evidence does the writer use to support the topic sentence? Circle all that apply.

a research

b a quotation

c a personal experience

[1]coed: for male and female students together
[2]proponent: a person who supports an idea, plan, or cause

Research Institute of UCLA (HERI). The report compared freshman girls from girls-only schools to girls in coed schools and found a significant difference in confidence in their academic ability, public speaking skills, and computer skills. It is obvious that an all-girls environment leads to success (Sax et al.).

3   In addition, girls in single-sex classes do better in math and science and have more positive attitudes toward these subjects. One study in Canada looked at grade differences for girls in the final two years of high school (Shapka and Keating). The researchers compared the effects of girls-only and coed classes on math and science performance. They found that the grades for girls in same-sex classrooms were 5 percent higher than their peers[3] in coed classrooms. This is a noteworthy difference. The HERI study found that SAT scores on math and verbal skills were over 40 points higher for girls in single-sex education. These girls were much more likely to study engineering. These statistics show that girls-only schools could produce more successful women in the workforce, especially in the areas of technology and engineering.

4   Some critics of single-sex classrooms argue that single-sex education is dangerous because it reinforces gender stereotypes.[4] In their view, a same-sex environment makes girls and boys emphasize the differences in each other and adopt stereotypical behaviors. In other words, girls act more passively and boys act more aggressively. While it may be true that same-sex grouping **has the capacity** to make boys and girls aware of differences, we should not **draw the conclusion** that they behave stereotypically as a result. Some research has shown that, in fact, students behave in a less stereotypical way. Similarly, a study by Park, Behrman, and Choi looked at girls in single-sex and coed physics classes. They assigned girls to each class and found that those "in the all-girls classroom were less likely to regard physics as a boys' subject, compared to girls who had been randomly assigned to the coed classroom" (Park, Behrman, and Choi). In other words, the single-sex environment allowed girls to be free of the limits and expectations that they felt in the mixed gender classroom.

[3]peer: a person of the same age, social position, or abilities as other people in a group
[4]stereotype: a description of a particular group of people that is usually false or inaccurate

(CONTINUED)

---

3 Analyze Writing Skills

What mode does the writer use in paragraph 2 to make her point?

a   narrative

b   cause and effect

c   comparison and contrast

4 Analyze Writing Skills

In paragraph 3, which piece of evidence is strongest in your opinion? Why do you think so?

5 Analyze Writing Skills

How is paragraph 4 different from the previous two paragraphs? Circle its purpose.

a   to explain why girls-only classrooms are dangerous

b   to discuss the reasons why people might disagree with her

5   In **conclusion**, studying in a single-sex environment has important benefits. It can make girls be more self-confident and improve their grades in math and science, two subjects that can lead to jobs in growing fields. Girls deserve to have the opportunity to enjoy these benefits, no matter where they live. Girls-only classes must be available everywhere to make that possible.

Works Cited

Park, Hyunjoon, Jere R. Behrman, and Jaesung Choi. *Causal Effects of Single-Sex Schools on College Entrance Exams and College Attendance: Random Assignment in Seoul High Schools*. PSC Working Paper Series. U of Pennsylvania, Jan. 2012. Web. 24 Oct. 2014.

Sax, Linda J., et al. *Women Graduates of Single-Sex and Coeducational High Schools: Differences in Their Characteristics and the Transition to College*. Higher Education Research Institute, U of California, Los Angeles, 2009. Web. 28 Nov. 2014.

Shapka, Jennifer, and Daniel Keating. "Effects of a Girls-Only Curriculum During Adolescence: Performance, Persistence, and Engagement in Mathematics and Science." *American Educational Research Journal* 40.4 (2003): 929–60. Print.

> **6 Analyze Writing Skills**
>
> Underline the writer's call to action or recommendation in the final paragraph.

ACTIVITY 3.1 Check Your Understanding

Answer the questions.

1 According to the writer, what advantages do girls-only classes provide?

2 What is the writer's opinion about math and science classes for girls?

3 Has the writer convinced you that all-girls schools make girls more successful? Why or why not?

ACTIVITY 3.2 Outline the Ideas

Complete the outline for "Why Girls Should Learn Alone" using the phrases in the box.

critics – single-sex classes reinforces stereotypes

HERI report

less shy

participated more

physics – not only for boys

Park, Behrman, and Choi – does not reinforce stereotypes

math and verbal skills – 40 points higher

ESSAY OUTLINE

I. Introduction   *Hook + background infor + Thesis + 2 reasons*

Thesis Statement

Girls should learn in girls-only classes *[I] [C]* because girls become more self-confident *[①]* and

perform better in math and science. *[②]*

Body Paragraph 1: First Point

II. More confidence   *Topic sentences*

Evidence

Supporting Idea 1

A. Personal experience at a girls-only high school

Detail

1. Less shy without boys in class

Sub-detail

Why a.   Free to express ourselves and take risks

Sub-detail

more
b. Participated in class more, become more confidence

Supporting Idea 2   *Commentary*

B. Research by UCLA HERI report

Detail

more or detail 1. Compared freshman girls from mixed sex and girls-only schools   *Why is Quote important*

Sub-detail

a.   Difference in confidence, public speaking skills, computer skills   *why support*

Body Paragraph 2: Second Point

III. Do better in math and science and more positive attitudes   *Topic*

Supporting Idea 1

A. Shapka and Keating study   *Research + Evidence*

Detail

1. Compared effects of girls-only and coed classes in math and science

Sub-detail

a.   Grades were 5 percent higher

Supporting Idea 2

B. HERI report

Detail

1. Score on math and verbal skills were over 40 points higher

Detail

2. More likely to plan for careers in technology and engineering   *Comm*

(CONTINUED)

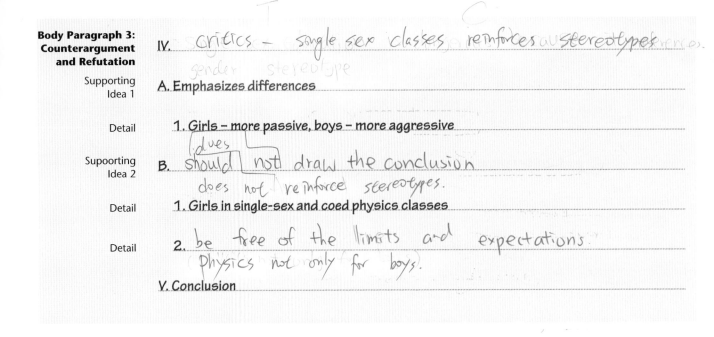

Body Paragraph 3: Counterargument and Refutation

IV. ~~Critics~~ single sex classes reinforces ~~a~~ stereotypes ~~rences~~.
gender stereotype

Supporting Idea 1

A. Emphasizes differences

Detail

1. Girls – more passive, boys – more aggressive

dues

Supporting Idea 2

B. should not draw the conclusion
does not reinforce stereotypes.

Detail

1. Girls in single-sex and coed physics classes

Detail

2. be free of the limits and expectations
Physics not only for boys.

V. Conclusion

B Argumentative Essay with Refutation

The purpose of an argumentative essay is to convince the reader of your ideas by making clear and strong arguments for them. In addition, you will also need to explain why your argument is better in some way than your opponent's arguments. This skill is called **refutation**.

An argumentative essay that includes refutation has the following structure:

- An **introductory paragraph** that introduces the topic and necessary background information, leading readers to the thesis statement.

- Two or more **body paragraphs** that build the argument by explaining each point, or reason, and giving clear evidence to convince the reader that the point or reason is valid.

- A final body paragraph which raises a **counterargument** and a **refutation** that explains the counterargument's weaknesses and tells why your argument is more valid.

- A **concluding paragraph** that restates the thesis and ends with a suggestion, prediction, or call to action.

Look at the Student Model essay on pages 220–222. Read the summary sentences for each paragraph below. Number them in the same order as they appear in the essay.

.... a Even though some people think that coed classrooms reinforce stereotypes, evidence suggests that the opposite is true.

.... b Girls develop a stronger self-confidence in themselves and their abilities because they are free to be themselves.

.... c Girls-only classes have clear advantages over coed classes, which is why girls in all schools deserve access to them.

....1.... d Increased self-confidence and higher performance in math and science are the two main advantages of girls-only classes.

.... e When girls learn math and science in girls-only classes, they get better grades and are more likely to pursue careers in these areas.

INTRODUCTORY PARAGRAPH

An introductory paragraph for argumentative essays has a few important features:

- The hook helps writers attract the attention of the reader.

  Can learning in girls-only classrooms help girls be more successful? I believe it can.

- The **background information** helps readers understand the topic and shows them why the topic is relevant and important. When choosing your background information, it is important to be aware of your audience – including their knowledge of the topic and range of views. For background information to be effective, consider your readers and ask yourself these questions:

  – What do my readers know about the topic? How much do I have to explain?

  In contrast to coed classes, single-sex education means that only students of one gender will be in a class together. In some countries, all schools are single-sex. In other countries, such as the United States, students can choose a single-sex school only if there is one close by. The number of single-sex schools is rising in the United States, but educators disagree on the benefits of them.

  – What common perceptions and views on the topic do my readers have?

  Proponents say that girls-only classes remove the social pressures that girls feel. Opponents say that they make girls less competitive and act stereotypically.

- The **thesis statement** states your position or point of view and usually your main reasons, which you will develop in the body paragraphs.

  In my opinion, girls should learn in girls-only classes because they become more self-confident and perform better in math and science.

Reflect on the prompt and think about the audience for your essay. Write four or five sentences that answer the questions and make your introduction effective.

WRITING PROMPT: Should boys learn in an all-male environment?

1 What do my readers know about the topic? How much do I have to explain about it?

....

....

....

2 What common perceptions and views do my readers have regarding the topic?

....

....

....

ACTIVITY **3.5** Apply It to Your Writing

Think about your audience and answer the same questions from Activity 3.4 about the topic for your writing prompt on page 215.

....

....

....

....

....

THESIS STATEMENT

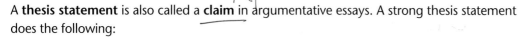

A **thesis statement** is also called a **claim** in argumentative essays. A strong thesis statement does the following:

- It answers the question in the prompt.
- It contains the topic, the writer's point of view, and the main reasons for it. Those main reasons are then covered one by one in the body paragraphs.
- It is narrowly focused. If your thesis statement is too general, it will be hard to come up with good reasons and evidence to support it.
- It contains only one point of view. To write an effective argumentative essay, you must decide what you believe and try to persuade readers of that one idea only, not other ideas or points of view.

Avoid writing weak thesis statements by following the rules below:

Rules for Creating Strong Thesis Statements

1 Do not simply introduce the topic.

   Weak: *I am going to write about single-sex education because I am interested in that topic.*

   Strong: *In my opinion, girls should learn in girls-only classes because they become more self-confident and perform better in math and science.*

2 Do not just state an opinion that is vague.

   Weak: *Cyberbullying is a bad thing for children.*

   Strong: *Cyberbullying destroys self-esteem, creates anxiety, and inhibits the social development of children.*

3 Do not just make statements of fact that everyone would agree with.

   Weak: *Social media is a very common way to communicate.*

   Strong: *Social media is a useful tool for influencing political, moral, and social opinions.*

ACTIVITY 3.6 Notice

Read the thesis statements below. Write *W* if the argument is weak and *S* if the argument is strong. Write the reasons why each statement is strong or weak.

W 1 Today I can see more and more children using social media to connect with their friends and relatives.

   First person

S 2 Teenagers need to learn email etiquette because it will have positive effects on their personal and professional lives in the future.

   Cause effect

W 3 Many people think teaching children at home is a good idea because of all the problems in local schools.

   Many people is not academic.

S 4 Requiring people to use their real names on social networking sites would make children safer, prevent scams, and allow people to connect with old friends more easily.

Clear

W 5 I am interested in learning why parents do not have more influence on their children as they get older.

first person

ACTIVITY **3.7 Practice**

Work with a partner. Choose a weak thesis statement in Activity 3.6 and make it stronger by taking out first-person pronouns and replacing vague opinions with specific reasons.

BUILDING STRONG ARGUMENTS IN BODY PARAGRAPHS

The argument is developed in the body paragraphs, where writers give reasons that support their point of view. For each body paragraph, writers include a topic sentence that identifies the reason from the thesis. Look at these examples from the Student Model:

First of all, girls in girls-only classes develop a confidence in themselves that stays with them.

In addition, girls in single-sex classes do better in math and science and have more positive attitudes toward these subjects.

To make an argument strong and convincing, each reason is supported by evidence such as examples, facts, statistics, research, quotations, and personal experience. Below are examples of the types of evidence that writers use to support the arguments in their body paragraphs, some of which are from the Student Model.

- **Facts:** Facts are ideas that can be proven or are accepted as true. They make your arguments seem more logical.

  Given that those fields have more men than women working in them, it is important to see this benefit of girls-only classes changing cultural attitudes.

- **Statistics:** Statistics are numbers and data that come from research, surveys, and polls. They make your arguments seem more credible.

  They found that the grades for girls in same-sex classrooms were 5 percent higher than their peers in coed classrooms.

- **Quotations:** Quotations are the exact words of another person, usually an expert, authority, or other respected individual. They make your arguments more valid. Writers can also paraphrase quotations and cite the source.

   They assigned girls to each class and found that those "in the all-girls classroom were less likely to regard physics as a boys' subject, compared to girls who had been randomly assigned to the coed classroom" (Park, Behrman, and Choi).

   When the researchers randomly assigned girls to each class, they learned that the single-sex environment made girls feel like they were as capable as boys when it came to understanding physics.

- **Examples:** Examples are specific stories or cases that illustrate a point. They help the reader imagine and understand what you mean.

   Maria Amelia, a high school senior, was a star student in math. When her teacher told her that she should study physics in college, she was shocked and looked embarrassed. The teacher had several discussions with her and found out that Maria Amelia did not feel comfortable being in a mostly male career. She decided she would be an accountant because it was more acceptable to her family.

- **Personal experience:** Personal experiences are stories that happened to you or someone you know. They make your arguments more real and believable.

   When I was younger, I attended a girls-only high school in Ecuador. Without boys in class, we were less shy. We felt free to express ourselves and take risks. Personally, I started to participate in class more, and the more I did, the more confident I became. This is true of many of my friends, too, and this confidence remained after we graduated.

In an argumentative essay, strong evidence is key for convincing your readers to agree with your point of view. Strong evidence is specific and relates directly to the topic sentence of the body paragraph. Weak evidence is general and does not relate to the topic sentence. Read the examples below. Notice how the weak evidence does not show how girls do better in math and science or have better attitudes:

Topic sentence: In addition, girls in single-sex classes do better in math and science and have more positive attitudes toward these subjects.

Weak: Girls usually get better grades than boys in their classes. They try harder because they like to do well.

Strong: One study in Canada looked at grade differences for girls in the final two years of high school (Shapka and Keating). The researchers compared the effects of girls-only and coed classes on math and science performance.

To find strong evidence, ask yourself these questions:

- What facts or statistics would most likely convince my reader?
- What quotations or examples clearly support my point of view?
- What personal experiences would make my point of view more persuasive?

Read the writer's body paragraph for an argumentative essay on the effects of social media on businesses. Then answer the questions.

Topic Sentence First of all, social media allows companies to reach a worldwide audience, which improves profits. *Fact* All major companies today use various types of social media to improve their customer base, such as Facebook, Twitter, and Instagram. They know that millions of people visit these sites every day, which can translate into millions of dollars for their company. *a quote* A recent study found *statistic* that customers who visit a company's social media site will bring in 5.6 percent more revenue for the company compared to customers who never participate ("Businesses Increase Revenue"). They state that is because social media improves the customer's experience. It also creates a stronger sense of community among customers. In other words, customers feel more loyal to the company because they feel valued; therefore, they are more likely to visit the site and spend their money. *summary of research* Considering that a company's social media site reaches a much larger audience than a store would using traditional marketing, this generates much higher profits as well. *commentary*

Conclusion

1 Circle the thesis statement that the writer's body paragraph supports.

   a Social media increase costs for businesses because staff is needed to interact with millions of customers online.

   (b) Social media helps businesses because they are able to attract more customers and figure out what customers want more easily.

2 Circle the kinds of evidence the writer uses to support his ideas. Then underline the evidence in the paragraph.

   (a) facts   (d) a summary of research

   (b) statistics   (e) examples

   (c) a quote   f a personal experience

ACTIVITY 3.9 Match

Read the writing prompt, thesis, and body paragraph topic sentences. Match the evidence to the body paragraphs. Write the letter.

WRITING PROMPT: Should parents monitor their children's text messages?

Thesis statement: *Parents should not monitor their children's text messages because it can hurt the relationship between them and cause their children to rebel.*

Body paragraph 1 topic sentence: Close monitoring of texts can damage the trust between parents and children.

Evidence: _____ b c d

Body paragraph 2 topic sentence: If parents monitor their children's texts, there is a higher chance that children will rebel and make poor decisions.

Evidence: _____ a c

a "Kids need to have a separate life their parents don't know all about," says Dr. Schlozman. "If you don't give them any privacy or independence, they may engage in riskier behaviors."

b Child psychologist James Lehman points out that monitoring children who are always responsible and follow their parents' rules will send the wrong message that they can never be trusted.

c Children may try to find other ways to contact their friends privately, which could be more dangerous. For example, they may lie to their parents, saying they need to stay late at school when in truth they are secretly meeting their friends somewhere else.

d In my experience, most children want to do the right thing and gain their parents' confidence, but sometimes parents feel like they must control everything, including their children's text messages. As a result, children do not feel trusted.

ACTIVITY 3.10 Evaluate Evidence

Read the writer's topic sentence, which identifies one reason why social media harms companies. Then evaluate the evidence below. Write *W* for weak and *S* for strong. Explain your answers to a partner.

Topic sentence: Businesses can lose money when their employees spend time on social networking sites at work.

1 ___S___ a A study by Nucleus Research reports that businesses lose 1.5 percent in productivity because of employees who use social media at work.

___W___ b Nucleus Research surveyed 237 randomly selected office workers in the United States and found that 77 percent had a Facebook account.

2 ___W___ a Most employees visit social networking sites when they are bored at work or unsatisfied with their job.

___S___ b When employees visit social networking sites at work, they end up wasting their employer's time.

3 ....W.... a My friend Susan works at a bank, and she is always checking her friends' posts on her Facebook account.

........(S)...... b My friend Susan is always checking her Facebook posts when she is supposed to be calling customers.

ACTIVITY 3.11 Apply It to Your Writing

Choose one of your supporting reasons from Activity 1.2 on page 215. Write it in the chart below. Then check (✓) two or three different kinds of evidence you want to use to support your reason. Add your evidence to the chart.

Reason:		
☐	A fact	
☐	A statistic	
☐	A quotation	
☐	An example	
☐	A personal experience	

P3

COUNTERARGUMENT AND REFUTATION

In an argumentative essay, the final body paragraph often presents a **counterargument**, or opposing argument, and a **refutation**, or reasons why the argument is weak. This technique makes an argument stronger and more persuasive because it shows that the writer is knowledgeable about the topic and has considered other points of view. Therefore, it is a good writing skill to master.

Follow these steps to develop a counterargument and refutation:

Topic Sentence 1 Introduce the counterargument. Explain the argument and identify the people who believe it. *supporting Idea 1*

> Some critics of single-sex classrooms argue that single-sex education is dangerous because it reinforces gender stereotypes.

Support Idea 2 Describe the evidence or reasons people give for this counterargument. *Detail*   *why they*

detail > In their view, a same-sex environment makes girls and boys emphasize the differences in each   *think*
Detail > other and adopt stereotypical behaviors. In other words, girls act more passively and boys act   *that*
Detail > more aggressively.   *details*

Explain the reason

[handwritten: Acknowledge what is true]

[handwritten: pport Idea] 3 Acknowledge any part of the argument that may be true or partly true and explain why. Then

[handwritten: Detail] refute the counterargument by calling attention to a weakness based on evidence or reasoning.

[handwritten: Detail] A refutation should be based on evidence, logic, and objective facts, not emotions or bias.

While it may be true that same-sex grouping has the capacity to make boys and girls aware of differences, we should not draw the conclusion that they behave stereotypically as a result. Some research has shown that, in fact, students behave in a less stereotypical way. Similarly, a study by Park, Behrman, and Choi looked at girls in single-sex and coed physics classes. They assigned girls to each class and found that those "in the all-girls classroom were less likely to regard physics as a boys' subject, compared to girls who had been randomly assigned to the coed classroom."

[handwritten: Concluding sentence] 4 Conclude by showing how your evidence disproves the counterargument.

In other words, the single-sex environment allowed girls to be free of the limits and expectations that they felt in the mixed gender classroom.

ACTIVITY **3.12** Write Counterarguments

State the counterargument using the phrase in parentheses. Then write facts, examples, or other evidence that someone might use to support the counterargument.

1 Social media harms businesses. (Some people claim that)

Some people claim that social media harms businesses. For example, when someone famous shares a negative review about a company on Twitter, it can make their followers decide to stop buying their products.

2 Coed classes prepare children better for the real world. (Some critics say that)

3 Online friends are not "real" friends. (Some opponents state that)

4 Schools have a responsibility to stop cyberbullying. (Critics may argue that)

5 Competition is healthy in the workplace. (Some people claim that)

Read each counterargument. Acknowledge the argument using the phrase in parentheses. Then write a refutation.

1 Some people say that social media harms businesses. For example, when someone famous shares a negative review about a company on Twitter, it can make their followers decide to stop buying their products. (While this may be true up to a point …)

   While this may be true up to a point, the fact is that negative press can help a company, too. Receiving a very public negative review gives companies a rare but useful opportunity to apologize to the world and show that they truly care about their customers. This may convince people that the company has high values and deserves their business even more.

2 There are some who say that teenagers should never engage in conversations or texts without their parents' supervision. In their opinion, teenagers cannot be trusted to use their cell phones responsibly. (Although it is true that some teens abuse this responsibility, …)

3 Supporters of online classes argue that they prepare students better for the twenty-first century than traditional classes do. They often cite the fact that in more and more workplaces, employees are expected to collaborate on projects via email and online platforms. (I agree that … . However, it is simply not true that …)

4 Critics argue that companies should not ask to view people's Facebook pages when they are hiring new employees. They claim that it is unfair to job applicants, and it violates their personal privacy. (That may be so, but …)

....

....

....

....

....

....

CONCLUDING PARAGRAPH

A concluding paragraph in argumentative essays contains the following unique elements:

- It states reasons why the writer's point of view is more valid than the opposing views.

  In conclusion, studying in a single-sex environment has important benefits. It can make girls be more self-confident and improve their grades in math and science, two subjects that can lead to jobs in growing fields.

- It emphasizes the importance of the topic being argued.

  Girls deserve to have the opportunity to enjoy these benefits, no matter where they live.

- It ends with a strong comment, recommendation, or call to action.

  Girls-only classes must be available everywhere to make that possible.

 **3.14** Notice

Read the conclusion below from an essay about using real names in social networking. Underline the restated thesis. Circle the recommendation or call to action. Put boxes around the three arguments.

In conclusion, social media companies may have different policies, but that does not mean that they cannot have one in common. Requiring people to use real names online makes children safer on social media and prevents scammers from taking advantage of people. It also allows people to find old friends and connections easily, which is the most common use of social media sites. For social media to work well for users, all social media sites must agree to a shared policy that requires users to use real names and validate identities when registering.

In this section you will learn the writing and grammar skills that will help make your writing more sophisticated and accurate.

Ⓐ Writing Skill 1: Audience and Appeal

After writers build a strong argument, the next step is choosing the right approach that would appeal to their audience.

The approach will depend on your purpose, audience, and point of view.

- **Purpose**: What do you want your audience to do? Accept your view? Change their mind? Take action?
- **Audience**: Who are you writing for? What do you have in common? What do they know about the topic?
- **Point of view**: Why is this topic important to you? Do you want the audience to see you as an ally? An activist? An expert?

How you persuade your reader also changes according to your purpose, audience, and point of view. Will you use logic, values, or emotions to convince them?

- **Logic**: *Children should learn in coed classrooms because <u>many teachers do not have training in how to teach a girls-only or boys-only class.</u>*
- **Values**: *All children should learn in coed classrooms because <u>equality is a basic principle of public education.</u>*
- **Emotion**: *All children should learn in coed classrooms because <u>it is the right thing to do. You would want it for your precious child.</u>*

Finally, for your argument to be effective, your audience needs to trust you. You can build trust by showing you are balanced, open to other views, or an expert on the subject.

- **Balanced**: *There are <u>some girls who learn better with female peers,</u> and <u>others who succeed perfectly well in coed classrooms</u>.*
- **Open**: *Although <u>some people think coed classrooms cause too much competition between girls and boys</u>, they actually make students feel equal when taught correctly.*
- **Expert**: <u>*According to a recent report*</u>, *students in coed classrooms perform just as well as those in single-sex classes.*

4.1 Notice

**Work with a partner. Read the sentences from "Why Girls Should Learn Alone."
Then circle the answer.**

1 "Girls-only classes must be available everywhere to make that possible."

   The writer wants the audience to **accept her view / change their mind / take action**.

2 "In some countries, all schools are single-sex. In other countries, such as the United States, students can choose a single-sex school only if there is one close by."

   The writer is writing for someone who knows **a lot / very little** about the topic.

3 "The HERI study found that SAT scores on math and verbal skills were over 40 points higher for girls in single-sex education. These girls were much more likely to study engineering."

   The writer wants to be seen by the reader as **an ally / activist / expert**.

4 "Girls deserve to have the opportunity to enjoy these benefits, no matter where they live."

   The writer is using **logic / values / emotion** to convince the reader.

5 "Some critics of girls-only classes argue that separating boys and girls is dangerous because it reinforces gender stereotypes."

   The writer is building trust by being **balanced / open / emotional**.

4.2 Apply It to Your Writing

YOUR TURN

Look at the ideas you wrote about your prompt in Section 1 on page 215. Use the guide above to help you. Answer the questions on a separate sheet of paper.

1 What do you want your reader to do? *accept my view / sympathetic response*

2 Who are you writing for? *ordinary people, Bryan*

3 Why is this topic important to you? *it's an issue. / I want to let more pp know then solve it*

4 Will you use logic, values, or emotions to convince your readers?

5 How will you build trust with your reader? *Yes.*

research. eg ...

B Writing Skill 2: Language for Introducing Counterarguments and Refutation

When writers introduce counterarguments and refutation in their writing, they often use the following words and phrases.

Words to describe people: *critics, opponents, proponents, supporters*	*Although there are many benefits to online classes, there are still many **critics/opponents** who question their effectiveness.* ***Proponents/Supporters** of online classes say they make learning more dynamic.*
Words to describe positions: *be for/against, be in favor of*	*Many private universities **are for / are in favor of** making more classes online.* *Some professors **are against** this proposal and believe traditional courses help students learn better.*
Words to refer to ideas: *argument, belief, claim, fact, problem*	*This **fact** reflects their **belief** that online courses are more attractive to students because they offer students more flexibility.* *The teachers' union makes the **argument/claim** that online classes create **problems** for teachers.*
Counterargument/Refutation language: *while/although it is true that ..., this may be so, but ..., it is simply not true that ...*	***While/Although it is true that** online courses provide a dynamic learning environment, they are not suited to all students.* *The author suggests that online classes make students responsible for their own learning. **This may be so, but** some students need the discipline that a traditional environment provides.* ***It is simply not true that** online classes are less interactive.*
Identifying a specific source: *According to ...*	***According to** researchers at MIT, students learn as much in online classes as they do in traditional classes.*

4.3 Combine Ideas

Complete the body paragraph with the words and phrases in the box.

according to	argument	critics	in favor of	this may be so

There are many companies that are .... banning social networking (1) sites at work. They make the .... that websites such as Facebook and (2) Twitter distract workers and cause them to waste too much time. ...., (3) but giving employees a little free time while at work may in fact make them more productive. .... researchers at the University of Illinois, when people spend a (4) long time doing one task, they can easily lose focus (Ariga and Lleras). However, when they take several short "mental breaks," it is easier for them to remain focused, and they perform better at extended tasks. It is not surprising that the main .... of social (5) networking at work are bosses and business owners. They believe that time away from work is time and money wasted, but it appears that this may not always be the case.

C Grammar for Writing: Complex Noun Phrases

In academic writing writers often use complex noun phrases to discuss complicated ideas in an efficient way.

Below are common ways to modify nouns to create complex noun phrases:

COMPLEX NOUN PHRASES	
1 Two common types of complex noun phrases have the following structures: Noun + relative clause Noun + prepositional phrase	NOUN + RELATIVE CLAUSE *Principals work hard to help <u>children</u> **who are the victims of cyberbullying.** NOUN + RELATIVE CLAUSE *Extra support is needed for <u>children</u> **at schools** to prevent bullying online or in real life.*
2 Relative clauses are sometimes reduced to an *-ing* or *-ed* by omitting the relative pronoun and the *be* form of the verb.	NOUN + *-ING* PHRASE *Principals help <u>children</u> ~~who are~~ **being bullied online.** NOUN + *-ED* PHRASE *Principals help <u>children</u> ~~who are being~~ **bullied online.***

ACTIVITY 4.4 Combine Ideas

Combine the sentences using complex noun phrases.

1 Companies worry about employees. Some employees waste time on Facebook.

....

2 Cell phone abuse is a concern. Parents with teenagers are concerned.

....

3 Today there are many popular websites. These websites are used for social networking.

....

4 The researchers compared girls. There were girls in single-sex and coed classes.

....

5 The report looked at boys. The boys were competing against girls.

....

6 The students were taking online classes. The classes were being offered by private universities.

....

Avoiding Common Mistakes

Research tells us that these are the most common mistakes that students make when using noun phrases in academic writing.

> **1 Do not omit the relative pronoun with subject relative pronouns.**
>
> *The girls ^ who were studying in single-sex classes performed better.*
>
> **2 Remember to use the correct verb form when you use an *-ing* or *-ed* verb phrase.**
>
> *The girls ~~studied~~ studying in single-sex classes performed better.*
>
> **3 Remember to use the correct relative pronoun for people.**
>
> *The girls ~~which~~ who studied in coed classes performed worse.*

ACTIVITY 4.5 Editing Task

Find and correct six more mistakes in the following paragraph.

    One reason cell phones make people worse at maintaining relationships is because of texting. First, people ^ who prefer to text instead of call will try to have whole conversations with someone in very short messages, which can cause confusion. Short texts cannot communicate what voices and conversations can. People talked on the phone can hear pauses and changes in tone, which results in clearer communication. For example, for a parent which wants to know if her child is safe, a phone call is very important. Beyond this, texting teaches and reinforces poor writing skills, which can affect those looked for jobs. For example, high schoolers text often use abbreviations and spell words incorrectly. This problem has recently been identified by U.S. universities. Many students which need better grammar skills now must take courses to improve their writing so they can make a good impression on future employers. Texting is just one way that cell phones have a negative effect on people want to maintain relationships and social skills.

ⓓ Avoiding Plagiarism

Graphs and charts are a useful addition to an essay, but they need to be cited correctly.

Q

I found some great information in a table about millennials and their use of social media, but I'm not sure how to cite the information. How do you cite information in charts and graphs?
– Hodan

A

Dear Hodan,

Charts and graphs are great sources of information! I'm glad you know that you need to cite them. Many people forget to do that. When you refer to a chart or graph, but don't include the graph in your paper, you should cite the source both in-text and in your Works Cited. If you include the chart or graph in your paper, you should label it. If you include a source as part of the label, you don't need to include that information in Works Cited.

Best regards,

Professor Wright

There are two ways to use the information from graphs and charts. Each requires a different citation style.

CITING GRAPHS AND CHARTS

If you include the graph or chart in your paper	• Set the graph or chart close to the text that refers to it. Label the graph or chart. Include *Fig.* + *number* and a short caption above the graph or chart. For example: *Fig. 1. Negative technology experiences in relationships* • Include information about the source below the graph or chart. *Source: Amanda Lenhart and Maeve Duggan, "Couples, the Internet, and Social Media: The Main Report." Pew Research Center. Pew Research Center, 11 Feb. 2014. Pew Research Internet Project. Web. 9 Aug. 2014.* • Refer to the figure in your paper and summarize the information in the graph or chart. *As figure 1 shows, 8 percent of married couples argue about time spent online.* • Do not include a citation in Works Cited if you write the source below the chart or graph.

If you use the information in a graph or chart but do not include the graph or chart in the paper	• Include an in-text reference, like all other citations. *According to a recent Pew Institute Research Project, technology has a negative effect on couples (Lenhart and Duggan).* • Include a citation in Works Cited. *Lenhart, Amanda, and Maeve Duggan. "Couples, the Internet, and Social Media: The Main Report." Pew Research Center. Pew Research Center, 11 Feb. 2014. Web. 9 Aug. 2014.*

 4.6 Notice

Work with a partner. Circle the three things that are included with this in-text chart to avoid plagiarism. What would you need if only the information in the chart were included in the paper?

Fig. 1

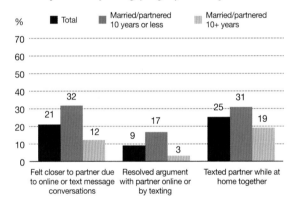

Positive technology experiences in relationships

Among internet users or cell phone owners in a committed relationship, the % who have experienced the following by length of relationship

Legend:
- Total
- Married/partnered 10 years or less
- Married/partnered 10+ years

Felt closer to partner due to online or text message conversations: 21, 32, 12
Resolved argument with partner online or by texting: 9, 17, 3
Texted partner while at home together: 25, 31, 19

PEW RESEARCH CENTER

Source: Amanda Lenhart and Maeve Duggan,
"Couples, the Internet, and Social Media: The Main Report." *Pew Research Center.*
Pew Research Center, 11 Feb. 2014. Web. 9 Aug. 2014.

As figure 1 shows, the longer a couple is together, the less they use the Internet and cell phone in their relationship.

In this section you will follow the writing process to complete the final draft of your essay.

STEP 1: BRAINSTORM

Work with a partner. Follow the steps below to brainstorm more ideas.

1 Before you start, notice how the writer of the Student Model brainstormed. She wrote many ideas. Then she circled three strong reasons she thought could support her claim. Finally, she wrote research questions to help her find facts and evidence to support her ideas.

WRITING PROMPT: Single-sex education is a controversial topic in the United States. In your opinion, is it beneficial for students – either girls or boys – to learn in a single-sex classroom?

Yes / Positive	No / Negative
• environment less distracting when separated	• competition between girls and boys is useful
• builds confidence in girls	• does not treat girls and boys equally
• do better in school	• reinforces stereotypes
• girls learn differently	• does not prepare girls for the real world

Research Questions:

1. Is a girls-only classroom less distracting? And does it really help?

2. Does a girls-only classroom build more confidence? What evidence is there?

3. Do girls really get better grades?

4. Do girls learn differently from boys?

2 Write the ideas that you wrote in Section 1, page 215, in the chart below. Include ideas from the Your Turns throughout the unit. Brainstorm more ideas.

Yes / Positive	No / Negative
•	• ....
....	....
•	• ....
....	....
•	• ....
....	....
•	• ....
....	....

Research Questions:

1 ....

2 ....

3 ....

4 ....

When you are finished, circle the three strongest points that support your thesis and write them here.

1 ....

2 ....

3 ....

STEP 2: DO RESEARCH: USING NON-TEXTUAL SOURCES IN RESEARCH

Non-textual sources, like graphs and charts, often include statistics, rankings, or other numerical information that can be effective evidence to support your writing. As with written support, it is important to evaluate the non-textual source to ensure it is relevant to your argument. You also must give credit to the **author** of the source with a proper citation.

Fatima used a graph as evidence for her response to this prompt: *Are gender roles important to society?* Read and find out how she did it.

I found a graph with excellent information about the number of female and male workers in different industries. After recording the source information (title, publication date, web address, author, etc.), I took notes about the graph including: **what** information the source includes, **why** this information is relevant to my argument, and **how** I plan to use the information in my essay. Then, I incorporated the information from the graph into my essay as support for my argument. Finally, I created a citation.

Fatima's Results

Thesis: Gender role expectations and trends in childhood influence career choices and opportunities in adulthood.

Title of graph: "Occupations by Gender in the UK"

Author(s): Office of National Statistics (ONS)   Publication Date: 2013

What? The graph in this article shows that female workers dominate administrative, customer service, & teaching – twice as many women as men in each field. Male workers dominate science & trade industries with at least three times as many men as women in each field.

Why? I want to compare the trends of subject interests and part-time jobs in high school to career choices later in life.

How? This information supports my paragraph about how job fields are unbalanced in their number of male & female workers, both in high school & adulthood.

Paraphrase (citation): Gender imbalance continues in the adult workforce with women outnumbering men in administrative, sales, and teaching fields by at least two to one. In contrast, men outnumber women in science and skilled trades by at least three to one (Office of National Statistics).

ACTIVITY **5.1** **Apply It to Your Writing**

Follow the steps Fatima took to use a non-textual source for your essay. Write the information in a chart.

STEP 3: MAKE AN OUTLINE

Complete the outline below with your ideas from the previous steps.

ESSAY OUTLINE

I. Introduction

Thesis Statement

Body Paragraph 1: First Point II.

Supporting Idea 1 A.

Detail 1.

Detail 2.

Supporting Idea 2 B.

Detail 1.

Detail 2.

Body Paragraph 2: Second Point III.

Supporting Idea 1 A.

Detail 1.

Detail 2.

Supporting Idea 2 B.

Detail 1.

Detail 2.

(CONTINUED)

Body Paragraph 3: **Counterargument** **and Refutation**	IV.	
Supporting Idea 1	A.	
Detail	1.	
Detail	2.	
Supporting Idea 2	B.	
Detail	1.	
Detail	2.	
	V. Conclusion	

STEP 4: WRITE YOUR FIRST DRAFT

Now it is time to write your first draft. Here are some suggestions on how to get started.

1 Reread your essay prompt and your outline to make sure that your ideas answer the prompt.

2 Use your outline and notes to make sure you make your claim and reasons clear.

3 Just write and let your thinking come out on the page.

After you finish, read your essay and check for basic errors.

1 Check that your paragraphs are each focused on a single reason and evidence for it.

2 Make sure that you have correctly used noun phrases.

3 Make sure your thesis statement and topic sentences are clear.

STEP 5: WRITE YOUR FINAL DRAFT

1 After you receive feedback on your first draft, review it carefully. Fix any errors.

2 Make a note of errors that were most frequent (misspellings, wrong verb tense, errors in using commas). Try to avoid them as you write.

3 Review the Academic Vocabulary and Academic Collocations from this unit. Are there any that you can add to your essay?

4 Turn to page 276 and use the Self-Editing Review to check your work one more time.

5 Write your final draft and hand it in.

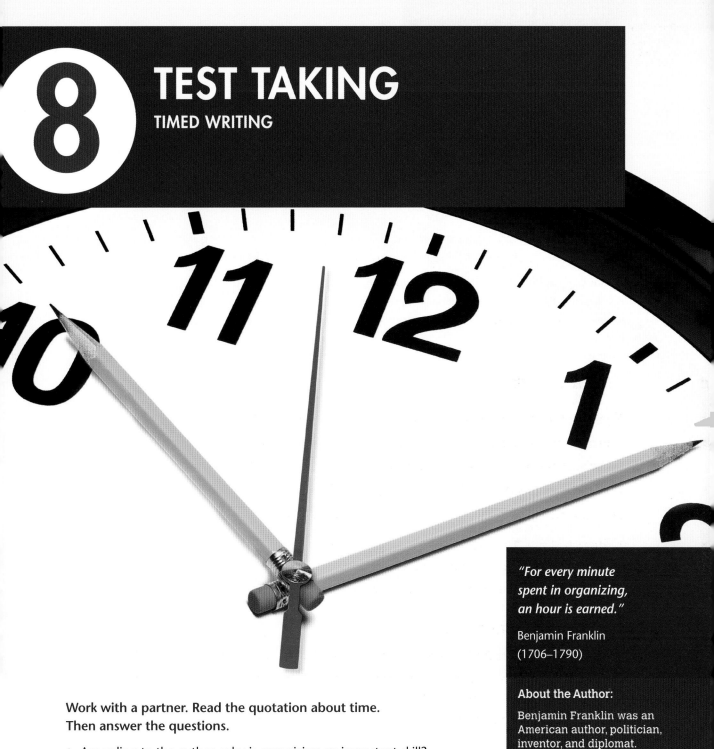

8 TEST TAKING
TIMED WRITING

"*For every minute spent in organizing, an hour is earned.*"

Benjamin Franklin
(1706–1790)

About the Author:

Benjamin Franklin was an American author, politician, inventor, and diplomat.

**Work with a partner. Read the quotation about time.
Then answer the questions.**

1 According to the author, why is organizing an important skill?

2 Are you a person who is organized? Give an example.

3 Before you write, how much time do you spend organizing your ideas?
Do you agree with the author that organizing ideas will "earn" you time?

WHY IS TIMED WRITING IMPORTANT?

There are many times in your academic life when you will be asked to write something within a limited time. This may range from short answers to questions on a quiz or test, to entire essays in response to a prompt. Timed writing is also used for college admissions, such as TOEFL, IELTS, and GRE. Occasionally, you may be required to provide a timed writing sample as part of a job application. In general, it is important for a college student to develop the skill of writing well under pressure.

WHY IS TIMED WRITING CHALLENGING?

Throughout this book, you have done a lot of writing. You have had time to think and discuss each essay before you started, and then rewrite your draft until it looked perfect.

Timed writing feels very different. Students who are good at timed writing have strategies to quickly get focused, get organized, and get writing. Students who do not do well at timed writing don't have those strategies, so they have more fear or worry. Here are some common concerns that students have:

- Pressure to do well: "Doing well on this test is really important for my future. There's **a lot of pressure!**"

- Anxiety: "I'm so nervous during a test I forget my vocabulary and grammar. I can't think!"

- Poor timing: "I forget to look at the clock, and I don't always finish!"

- Poor planning: "There's really no time to brainstorm or make an outline!"

- Perfection: "I want it to be perfect!"

All of these concerns are common among everyone who does timed writing, both native speakers and non-native speakers. Knowing your concerns about timed writing can guide you in learning the right strategies to help you succeed.

In this unit, you will learn ways to use your time wisely and efficiently. You will develop skills to write the best essay in a short period of time.

 1.1 Reflect

Work with a partner. Discuss the concerns above that are true for you. Are there other things about timed writing that are difficult for you? Do you have any strategies for dealing with the challenges of timed writing?

An important skill in timed writing is to quickly understand the prompt and decide the best type of essay to write. Below are the four steps that writers use to do this and an example of a writer thinking through the steps using the writing prompt that follows. These steps should take less than a minute.

WRITING PROMPT: Many students enjoy studying from home in an online college class. Others prefer to be in a traditional classroom, working with other students and the professor. ① How are these types of classes similar or different? ② Which type of class do you prefer?

HOW TO ANALYZE THE PROMPT

Step 1: Decide what the topic is. Circle the key words.

"I need to write about both online classes and classes in a traditional classroom."

Step 2: Be sure you understand the question. In your mind, restate the question as a statement.

"Online college classes and classroom classes have similarities and differences."

Step 3: Notice if there is more than one part to the question. Number each part.

"There are two parts. I need to talk about how these classes are similar or different and I need to give my opinion."

Step 4: Look at the language in the question. Decide what kind of essay (narrative, problem-solution, comparison and contrast, etc.) that you will write. Underline the words that help you decide.

"The words 'similar or different' tell me this is a comparison-and-contrast essay."

Below are words that are commonly used to indicate specific essay types. However, as you will see, some words can indicate different types of essays depending on the circumstance in which they are used, for example, the word *change*.

IF YOU SEE THESE WORDS AND PHRASES ...	YOU USUALLY WRITE THIS TYPE OF ESSAY:
describe, tell about a time when you	narrative
affects, benefits, change (as a result of situation of action), effects, impact, influence, leads to, reasons, results	cause and effect
best, better, change (over a period of time), compare, differ, different, similar	comparison and contrast
change (in terms of proposal, fix or remedy), solve, some ways, stop, what can be done	problem–solution
agree, believe, disagree, should, to what extent	argumentative

2.1 Recognize Types of Essays

Match the writing prompts with the correct types of essay. Write the letter. Underline the key words in the prompt that helped you decide.

a. argumentative   c. comparison and contrast   e. problem–solution
b. cause and effect   d. narrative

.... 1 College should be more than just a place for job training. It should also teach people to be good global citizens. To what extent do you agree?

.... 2 People communicate with each other very differently than in the past. How has human communication changed in the past 10 years?

.... 3 What would the impact on education be if teachers were paid well, like bankers and lawyers?

.... 4 Sports programs for children, such as soccer and football, have become more dangerous and more competitive. What are some ways that schools can change this situation?

.... 5 Describe a time when you did something helpful or special for another person. How did you feel about what you did?

2.2 Analyze Prompts

Work with a partner. Choose one writing prompt below and analyze it according to the four steps to analyze a prompt.

1 Historic buildings should be preserved instead of being torn down, even if it is expensive to maintain them. Do you agree or disagree with this statement?

2 How does growing up in a city differ from being raised in a small town?

Many times the prompt may have one dominant type of essay, but it may also require you to use features of other types of essays in your writing to answer other questions or to make your points clearer and more convincing.

Read the prompt below and underline the words that indicate types of essays. Decide which type will be the dominant one and then think about which features of other types that you would use. Often, the first question in the prompt tells you the type of essay to write.

WRITING PROMPT: Describe a time when you had to make an important decision. What was the decision? How did you make it? How did the decision affect you and important people in your life?

As you can see, the prompt requires that you tell the story about an important decision that you have made, so you should use a narrative mode, but you will also use cause and effect to explain how it affected your life.

Work with a partner. Choose one of the following prompts, and on a separate sheet of paper complete the steps to analyze it. Which essay type is dominant? Which features of other essays will you also use?

1 Some people say that we learn more from our mistakes than from our successes. Describe an occasion when either you or someone you know made a mistake. Explain what was learned from the mistake and its impact.

2 Compare the ways two different generations communicate, for example, someone born before 1970 and someone born after 1995. How are they different? In your opinion, have these differences changed family relationships?

One of the biggest mistakes that writers make is not planning their writing process well. They do not plan how much time they will spend during each step of the process, and they do not take the time to brainstorm or make an outline before they write.

Taking a few minutes to plan your time and organize your ideas before you start writing will save you time later during your writing. It will also make your writing better and your essay more organized.

Imagine you are driving to a new neighborhood for a job interview and you have very little time. Would you just start driving and figure it out on the way? Would you risk getting lost? Probably not. You would probably look at a map or use a GPS to find the easiest way to get there. Writing under pressure is the same. Plan first, write second.

Below is the list of steps for timed writing and suggested times for each step in different writing situations. This will help you decide how much time to allot for each step. A good rule is to use 10 to 15 percent of your time for planning.

Steps	Timed Writing Situations			
	30 minutes	45 minutes	60 minutes	90 minutes
1 Plan your time.	less than a minute	less than a minute	less than a minute	less than a minute
2 Analyze the prompt.	less than a minute	less than a minute	less than a minute	less than a minute
3 Brainstorm.	2 minutes	3 minutes	4 minutes	5 minutes
4 Outline.	2 minutes	3 minutes	5 minutes	7 minutes
5 Write your essay.	20 minutes	30 minutes	40 minutes	65 minutes
6 Proofread.	4 minutes	7 minutes	9 minutes	11 minutes

After you have planned your time and analyzed your prompt, you will be ready to brainstorm ideas. Below is a quick review of different ways to brainstorm.

YOU CAN USE ...	IF YOU ARE WRITING ABOUT ...
a cluster diagram (see page 15 for an example)	reasons, advantages/disadvantages, ways, etc.
a three-column chart (see page 49 for an example)	a narrative

arrows to show connections (see page 81 for an example)	cause and effect
a Venn diagram (see example below)	comparison and contrast
a chart that lists solutions (see page 144 for an example)	a problem and its solutions
a two-column chart (see page 215 for an example)	an argumentative position

Another brainstorming technique you could try is freewriting – or writing all your ideas quickly – to get your ideas flowing.

In timed writing situations, brainstorms will be quick. Often writers use individual words, short phrases, symbols, and abbreviations so that they do not waste time.

Read the example brainstorm for the prompt below in the Venn diagram. Notice how the writer uses symbols such as ↓ and $ instead of words to write her ideas down as quickly as possible.

WRITING PROMPT: How does a small, natural foods store compare with a large supermarket that is part of a national chain in terms of what the business contributes to a community? Which one is better for your community? Explain.

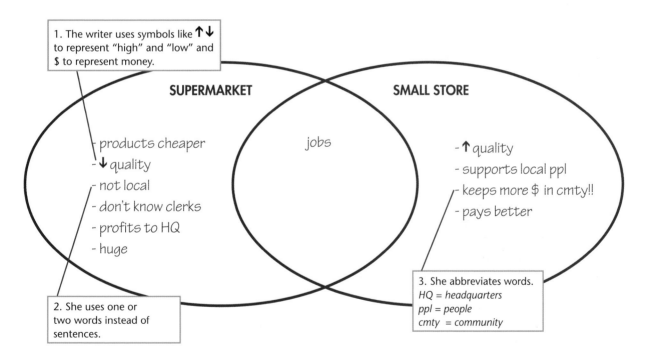

After brainstorming, two things should be very clear:

- Your thesis – including the points that you will cover.
- Support for each point in the body paragraphs.

ACTIVITY 3.1 Practice Brainstorming

Read the prompts below. Discuss with a partner which way you would use to brainstorm. Your partner may have a different idea from yours.

1 How are working alone and working in a group different? Which do you generally prefer?

2 Many cities have good public transportation, but people choose to drive alone in their own car, increasing traffic congestion. What are some ways to encourage people to change their habits? Which one would be the most effective?

The next task is to quickly organize your ideas in an outline. Preparing a quick outline will give you confidence that you have the ideas to answer the prompt well.

Read the example outline below and notice that the writer uses only words, phrases, and symbols to help her remember her ideas when she writes.

OUTLINE

I. Intro

Thesis Small, natural foods stores are better for a community because they support the local

people, provide good quality foods, and keep the profits in the community.

II. Support local ppl

    1. Local suppliers ex: farmers, busn. owners, part of cmty

III. Quality

    1. Organic, natural, healthier. Ex: my store

IV. Profits in cmty

    1. Invests in ed programs for kids, support local econ

Remember to refer back to your outline as you write.

ACTIVITY 3.2 Practice Brainstorming and Outlining

Create a brainstorm and outline for each prompt. Work quickly. Compare your brainstorms and outlines with your partner.

1 More and more people are volunteering in many different kinds of organizations. Is volunteerism necessary in the world?

2 "School is not a major part of a child's education, and it should not be." To what extent do you agree or disagree with this statement?

As you write your essay, it is important to be aware of three common pitfalls of writers that can cause poor results:

- They do not plan their time well.
- They waste time during their writing.
- They forget about the time.

What you have learned so far should help you avoid these traps. However, because they are so common, it may be helpful to remind yourself of them and follow the tips below:

1 Plan your ideas well so that you do not feel midway through that you have nothing to say or that in the end you did not really answer the prompt. Follow the tips below to feel confident about what to write and how to write it:

DO	DON'T
1 Take the time to understand the prompt and what your thesis should include. Include the key words from the prompt in your thesis.	Don't read through the prompt quickly without analyzing it.
2 Take the time to brainstorm and do a quick outline of ideas.	Don't start writing before you brainstorm and make an outline.
3 Use a new paragraph for each idea.	Don't focus on more than one idea in each paragraph.

2 Use your time well so that you do not spend too much time on things that will not improve your score. Consider this comment from earlier in this unit: "I want it to be perfect." That person wastes time trying to write a perfect essay. Follow the tips below to stay focused on writing your ideas well:

DO	DON'T
1 Cross out mistakes. Insert a missing word with a carat (^).	Don't spend time erasing.
2 Forget about a hook or title if it is not necessary for the test you are taking. Keep the introduction brief.	Don't spend a lot of time on the introduction.
3 Choose a position and stick with it.	Don't change your mind.

3 Keep track of your time so that you do not discover that there is no time to write a conclusion or proofread for errors. Follow the tips below to keep you on track and on time:

DO	DON'T
1 Make a note as to what time the test ends.	Don't ignore the clock.
2 Plan how much time to spend on each step (see p. 254 for suggested times). Check the clock regularly.	Start writing immediately.

(see p. 254 for suggested times)

ACTIVITY **4.1** Reflect

Put a star next to the "Dos and Don'ts" above that apply to you. Discuss what you plan to do differently in the timed writing task that follows in Section 6, Activity 6.2.

5 PROOFREAD

In timed writing, you are writing quickly. You may not notice that you have made some very basic mistakes. That is why it is important to leave time at the end to re-read your essay and check for errors. Most of the mistakes that writers make are grammar structures that they know. Take the time to find and correct those mistakes!

You may already know that there are certain mistakes you commonly make in writing. Pay attention to those when you proofread.

Use the acronym STAMP to help you correct the most common mistakes that writers make:

S is for plural *-s* on count nouns and *-s* on third-person singular verbs. It is also a reminder NOT to add an *-s* on adjectives before plural nouns.

> Missing plural *-s*: *Children who watch a lot of TV program^s see a lot of advertisement^s.*
>
> Missing third person *-s*: *If a celebrity like^s a certain brand of shoes, teens want those shoes.*
>
> No *-s* on adjectives: *I was surprised by his strong~~s~~ reactions against technology.*

T is for using correct verb **tenses** and forms of tenses.

> Correct tense: *In recent years there ~~are~~ [have been] studies showing the effects of technology on children.*
>
> Correct form: *More children are ~~been~~ [being] treated for addiction to technology.*

A is for the **article** (or determiner) before all single count nouns. Also, remember to use *the* for the second mention of the noun.

> Article before count nouns: *When children see ^[an] advertisement for unhealthy snacks, they may develop poor food habits.*
>
> "The" for second mention: *Likewise, if a child sees an expensive toy on television, he may not understand ~~a~~ [the] toy is too costly for his parents to buy.*

M is for **missing** subjects and verbs and for fragments.

> Missing verb: *I think that parents ^[are] responsible for controlling what their children watch on television.*
>
> Fragment: *Although advertising will always be in our lives~~.~~[, we] ~~We~~ can learn to control our impulses.*

P is for errors in **punctuation**.

> Wrong use of comma: *Even though, many advances in technology will have a good effect on society, scientists have concerns about some of its negative effects.*
>
> Run-on sentence: *Companies should be more responsible in advertising to children, they should limit the amount of advertising during children's programming.*
>
> . They ^

Finally, check for words that you often misspell. Research tells us that the words below are most commonly misspelled on academic tests:

believe	different	government	percentage	until
definitely	environment	nowadays	their	

As you make corrections, either insert words using a carat below (^) and the word above, or cross out the error with one, single line and write the correction above. In all cases, write as neatly as possible.

 5.1 Reflect

Which of the STAMP mistakes listed above do you often make? What other kinds of mistakes do you make when you write?

 5.2 Practice

Work with a partner. Practice spelling the commonly misspelled words.

In this section you will see how a student approached a prompt for a timed writing by following the steps in this unit. After you study the Student Model, you will apply all of these steps to your own timed writing task.

A Student Model

Follow the steps of the student writer as she writes an essay for a 45-minute timed writing test. Then answer the questions in Activity 6.1 on page 263.

STEP 1: THE STUDENT SPENDS ONE MINUTE TO PLAN HER TIME.

"I have 45 minutes, so I can spend this much time on each step."
Analyze the prompt: 1 minute or less
Brainstorm: 3 minutes
Outline: 3 minutes
Write: 30 minutes
Proofread: 7 minutes

STEP 2: THE STUDENT ANALYZES THE PROMPT.

1. The student circles key words.

2. She numbers the parts of the question.

WRITING PROMPT: Choosing a college or university is a difficult decision for many students. ① What are the advantages or disadvantages of a large university compared to a small college?

② Which would you prefer to attend?

3. She reads the question again and underlines the words that tell her what type of essay to write: comparison and contrast essay. She decides to do a point-by-point essay.

4. In her mind she restates the question to be sure she understands it: "Compare a big university and a small college. Say which one I would like to go to."

STEP 3: THE STUDENT BRAINSTORMS IDEAS. SHE CHOOSES A CHART TO COMPARE THEM.

Brainstorm

1. She uses exclamation points to indicate strong ideas and question marks to indicate weaker or less certain ideas.

2. She circles the strongest ideas. Each idea will be a separate body paragraph.

	Large univ.	Small coll.
$$	same (?) $3,000/ sem.	same (?)
Size of Classes	too big!! 150!	better, smaller <25
Extracurr activ	better, more to do, film club	
Profs	more famous (?)	patient
Help / admin.	bad exp. – rude on phone, busy	nicer!!
Famous sports teams	yes	no
Mtg ppl	only ppl from my country!!!	easier (shy)

STEP 4: THE STUDENT WRITES A SHORT OUTLINE. SHE STARTS WITH HER THESIS AND THEN ORGANIZES HER IDEAS. SHE ADDS NEW IDEAS THAT OCCUR TO HER AS SHE WRITES.

> 1. The student starts with her thesis.

Thesis: A smaller college is more attractive because of the smaller class size, availability of administrators to help students, and opportunities to meet people from diverse backgrounds.

I. Class size

> 2. She writes quick notes and abbreviations. She doesn't write out full sentences.

    big univ = too big; can't talk to profs or others; ex: bro's class

    at UW compare sm. coll = Reed, office hrs. / help

II. Admin. help

> 3. She expands her brainstorm with brief examples and details in each paragraph.

    big univ = too busy; ex- visa prob → delay

III. Mtg ppl

    big univ = lots of clubs; not good, shy ppl; only my country people

    sm coll = events for all

STEPS 5 AND 6: THE STUDENT WRITES HER ESSAY AND THEN PROOFREADS.

> 1. A simple introduction gives the writer's thesis and her key points. It is brief and to the point.

    When a student chooses where to go to college, the size of the school is an important consideration. Most people are drawn to large, famous universities, but in my opinion, there are more advantages to attending a smaller college. It is more attractive because of the smaller class size, availability of administrators, and opportunities to meet people.

    One disadvantage of a large university is the size of freshman ~~classes, they~~ classes. They are often very large, and the students do not ever talk with the professor. Classes are usually lecture style, and there is no chance to discuss the topics with others in the class. When my older brother studied at the University of Washington, his first class had 800 students. The professor was quite famous, but my brother only talked to teaching assistants. By contrast, most of the classes at Reed College include discussions between students and their professors. Also, there is a chance to visit professors during their office hours and get personal help if something is confusing.

> 2. The writer makes simple and clean corrections. She knows from her instructor's feedback that she often forgets articles and the third person -s, so she looks for that error carefully. She sees other mistakes as well.

Big universities have many people available to help students, but ~~they~~ *there* are so many

students that it is often hard to get an appointment. If you need to see an adviser or

someone to help with a visa problem, you have to wait to see them. In a small college,

on the other hand, an adviser keep*s* drop-in office hours, so you can usually see an

administrator the same day. This is really important for international ~~students. Who~~ *students who* may

need to have their visa question answered right away.

Finally, although big schools may offer a lot of different clubs, if a person is shy, *it* may

be hard to join new groups and meet people. Usually, on large campuses, international

students join the student group from their country, but they don't meet other people. In

smaller colleges, however, there are often events that are organized for all freshmen. The

organizer make*s* sure everyone is invited and feel*s* welcome. It make*s* it easier to meet new

people and make friends.

Overall, there are more advantages to a small college than to a huge university.

Getting an education at a small college would be preferable to me because of the

smaller classes, administrative help, and ease of making friends.

> 3. The conclusion restates the thesis and key points. It is short. There is no new information.

ACTIVITY 6.1 Notice

Answer the questions below with a partner.

1 What does the student writer do first?

2 What does the student writer do last?

3 How much time does she spend planning?

4 How much time does she spend writing her essay?

B Your Turn

Before you write, review the points in each section in this unit. The more you practice these

steps, the faster you will write and the better your timed writing will be.

**Choose one prompt from the list below and use the steps to write a timed essay.
Record the time you *plan* to spend in the chart below. At the end, record the time you
actually spent.**

1 Journalists often report on large riots or protests in the streets. What effect does their
  reporting have? Is the effect mostly positive or negative?

2 Stress has become a common problem in modern societies. People try to do too much and
  also feel there are a lot of demands on their time. What are some solutions for this problem?
  What can employers do to help? What can people do themselves?

3 "All schools should include art and music throughout a child's education." Do you agree or
  disagree with this statement?

	Time planned	Time spent
Total Time		
STEP 1: Plan time.		
STEP 2: Analyze prompt.		
STEP 3: Brainstorm.		
STEP 4: Write outline.		
STEP 5: Write essay.		
STEP 6: Proofread essay.		

Write your essay here:

SELF-EDITING REVIEW

1 ACADEMIC ESSAYS PSYCHOLOGY: CONSUMER BEHAVIOR

Self-Editing: Review Your Work	Completed
1 Check one last time that your thesis statement is clear and answers the writing prompt.	
2 Have you cited your sources so that your readers will know where your evidence comes from? Underline all your citations to make sure.	
3 If you use the exact words from a source, make sure you put the words in quotes and cite the source. Try to use your own words whenever possible (but still cite the source).	
4 Underline the Academic Vocabulary words and Academic Collocations you used. Make sure you used at least two words and one collocation.	
5 Underline gerunds and infinitives and make sure you avoided any mistakes.	
6 Look for mistakes that you typically make, such as using the wrong verb tense or form of the verb, missing *a/an* and *the*, or errors in using commas.	

Self-Editing: Review Your Work	Completed
1 Check one last time that your theme or thesis statement is clear and answers the writing prompt.	
2 Underline the Academic Vocabulary words and phrases you used. Make sure you used at least two words and one phrase.	
3 Underline any past perfect, past progressive, and past perfect progressive verb forms and make sure you avoided any mistakes.	
4 Check sentences that use parallel structure. Are they correct?	
5 Underline sentences in your essay that are written using the different sentence varieties you learned about in this unit.	
6 Make sure you have at least one quotation. Is it punctuated correctly?	
7 Look for mistakes that you typically make, such as using the wrong verb tense or form of the verb, missing *a/an* and *the*, or errors in using commas.	

Self-Editing: Review Your Work	Completed
1 Check one last time that your thesis statement is clear and answers the writing prompt.	
2 If you did research, check that you included sources in your essay and you have included a Works Cited. See page 39 for more information.	
3 If you paraphrased sources, check (or have a partner check) that you have not plagiarized your original sources. If working with a partner, show your partner your original sources and notes.	
4 Underline the Academic Vocabulary words and Academic Collocations you used. Make sure you used at least two words and one collocation.	
5 Circle places where you used the language of cause and effect. Make sure this happens in every paragraph of your essay.	
6 Underline verbs in the present perfect or present perfect progressive and make sure you avoided any mistakes.	
7 Read your essay one last time to make sure you do not have any fragments, run-on sentences, or comma splices.	
8 Look for mistakes that you typically make, such as using the wrong verb tense or form of the verb, missing *a/an* and *the*, or errors in using commas.	

Self-Editing: Review Your Work	Completed
1 Check one last time that your thesis statement is clear and answers the writing prompt.	
2 If you did research, check that you included sources in your essay and you have included a Works Cited. See page 39 for more information.	
3 If you paraphrased sources, check (or have a partner check) that you have not plagiarized your original sources. If working with a partner, show your partner your original sources and notes.	
4 Underline the Academic Vocabulary words and phrases you used. Make sure you used at least two words and one phrase.	
5 Underline any appositives that you used and make sure that you have avoided any mistakes.	
6 Circle any vocabulary that you used for showing similarities and differences.	
7 Draw an arrow in the margins pointed at any of the techniques you used for coherence.	
8 Look for mistakes that you typically make, such as using the wrong verb tense or form of the verb, missing *a/an* and *the*, or errors in using commas.	

Self-Editing: Review Your Work	Completed
1 Check one last time that your thesis statement is clear and answers the writing prompt.	
2 If you did research, check that you have relied on up-to-date information and cited all your sources. See page 173 for more information.	
3 Make sure that you acknowledge and refute at least one alternative solution to show your solution is the best one.	
4 Underline the Academic Vocabulary words and Academic Collocations you used. Make sure you used at least two words and one collocation.	
5 Underline the *it* constructions and make sure you avoided any mistakes.	
6 Look for mistakes that you typically make, such as using the wrong verb tense or form of the verb, missing *a/an* and *the*, or errors in using commas.	

Self-Editing: Review Your Work	Completed
1 Check one last time that your thesis is clear.	
2 If you did research, check that you included sources in your essay and you have included a Works Cited section. See page 39 for more information.	
3 Underline the Academic Vocabulary words and phrases you used. Make sure you used at least two words and one phrase.	
4 Make sure you have used the strategies for summarizing that were presented in this unit.	
5 Underline any noun clauses that you have written, and make sure that you have avoided any mistakes.	
6 Double underline the use of *this* + noun and pronouns to avoid overusing key words.	
7 Look for mistakes that you typically make, such as using the wrong verb tense or form of the verb, missing *a/an* and *the*, or errors in using commas.	

Self-Editing: Review Your Work	Completed
1 Check one last time that your thesis statement is clear and answers the writing prompt.	
2 If you did research, check that you have cited all your sources, including non-textual ones. See pages 39 and 246 for more information.	
3 Underline the Academic Vocabulary words and Academic Collocations you used. Make sure you used at least two words and one collocation.	
4 Underline the noun phrases and make sure you avoided any mistakes. Try to reduce relative clauses to -*ing* and -*ed* phrases and replace long verb phrases with shorter noun phrases where you can.	
5 Look for mistakes that you typically make, such as using the wrong verb tense or form of the verb, missing *a/an* and *the*, or errors in using commas.	

SOURCES

The following sources were consulted during the development of Final Draft *Student's Book 4.*

UNIT 1

Carlson, Nicholas. "This Post Has All the Black Friday Stats You Need to Sound Smart in Meetings." *Business Insider*. Business Insider, 3 Dec. 2013. Web. 15 Mar. 2015.

Levin, Adam. "The 4-Letter Word That Can Ruin Your Credit." *Huffington Post*. Huffington Post, 27 Feb. 2014. Web. 15 Mar. 2015.

"Mobile Technology Fact Sheet." *Pew Research Center*. Pew Research Center, n.d. Web. 15 Mar. 2015.

Sontag, Susan. *The Volcano Lover: A Romance*. New York: Picador, 1992. Print.

Yarrow, Kit. "Why Clearance Sales Are Psychologically 'Irresistable.'" *Psychology Today*. Psychology Today, 17 Jan. 2013. Web. 15 Mar. 2015.

UNIT 2

"Albert Einstein: Biography." *Bio*. A&E Television Networks, 2015. Web. 15 Mar. 2015.

"Australia's Immigration History." About. *Waves of Migration*. Australian National Maritime Museum, 2015. Web. 15 Mar. 2015.

"Chinese Exclusion Act." *Wikipedia*. Wikipedia, n.d. Web. 15 Mar. 2015.

Ferguson, Craig. *American on Purpose: The Improbable Adventures of an Unlikely Patriot*. New York: Harper, 2009. Print.

"Immigration to Australia." *Wikipedia*. Wikipedia, n.d. Web. 15 Mar. 2015.

"The Joss House at Weaverville." History and Heritage. *California State Parks' 150th Anniversary*. California Dept. of Parks and Recreation, n.d. Web. 15 Mar. 2015.

"Marie Bashir." *Wikipedia*. Wikipedia, n.d. Web. 15 Mar. 2015.

"Nicholas Shehadie." *Wikipedia*. Wikipedia, n.d. Web. 15 Mar. 2015.

UNIT 3

Bochner, Stephen. "Culture Shock Due to Contact with Unfamiliar Cultures." *Online Readings in Psychology and Culture* 8.1 (2003): n. pag. Web. 15 Mar. 2015.

"China's Overseas Population: Leveraging a Critical Asset." Sign of the Times. *GreaterPacific*. Greater Pacific Capital, Sept. 2013. Web. 15 Mar. 2015.

Frighetto, Jennifer, and Elizabeth Wolf. "Global Consumers More Likely to Buy New Products from Familiar Brands." *Nielsen*. Nielsen Company, 22 Jan. 2013. Web. 15 Mar. 2015.

"The Growing U.S. Hispanic Population: Impact on the U.S. Economy and Business." Briefing. *U.S. Dept. of State*. Foreign Press Center, New York, 24 May 2012. Web. Transcript. 15 Mar. 2015.

Guisepi, R. A., ed. "The Story of Hispanics in the Americas." The Americas: Hispanics. *International World History Project*. History World International, n.d. Web. 15 Mar. 2015.

Harris, Amy. "The History of Airline Industry." Travel Tips. *USA Today*. USA Today, n.d. Web. 1 Dec. 2013.

Huesca, Robert. "How Facebook Can Ruin Study Abroad." Commentary. *Chronical of Higher Education*. Chronicle of Higher Education, 14 Jan. 2013. Web. 1 Dec. 2013.

Jiménez-Castellanos, Oscar, Mary Carol Combs, David Martínez, and Laura Gómez. *English Language Learners: What's at Stake for Arizona?* Arizona State U, Morrison Institute for Public Policy, Mar. 2013. Web. 15 Mar. 2015.

"Migration: A World on the Move." Topic. *UNFPA.org*. United Nations Population Fund, n.d. Web. 15 Mar. 2015.

Ncube, Mthuli. "Urbanization of Africa." *AFDB.org*. African Development Bank Group, 2012. Web. 15 Mar. 2015.

"Open Doors 2013: International Students in the United States and Study Abroad by American Students Are at All-Time High." Press Release. *Open Doors*. Institute of International Education, 11 Nov. 2013. Web. 15 Mar. 2015.

"The Outs and Ins of Rural Migration." Fact Sheet. *The Center for Rural Pennsylvania*. Center for Rural Pennsylvania, 2007. Web. 15 Mar. 2015.

Redden, Elizabeth. "International Study Up." *Inside Higher Ed*. Inside Higher Ed, 11 Nov. 2013. Web. 1 Dec. 2013.

"Skype Grows FY Revenues 20%, Reaches 663 mln Users." *Telecompaper.com*. Telecom.paper, 8 Mar. 2011. Web. 1 Dec. 2013.

Walsh, Bryan. "Urban Planet: How Growing Cities Will Wreck the Environment Unless We Build Them Right. *Time*. Time Inc., 18 Sept. 2012. Web. 15 Mar. 2015.

UNIT 4

Farb, Peter, and George J. Armelagos. *Consuming Passions: The Anthropology of Eating*. Boston: Houghton, 1980. Print.

Greenberg, Elizabeth. "Chameleon: How Chinese Food Has Adapted to Its Surroundings Worldwide." *China Insight*. China Insight, 29 June 2010. Web. 15 Mar. 2015.

Lee, Jennifer 8. *The Fortune Cookie Chronicles: Adventures in the World of Chinese Food*. New York: Hachette, 2008. Print.

Waters, Alice. "Alice Waters Says the Future of Food Is Sustainable and Locally Sourced." *WSJ.com*. Wall Street Journal, 7 July 2014. Web. 15 Mar. 2015.

UNIT 5

"Caregiving." *FCA*. Family Caregiver Alliance, 21 Jan. 2014. Web. 15 Mar. 2015.

Lenhart, Amanda, et al. "Teens, Kindness and Cruelty on Social Network Sites: How American Teens Navigate the New World of Digital Citizenship." *Pew Research Center*. Pew Research Center, 9 Nov. 2011. Web. 15 Mar. 2015.

UNIT 6

Head, Alison J., and Michael B. Eisenberg. "College Students Eager to Learn but Need Help Negotiating Information Overload." *Seattle Times*. Seattle Times, 3 June 2011. Web. 15 Mar. 2015.

"Sir Tim Berners-Lee: Web Inventor and Founding Director of the World Wide Web Foundation." About. *Webfoundation.org*. World Wide Web Foundation, n.d. Web. 15 Mar. 2015.

UNIT 7

"Advantages for Girls." *Singlesexschools.org*. National Association for Single Sex Public Education (NASSPE), n.d. Web. 15 Mar. 2015.

Ariga, Atsunori, and Alejandro Lleras. "Brief and Rare Mental 'Breaks' Keep You Focused: Deactivation and Reactivation of Task Goals Preempt Vigilance Decrements." *Cognition* 118.3 (Mar. 2011): 439–43. Print.

"Businesses Increase Revenue with Social Media." *Phys.org*. Phys.org, 25 Mar. 2013. Web. 15 Mar. 2015.

Chandler, David L. "Study: Online Classes Really Do Work." *MIT News*. MIT News, 24 Sept. 2014. Web. 15 Mar. 2015.

"Chapter 5: Balancing Work and Family." *On Pay Gap, Millennial Women Near Parity—For Now. Pew Research Center*. Pew Research Center, 11 Dec. 2013. Web. 15 Mar. 2015.

Lenhart, Amanda, and Maeve Duggan. "Couples, the Internet, and Social Media: The Main Report." *Pew Research Center*. Pew Research Center, 11 Feb. 2014. Web. 9 Aug. 2014.

INDEX

Words that are part of the Academic Word List are noted with an **A** in this index.

A

academic essays, 13–46
    cluster diagrams, 14–15, 41–42
    essay structure, 24–31
    grammar, 35–38
    plagiarism, 39–40
    research, 43
    self-editing review, 270
    vocabulary and collocations, 16–17
    writing skills, 32–34

academic integrity pledge, 39

acknowledging and refuting opposing solutions, 165–166

adjust **A**, 48, 50, 53, 55–57, 74, 101

alter **A**, 114, 117, 120

alternative **A**, 16, 18–19, 38, 43, 159–160, 165–166, 182, 194, 202

alternative approach, 17, 22, 31

ambition, 50, 52, 55, 63

annotating, 196–197, 207

anticipate **A**, 50, 52, 54

anxiety, 84, 146–149, 151, 153, 156, 182, 227

apparent **A**, 146–147, 151

appositives, 134–135

are likely to, 21, 86, 115–116, 149, 182, 221, 229–230, 233

argumentative essays, 213–248
    argumentative charts, 214–215, 244–245
    essay structure, 224–235
    grammar, 240–241
    plagiarism, 242–243
    research, 246
    self-editing review, 276
    vocabulary and collocations, 216–217
    writing skills, 236–239

at the same time, 181–182

attribute **A**, 151, 180, 182, 184

audience and appeal, 236–237

B

background information, 24–27, 122, 154, 190–191, 224–226

block organization, 122–124

body paragraph, 24, 28–31, 62–65, 92, 125–126, 154–160, 190, 224, 228, 230–231

brainstorming, review and practice, 254–256
    graphic organizers:
    cause-effect graphic organizers, 80–81, 106–107
    charts: argumentative, 214–215, 244–245
        narrative, 48–49, 74–75
        problem-solution, 144–145, 171–172
        summary-response, 178–179
    cluster diagrams, 14–15, 41–42
    Venn diagrams, 112–113, 138–139, 255

C

capacity **A**, *182, 216, 218*
    have the capacity, 216–217, 221, 233

cause and effect essays, 79–110
    cause-effect graphic organizer, 80–81, 106–107
    essay organization, 89–96
    grammar, 100–103
    plagiarism, 104–105
    research, 108
    self-editing review, 272
    vocabulary and collocations, 82–83
    writing skills, 97–100

cause-effect graphic organizer, 80–81, 106–107

characters, 58, 61

charts: argumentative, 214–215, 244–245
    narrative, 48–49, 74–75
    problem-solution, 144–145, 171–172
    summary-response, 178–179

citation
    in research, 76, 108; to avoid mistakes, 208; of non-textual sources, 246
    to avoid plagiarism, 39–40, 72–73, 169; of graphs and charts 242–243

TEXT CREDITS

The authors and publishers acknowledge the following sources of copyright material and are grateful for the permissions granted. While every effort has been made, it has not always been possible to identify the sources of all the material used, or to trace all copyright holders. If any omissions are brought to our notice, we will be happy to include the appropriate acknowledgments on reprinting.

Text on pp. 18–19 adapted from "Does Buying Nothing Do Anything?" by Scott Harris. Reproduced with permission.

Text on pp. 52–53 adapted from "My Turn: An Immigrant's Silent Struggle" by Robert Kosi Tette,www.newsweek.com/my-turn-immigrants-silent-struggle-83929. Reproduced with permission of Robert Kosi Tette.

Text on pp. 84–85 adapted from "Moving Is Tough for Kids" by Nancy Darling, www.psychologytoday.com/blog/thinking-about-kids/201007/moving-is-tough-kids. Reproduced with permission of Nancy Darling.

Text on pp. 116–117 adapted from "The Cost of a Global Food Chain" by Robert Gottlieb, http://articles.latimes.com/2010/oct/20/opinion/la-oe-gottlieb-garlic-globalization-20101020. Reproduced with permission of Robert Gottlieb;

Text on pp. 148–149 adapted from "It's Not a Tumour! The Psychology Behind Cyberchondria" by Britt Peterson, www.newsweek.com/its-not-tumor-psychology-behind-cyberchondria-64071. Reproduced with permission of Britt Peterson.

Text on pp. 182–183 adapted from "Overcoming Information Overload" by Margarita Tartakovsky, http://psychcentral.com/blog/archives/2013/01/21/overcoming-information-overload/. Reproduced with permission of Margarita Tartakovsky.

Text on pp. 184–185 adapted from "Stop Knocking Curation" by Steven Rosenbaum, www.cjr.org/the_kicker/leave_curation_alone.php. Reproduced with permission of *Columbia Journalism Review*.

Text on pp. 211–212 adapted from "Face Time vs. Screen Time: The Technological Impact on Communication" by Chandra Johnson, http://national.deseretnews.com/article/2235/face-time-vs-screen-time-the-technological-impact-on-communication.html. Reproduced by permission of Deseret News National.

Text on pp. 218–219 adapted from "Online Friends, Real or Not? Discussing Dunbar's Number and Social Media" by Dawn Branley, https://thecyberpsyche.wordpress.com/2013/08/14/online-friends-real-or-not-discussing-dunbars-number-and-social-media/. Reproduced by permission of Dawn Branley.

The publisher has used its best endeavors to ensure that the URLs for external websites referred to in this book are correct and active at the time of going to press. However, the publisher has no responsibility for the websites and can make no guarantee that a site will remain live or that the content is or will remain appropriate.

CORPUS

Development of this publication has made use of the Cambridge English Corpus (CEC). The CEC is a multi-billion word computer database of contemporary spoken and written English. It includes British English, American English and other varieties of English. It also includes the Cambridge Learner Corpus, developed in collaboration with the University of Cambridge ESOL Examinations. Cambridge University Press has built up the CEC to provide evidence about language use that helps to produce better language teaching materials.

ART CREDITS

NOTES

NOTES